TikTok Broadway

TikTok Broadway

Musical Theatre Fandom in the Digital Age

TREVOR BOFFONE

OXFORD
UNIVERSITY PRESS

Oxford University Press is a department of the University of Oxford. It furthers
the University's objective of excellence in research, scholarship, and education
by publishing worldwide. Oxford is a registered trade mark of Oxford University
Press in the UK and certain other countries.

Published in the United States of America by Oxford University Press
198 Madison Avenue, New York, NY 10016, United States of America.

© Oxford University Press 2024

All rights reserved. No part of this publication may be reproduced, stored in
a retrieval system, or transmitted, in any form or by any means, without the
prior permission in writing of Oxford University Press, or as expressly permitted
by law, by license, or under terms agreed with the appropriate reproduction
rights organization. Inquiries concerning reproduction outside the scope of the
above should be sent to the Rights Department, Oxford University Press, at the
address above.

You must not circulate this work in any other form
and you must impose this same condition on any acquirer.

Library of Congress Cataloging-in-Publication Data
Names: Boffone, Trevor, author.
Title: TikTok Broadway : musical theatre fandom in the digital age / Trevor Boffone.
Description: New York : Oxford University Press, 2024. |
Includes bibliographical references and index.
Identifiers: LCCN 2023057139 (print) | LCCN 2023057140 (ebook) |
ISBN 9780197743676 (hardback) | ISBN 9780197743683 (epub)
Subjects: LCSH: TikTok (Electronic resource) |
Musicals—21st century—History and criticism. | Fans (Persons) |
Broadway—(New York, N.Y.)—History—21st century.
Classification: LCC HM743.T55 B64 2024 (print) | LCC HM743.T55 (ebook) |
DDC 302.30285—dc23/eng/20240118
LC record available at https://lccn.loc.gov/2023057139
LC ebook record available at https://lccn.loc.gov/2023057140

DOI: 10.1093/oso/9780197743676.001.0001

The manufacturer's authorised representative in the EU for product safety is
Oxford University Press España S.A. of El Parque Empresarial San Fernando
de Henares, Avenida de Castilla, 2 – 28830 Madrid (www.oup.es/en or
product.safety@oup.com). OUP España S.A. also acts as importer into Spain
of products made by the manufacturer.

To Pickles and Teddy, the most Jellicle cats at the Jellicle ball.

Contents

Preface ix
Acknowledgments xv
Author Bio xix

Introduction: The Great Digital Way 1

1. Marketing Musicals the TikTok Way: The Unexpected Case of *Beetlejuice* 34

   Interlude: All the Way from TikTok?! Damn!: Amber Ardolino's Digital Stage Door 59

2. Stealth Musicals: The TikTok Broadway Archive from *Heathers* to *Six* 67

   Interlude: TikTok Self-Tapes: The Muny *Legally Blonde* Dance Call 85

3. DIY Diva Drag: *Wicked*'s Elphaba on the TikTok Stage 92

   Interlude: *Mamma Mia!* Here We Cosplay Again 117

4. Anyone Can Cook, Anyone Can Create: *Ratatouille: The TikTok Musical* 123

   Interlude: We ~~Don't~~ Talk about TikTok: The Cultural Power of *Encanto* 153

   Conclusion 160

Notes 167
Bibliography 195
Index 207

Preface

At the request of my high school students, I took the plunge and downloaded TikTok in fall 2018. Being the theatre nerd that I am, I immediately searched for musical theatre songs on the app. Not surprisingly, there weren't many. But, by summer 2019, things had changed. Songs from *Beetlejuice* (2019), *Heathers: The Musical* (2014), and *Six* (2019) had become part of the mainstream on TikTok. In 2019, or the so-called Golden Age of TikTok (aka when the app was still largely a Gen Z affinity space), it was impossible to avoid a trio of teens bouncing their hips and lip-syncing the "Martha Dumptruck in the Flesh" section of the song "Big Fun" from *Heathers: The Musical*, a teenage girl channeling Anne Boleyn in the girl-power hit musical *Six*, or someone in Lydia Deetz cosplay recreating "Say My Name" from *Beetlejuice*. While musicals would become part of the digital TikTok ecosystem, when I joined TikTok, this was not the case. Moreover, the musicals I was interested in were absent. There was no *Company* (1970). No *Passing Strange* (2008). No *In the Heights* (2008). There wasn't even *Hamilton* (2015). But, to my surprise, someone had uploaded plenty of sound clips from one of my favorite musicals—*Fun Home* (2015), Jeanine Tesori and Lisa Kron's 2015 Tony Award–winning Best Musical, based on Alison Bechdel's graphic memoir about her closeted father's death (read: suicide) just weeks after Bechdel's coming out.

After I'd been lurking on TikTok for a few months, it was time to join in on the fun and begin making my own content. I could have "Changed My Major to Joan." I could have sang about my "Ring of Keys" ah-ha moment. And I could have proclaimed "Come to the Fun Home." But I decided that I wanted to go "Flying Away" and play airplane. You know, the game we all played as kids. Our parents would lie on their back, legs extending upward, as we rested our stomachs on their feet and assumed a flying position. I wanted to do that. No, seriously, I wanted to fly like an airplane while someone supported me, just as young Alison does with her father, Bruce, in *Fun Home*. Perhaps I wanted to channel my own nostalgia of my father, who had unexpectedly died just months prior, or maybe I was trying to game the TikTok algorithm and get "TikTok famous," but I knew that I needed to play airplane with one of my students. Now, the easiest route would have been for me to lie on my back, extend my legs upward, and have a petite student "fly." But that, folks, is cringe. Cringe doesn't get you clout. It doesn't get you TikTok street cred. What makes you TikTok famous is a student channeling Bruce Bechdel and me, a whole grown adult, flying with my student's support. The lucky student in this case? Avanté. He quickly volunteered. He was determined to support all 175 pounds of me (funny how writers lose a few pounds when writing a book, huh?) as I embodied small Alison, set to the lyrics "I want to play airplane." We tried. We laughed. We tried again. Other students looked on (they also laughed). While we were ambitious, we were *not* successful. Regardless of our failure to create a successful *Fun Home*–inspired TikTok, we had engaged in something that would soon become a phenomenon on the short-form video app. We had engaged with musical theatre TikTok.

My journey with musical TikTok didn't begin with that failed attempt at a viral *Fun Home* TikTok. Not even close. When I began working at Bellaire High School in fall 2018, my arrival on campus was met with another arrival that would have a far wider reach than I or any other teacher could have dreamed of. In August 2018, TikTok—owned by the Chinese conglomerate ByteDance—entered the US market, merging with the short-form video app Musical.ly. TikTok was an immediate cultural force at Bellaire. The songs became the soundtrack to our school's hallways. The trends became popular memes that students jokingly referenced during class. And an entire generation's attention span became roughly fifteen seconds. This was the environment in which my teaching began to flourish. Even though I had taught since finishing my undergrad in 2008, TikTok provided me with the tools to elevate my teaching. As I document in my book *Renegades: Digital Dance Cultures from Dubsmash to TikTok*, I began using the app to bring my students' personalities and cultures into the classroom. TikTok gave us the tool kit to build stronger, more authentic relationships, and engage in intergenerational bonding. The result was transformational and led to a host of surprises that saw my students and me performing live on *Good Morning America* at the end of the 2018–19 school year. Much to my surprise, the momentum never came to a screeching halt. Our TikToks—not to mention our Dubsmashes and Trillers—became synonymous with Bellaire High School.[1]

As my students and I continued to make regular local and national media appearances performing popular hip-hop dances, I noticed that one of my other interests was also growing on TikTok—musical theatre. Now, while my students and I stuck with R&B, rap, and pop-music dance challenges, I'd come home from school, take off my shoes, snuggle up with my cat Teddy on the sofa, and mindlessly scroll TikTok to unwind. In between the Microwave Challenge, set to "Slow Dancing in the Dark" by Joji, and the dance challenge to "Old Town Road" by Lil Nas X, I'd see musical theatre TikTok after musical theatre TikTok.[2] The more I interacted with musical theatre TikTok, the more I saw. I started small, mostly with the original—the OG—TikTok trio of *Beetlejuice: The Musical*, *Heathers: The Musical*, and *Six*. By the time the 2020 fall semester began, over a year later, there was so much musical theatre content that it became almost impossible to keep up with everything. It was the *Newsies* "Seize the Day" Challenge, in which TikTokers reenacted Christopher Gatelli's original Broadway choreography to the song. It was former theatre critic Broadway Bob leaking unseen footage of Patti LuPone singing "The Ladies Who Lunch" in the 2020-22 *Company* revival (spoiler: this one was Broadway Bob doing an exaggerated, if not shockingly accurate, Patti LuPone impersonation). It was Laura Benanti making fun of her bad haircut for the Tony Awards, set to the "Everybody Makes Mistakes" sound bite, and Kristin Chenoweth hitting high C's while doing colloquial quarantine tasks in her house. It was Mandy Patinkin dancing to turn out the vote for Joe Biden. It was the unlikeliest of TikTok musical trends—the collective creation of *Ratatouille: The TikTok Musical*.

And I was there for all of it.

Although it frequently morphs, the TikTok algorithm is a powerful program. The algorithm learns your preferences based on what you watch and interact with, quickly curating each TikToker's For You Page (FYP) into a unique experience. While some users may end up with predominately cooking-themed TikToks and others may get their fill of politics from the app, it didn't take long for TikTok to know what I wanted to see—musical theatre content, or what I call TikTok Broadway.

This book is the result of my journey to harmonize my TikToking and my musical theatre fanboying. The idea for this book first came to me while I was writing *Renegades* in spring 2020. I took notes in a Google Doc. I said I would go back to it later when I had more time. During this time, musical theatre content on TikTok grew at an exponential rate and began to thrive. By the time December 2020 rolled around and I had decided that maybe this research would just be an article or two and that the world didn't need this book, I realized that there was one person who did need TikTok Broadway—me.

I've always been a musical theatre fanboy. My earliest childhood memories are of watching the *Oklahoma!* (1955), *Grease* (1978), and *Bye*

Bye Birdie (1963) films on repeat. I may have grown up far from New York City, but I didn't need to live in the Northeast to have Broadway come to me. My parents would take me to national tours at the Saenger Theatre in New Orleans: *Bye Bye Birdie* (1960), *The King and I* (1951), *Grease* (1971), *Smokey Joe's Café* (1995), *Footloose* (1998). My CD player became home to the soundtracks to *Beauty and the Beast* (1991) and *Grease* (it was a recurring theme). Musicals were my comfort food. They were my happy place. They were a place where I felt seen, where I felt represented. Over time, my love for musicals grew. I dreamed of starring on Broadway, but that didn't pan out. I thought musical theatre had left me behind, that it would just be something I saw when visiting New York City. Little did I know that my journey through academia would lead me right back to the Great White Way. You see, musicals are part of my identity, and, as with any other part of one's identity, now is the time to unpack it.

In this book I (re)mix my TikToking practices and musical theatre fandom. While not entirely autoethnographic, *TikTok Broadway* does include my perspectives as a musical fan as well as my experiences as a TikToker.[3] Like other scholars engaging in fan studies, I enter this work as a participant observer. I am part of the TikTok musical theatre community. Although I have engaged with musical theatre TikTok by viewing, commenting on, favoriting, and sharing content, I have also created content. My TikToking adds to the archive and further blurs the lines between participant and observer. My understanding of TikTok is that of a scholar who experiences the platform from the creative side of things. I have not just learned about trends and aesthetics; I've executed them. I've not just read about the powerful (and mysterious) algorithm; I've seen firsthand how it works with the content I've created. And, I'm not just on TikTok; I have a large following that spills into other social media platforms. I am anything but anonymous. There is no denying this.

As such, this book follows a lineage of fan studies scholarship that includes, to cite fan studies scholar Matt Hills, narratives of self-discovery and self-awareness.[4] Fan studies scholar Mark Duffett goes a step further, suggesting that "having a fannish relation may mean greater knowledge, responsibility, accountability, sensitivity, and experience." And, perhaps most significantly, "we have moved to a point where we don't have to apologize for our investment in the popular media we study."[5] I suggest that my relationship to the fandom in question strengthens the work that follows. My role is not that of a cheerleader, but that of an objective insider-outsider.

Of course, ethics and positionality always factor into research. In fan studies, there is a robust conversation about the ethics of studying and writing about fan practices and communities.[6] I find these conversations valuable, and accordingly, they inform my work. That said, I find that much of this discussion does not apply to TikTok, given how public and how mainstream TikTok is. In the case of my book, the clips that I study have accumulated hundreds of thousands of views, even millions in some instances. Content has been cross-shared on other social media platforms. In some cases, such as *Ratatouille: The TikTok Musical*, the fan content has lived a life that extends far beyond TikTok. This is to say that TikTok facilitates a continuum of digital fan communities but is, nevertheless, distinct. It's not a closed community: it is inherently public. And, as this book details, virality enables musical theatre fan content to live a life far beyond *just* the fan community and, in the process, bring new people into the community.

The arguments in this book are informed by ethnographic findings from 2018 to 2022. My observations are based on daily engagement with TikTok over this period, sometimes as a spectator and other times as a creator. I engaged in informal and formal conversations with musical fans, theatre scholars, TikTokers, creators, and industry professionals, which have shaped the theories and frameworks that guide my study. These conversations have been invaluable to my understanding of how TikTok and the theatre community intersect.

TikTok has shifted US popular culture. What was once a niche digital community of teenagers in 2018 is now social media's most robust and thriving app. TikTok has influenced nearly every industry in the United States, theatre included. In what follows, I explore this phenomenon, revealing the nuanced ways that TikTok has changed how musical theatre fans view, interact with, and remix their favorite musicals. Whether it is the canon of so-called Golden Age musicals like *West Side Story* (1957) and *Cabaret* (1966), or more recent shows like *Hadestown* (2019) and *The Lightning Thief* (2014), musical theatre fans take to TikTok to perform their fandom. They make up a robust fan community that lives in a digital realm but spills out into the analog world. As TikTok continues to grow and musical theatre becomes increasingly mainstream, it's time to unpack how these two seemingly disparate worlds intersect. Musical theatre fans stand at the center of this crossroads. This book tells their stories.

Acknowledgments

I'm contingent. I don't receive any research support from any of my jobs. I didn't get any grants to do this research and write this book. I didn't have research leave or a research assistant. Nope. I wrote this book while teaching full-time as a high school teacher and adjuncting at two universities, both in person and online. Being contingent is hard af. Trying to be successful and publish books in a system that is not designed to support me has been demoralizing at times. It would have been easy to quit, but as I told myself every morning: "How lucky am I to be writing a book on musical theatre!" Indeed, this book has been a labor of love. The realities of being a contingent worker in academia aside, this project has not been without support. I am forever grateful for the various communities who have supported my bonkers idea to write a book about TikTok and musical theatre.

I've been fortunate to work with a terrific team at Oxford University Press. I especially thank my editor Norm Hirschy for believing in the value of this book from day one. I thank my project manager Ris Harp for guiding me through the publication process and relieving (so much of) my stress. I thank the three anonymous peer reviewers who greatly influenced revisions for this book. I couldn't have asked for better feedback. I extend a special thanks to Brandon Powers for helping with this book's conclusion.

I am indebted to Sarah Whitfield and Richard Glover at Wolverhampton University, Mary Jo Lodge at Lafayette College, Stacy Wolf at Princeton University, and Clare Chandler at the University of Lincoln, who invited me to present this research via Zoom. These formal and informal presentations held me accountable to get the writing done while also pushing me to deepen my understanding of musical theatre's intersections with social media. In a similar vein, I thank the virtual audience at the Song, Stage & Screen Conference in 2021 who watched me do Elphaba DIY Drag and then gave me incredibly helpful feedback that shaped many of the ideas in this book. Similarly, I owe my gratitude to the *Unobstructed Podcast*, Zachary Pincus-Roth of the *Washington Post*, Siobhan Burke of *Dance Magazine*, Margaret Fuhrer of *New York Times*, Alexandra Sternlicht from *Forbes*, and Britney

Crosson from the *Social Sunshine Podcast* for giving me a public platform to discuss this research.

My high school students, of course, continue to be my muses and sounding boards about Gen Z. I especially thank Curstin Brown, Katie Faour, Luke Parker, and J Stanfield for their support and interest in my research. I extend my thanks to the Bellaire High School community: Allison Underhill, Adrian Lopez, Sarah Humphrey, Micaela Segal de la Garza, Ebony Cooksey, Tania Andrews, Maria Gloria Borsa, Julie Burnside, Freddy Davalos, Esther Galo, Jenni Ho, Lisa McLendon, Sarah Miller, Samantha Quiroga, Michael Rossow, Hillary Schultz, and Brady Weldon.

The Music Theatre/Dance Focus Group of the Association for Theatre in Higher Education remains my scholarly home for all things musical theatre. I thank Grace Barnes, Lindsey Barr, Kaitlin Davis, Ryan Donovan, Brian Eugenio Herrera, Dustyn Martincic, Sam O'Connell, Adrienne Oehlers, Amy Osatinski, Phoebe Rumsey, Jessica Sternfield, Brian Valencia, Elizabeth Wollman, and Ron Zank for their feedback and ideas that have helped me to become a better scholar. Through MT/D I was fortunate to meet Barrie Gelles, Bryan M. Vandevender, and Laura MacDonald. I owe immense thanks to this trio for their friendship and shared love of musicals. Having scholarly buddies that I can send niche *Glee* memes, Skylar Astin thirst traps, and *Follies* hot takes to has made the long-writing days all the brighter. I received immense support from the "Afterlife and Its Consequences" Working Group at ASTR in both 2020 and 2021. I thank conveners Laura MacDonald and Bryan M. Vandevender for providing the space and Barrie Gelles, Stephanie Lim, Beth Osborne, Annie Potter, Dan Smith, Aaron C. Thomas, Victoria Thomas, and Stacy Wolf for their generosity. I was fortunate to attend the 2021 Mellon School of Theater and Performance Research at Harvard University, where I presented an early draft of this book's introduction. I thank Martin Puchner, Laura Dougherty, Elizabeth Hunter, Ariel Nereson, Gullermo Aviles Rodriguez, Michael Schweikardt, Jennifer Williams, and Samuel Yates for their detailed thoughts on my work. In a similar vein, I am indebted to Jane Barnette, Carla Della Gatta, Cristina Herrera, Lisa Jackson-Schebetta, Sarah Jerasa, Amy Osatinski, and Danielle Rosvally, who provided incredibly helpful feedback on various chapter drafts in this book.

The growing community of TikTok researchers has been fundamental to the development of this book. These brilliant scholars have pushed my thinking forward and made this project feasible. I especially thank Crystal Abidin, Tom Divon, Christian Lewis, Jess Maddox, and Jessica Sage

Rauchberg, Claudia Skinner, Krysten Stein, and D. Bondy Valdovinos Kaye for their support and camaraderie.

The entirety of this book was written after the COVID-19 pandemic began. Like many, I quickly found refuge in Zoom writing groups that not only helped me pass the time and stay connected, but also held me accountable to get the writing done. I especially thank fellow Zoom writers Jane Barnette, Shelby Brewster, Daniel Ciba, Meredith Conti, Susan Kattwinkel, William "Bill" Lopez, Lisa Nakamura, Ariel Nereson, and Danielle Rosvally.

I have been incredibly lucky to make some terrific friends along this journey. I especially thank Kevin Becerra, Josh Inocencio, Guadalupe Mendez, Jasminne Mendez, Emilio Rodriguez, Steward Savage, Abigail Vega, and Matt Wasson for the memes, long walks, game nights, meals, chisme, bochinche, margaritas, and collaboration.

I owe immense thanks to Danielle Rosvally aka my pandemic bestie. We met on Zoom and quickly bonded over our shared experiences as contingent scholars. Our friendship blossomed into the most aggressively Millennial relationship I have. Oh, and cats. Tons of cat pictures to help boost morale. Carla Della Gatta has been a similar pillar throughout the process of writing this book. Carla is always there for a ninety-minute phone call and cat pictures. Seriously, folks, cat pictures get me through the hard days. Speaking of cats, Cristina Herrera is not only a cat mom, but is an academic bestie extraordinaire. I am forever grateful for our friendship, collaborations, and willingness to read literally anything I send her. She's one of the best! Sarah Jerasa, despite being a dog mom, has been instrumental to my success. Just a few miles down the road from me in Houston, Sarah is always down for a co-working sesh, a hot meal, and a night out at the theatre.

I grew up in a musical theatre household. My parents loved musicals. Whether it was watching musicals on television, listening to cast recordings, or getting dressed up to attend a national tour at the Saenger Theatre in New Orleans, my parents ensured that I'd be our family's next theatre nerd. I thank my mother for being my biggest fan. I thank my late father for always encouraging me to be myself. My siblings are the best. I'm talking the best. My sister Frances is one of my favorite people to see a musical with. She is always down for Twizzlers, show merch, and lengthy post-show discussions over dessert. My brother Terry doesn't really love musicals and doesn't do the TikTok thing, but loves him some Dr. Boffone. Terry is one of the most vocal supporters I have. Thank you!

I have the two best research assistants a scholar could ask for. To Teddy HoneyBear and Pickles, thank you for your cuddles, therapeutic purrs, and support while writing this book. Speaking of the best, I extend my deepest love and thanks to Kayla, who has never once wavered in supporting my work. I know that I'm annoying when I want to talk about TikTok cultures and musicals at 6:00 am while you're still partially asleep. My bad. Just know that I only do it because I love you and have zero chill. Thank you!

A previous draft of Chapter 2 was published as "From *Heathers* to *Six*: Stealth Musicals and the TikTok Broadway Archive," *Studies in Musical Theatre* 15, no. 3 (2022): 175–89. A previous draft of Interlude 2 was published in "The Dance Call That Went Viral on TikTok," *American Theatre*, February 24, 2022, https://www.americantheatre.org/2022/02/24/the-dance-call-that-went-viral-on-tiktok/.

Author Bio

Trevor Boffone is a Houston-based content creator. He is a lecturer in the Women's, Gender & Sexuality Studies Program at the University of Houston. His work using TikTok and social media with his students has been featured on *Good Morning America*, *ABC News*, *Inside Edition*, and *Access Hollywood*, among numerous national media platforms. Insider named him to their 2020 Doers List, recognizing "trailblazers creating hope and inspiring us." Boffone is an extremely online Millennial who is addicted to TikTok (@official_dr_boffone), Instagram (@dr_boffone), and Twitter (@trevorboffone). He is the author of *Renegades: Digital Dance Cultures from Dubsmash to TikTok* (Oxford University Press, 2021), *Social Media in Musical Theatre* (Bloomsbury, 2023), and editor of *TikTok Cultures in the United States* (Routledge, 2022). Boffone is co-author of *Latinx Teens: US Popular Culture on the Page, Stage & Screen* (Arizona University Press, 2022). He is the co-editor of *Shakespeare and Latinidad* (Edinburgh University Press, 2022); *Encuentro: Latinx Performance for the New American Theater* (Northwestern University Press, 2019); *Seeking Common Ground: Latinx and Latin American Theatre and Performance* (Bloomsbury, 2021); and *Nerds, Goths, Geeks, and Freaks: Outsiders in Chicanx and Latinx Young Adult Literature* (University Press of Mississippi, 2020). He is currently co-writing a book on "Yassified Shakespeare" with Danielle Rosvally; Boffone and Rosvally are documenting the process on TikTok (@yassifiedshax).

Introduction

The Great Digital Way

In early March 2020, I sat in my high school classroom talking to Katie, one of my favorite students and a fellow musical enthusiast. Our topic of discussion? Our upcoming spring trips to New York City. While she was looking forward to seeing Jonathan Groff (her fave) in *Little Shop of Horrors*, I was more excited about Katrina Lenk and Patti LuPone in *Company*. Even as the realities of the COVID-19 pandemic became more apparent, we remained resolute. Regardless of what happened with the coronavirus, nothing was going to stop us from seeing these shows. Nothing.

We couldn't have been more wrong.

Within a few days, Broadway shut down. It went dark for what was supposed to be four weeks. The closure eventually lasted eighteen months, forming the longest dark period in Broadway history. Suddenly, live theatre ceased to exist. Live musicals stopped across the United States, from Philadelphia to Seattle, and Duluth to Bakersfield. Professional, community, educational, equity, non-equity, it didn't matter: it was all gone. What musical theatre fans had once taken for granted—live performance—was no longer a reality. Katie and I would never see *Little Shop of Horrors* and *Company*. In fact, we wouldn't even see each other again. Within a few days of Broadway shutting down, our school followed suit. Katie, a senior, wouldn't have a prom, a senior skip day, or even a graduation. Overnight, life had changed, and even as we collectively said, "when the pandemic is over," it was becoming apparent that we were in the middle of a massive sociocultural shift in the United States.

At the same time, musical theatre *was* flourishing, albeit somewhat unexpected—TikTok, the short-form video app that entered the US market in August 2018 and quickly became the most downloaded app in the country. Like many others, Katie included, I turned to TikTok as part of my daily quarantine routine. I'd find myself scrolling for hours every day, flipping through short videos from nearly every corner of TikTok. As I pacified my self-isolation boredom and soothed my pandemic anxieties on TikTok, I entered an escapist digital reality. The app's notoriously robust algorithm began to work, slowly filtering to me more content tailored to my specific interests. While scrolling through TikTok, I began to see videos of musical theatre fans remixing TikTok trends, putting Broadway spins on them. There were videos of Broadway divas such as Laura Benanti, Kristin Chenoweth, and Idina Menzel, who had recently joined the app and uploaded a variety of content showing off their comedy chops and knack for social media virality. And, of course, by March 2020, Broadway musicals began creating official TikTok accounts—some more successful than others.

I soon discovered *A Chorus Line* TikTok, the subculture of TikTok where fans of the groundbreaking musical express their fandom and interact with the dramaturgical world of the show. One video stood out, one that would mark a trend that brought me joy at a time when joy was hard to find. I had stumbled across Christopher Rice, a Broadway veteran and *A Chorus Line* alum who was performing in the national tour of *Hamilton* at the time of the shutdown and, like many, had downloaded TikTok to pass the time.[1] In this March 21, 2020, TikTok (see Figure I.1 and Figure I.2), Rice walks through an empty Berczy Park in Toronto as the crescendo builds to the beginning of "I Hope I Get It," the opening song of *A Chorus Line*, the 1975 musical conceived, directed, and choreographed by visionary Michael Bennett. Zach, the fictional musical within a musical's director-choreographer, tells the dancers to face away from the mirror just as Rice passes a mirror sculpture. The scene is set. Zach calls out, "From the top. A-Five, six, seven, eight!" Rice looks at the camera, smiles, and begins the show's signature choreography as Marvin Hamlisch's pulsating score crescendos. Although *A Chorus Line* opened forty-five years before Rice shot his video, Bennett's choreography remains the gold standard, and Rice's video accurately reflects it.[2] Occupying public space, bundled up in his winter coat, Rice exudes the excitement dancers feel when performing the show and the thrill audiences enjoy when witnessing "I Hope I Get It."

A Chorus Line tells the stories of seventeen dancers who are auditioning for a spot in the chorus line for an upcoming new Broadway musical. The show transpires in real time, during which we see these dancers form what Stacy Wolf calls a "temporary community," something replicated on TikTok.[3] As the final callback gets underway, each dancer is given an opportunity to tell their story and show off their talents in hopes of being one of the lucky eight dancers who will defy the odds and get cast. Notably, the show doesn't have a

Figures I.1 and I.2 Christopher Rice performs the choreography to "I Hope I Get It" in Berczy Park in Toronto. Posted March 21, 2020.

single protagonist. Even the musical's leading lady, Cassie, isn't a traditional leading role.[4] Cassie may be a fan favorite, but the show is truly about the collective.[5] Effectively, the same dynamics are at play on *A Chorus Line* TikTok. Just as "the gypsies work to satiate the director's curiosity by presenting personal narratives of varying lengths," so, too, do individual entries into the TikTok repertoire of *A Chorus Line* form a temporary community.[6]

Before I could even realize what was transpiring, TikTok was feeding me the repertoire, an endless stream of videos, all things *A Chorus Line*. These videos run the gamut of TikTok aesthetics and trends. *A Chorus Line* TikTokers engage with the musical's dramaturgy in various ways, marrying the show with popular TikTok trends. For example, actor Max Clayton (@maxmclayton) uploaded several videos from his time performing as Don in the 2018 City Center revival. In a December 17, 2020, video, Clayton does the "Tell me you're gay without telling me you're gay" challenge, stitching the prompt video with behind-the-scenes footage from the City Center sitzprobe of *A Chorus Line*. As Tony Yazbeck, playing Zach, calls out, "Facing away from the mirror. From the top. A-Five, six, seven, eight!" and the orchestra crescendos, the actors and fellow audience members erupt in cheers. The energy in the short video is palpable. It's infectious. In fact, I watched it no fewer than twenty times on repeat the first time I scrolled upon it.

Other TikTokers embody Cassie, who gets one of the musical's few solo numbers: "The Music and the Mirror." After dancer Matthew Aaron Liotine (@matthewaaronliotine) received a comment from a follower (i.e., fan) on one of his *A Chorus Line* TikToks, saying, "I'd pay millions to see you as Cassie," Liotine replied, "no need to pay millions" and posted a video of himself doing "The Music and the Mirror." In the August 25, 2020, video, he perfectly hits the choreography on his back patio. Per usual, the comment section hypes up Liotine: "the sustain on the pirouettes," "the accents," "that spotting tho," "BOOKED IT."[7] Bolstered by a wave of support, Liotine continued to post *A Chorus Line* videos in which he perfectly executes the choreography—while serving lewks (read: personal style), no less—the whole time building a dedicated following of TikTokers who vowed to see him onstage when the pandemic was over. TikTok had given him the chance to dance when no other viable options existed.

Although *A Chorus Line* TikTok features a variety of content making use of the app's vast array of effects, features, sound bites, and aesthetics, one trend has stood out. There is a growing body of TikToks featuring *A Chorus Line* alumni, like Christopher Rice, who have taken to the line to share the opening of "I Hope I Get It" as well as their signature dances from the show, from "I Can Do That" and "At the Ballet" to "One" and "The Music and the Mirror." Dancer Andrew N. Ruggieri (@andrewnataleruggieri) perhaps best exemplifies this. His account is filled with videos of him doing the choreography to "I Hope I Get It," onstage, off-stage, and in slow-motion instructional videos. Ruggieri performs several videos of "I Can Do That," the signature song of Mike, whom he played in the show's 2017–18 national tour. Ruggieri's TikTok has become a de facto *A Chorus Line* meeting place, linking the show's alumni and serving as a central place for the musical's fans to congregate. Ruggieri routinely states how much he loves the show, essentially becoming a fan while he shows off his talents as a bona fide musical theatre performer. But Ruggieri isn't alone in this work.

Soon there was a groundswell of *A Chorus Line* dancers using the platform to stay connected to the musical theatre community as well as to join the cohort of alums who had performed the show's landmark choreography eight times a week. Musical theatre scholar Warren Hoffman suggests that *A Chorus Line*'s "magic and staying power was due to Michael Bennett, whose staging was so integral to the show's concept and structure that even today most productions of the musical still re-create his work."[8] And, just as professional dancers use TikTok to perform Michael Bennett, so, too, do their followers as well as other fans of the musical. A quick search through the hashtag #AChorusLine reveals tens of thousands of videos of young dancers recreating Bennett's "I Hope I Get It" choreography. Each video is unique, yet one thing remains the same throughout the repertoire. Every dancer radiates energy. Their facial expressions reveal the joy they feel standing on the line. Their captions further convey their love for the musical, something matched in the comments section, where many question whether any musical theatre kid doesn't know the opening to "I Hope I Get It." The consensus is a definitive no.

Performing during a time when live performance—at least as many musical theatre practitioners had previously practiced it—had stopped, these dancers began using TikTok as a strategic site to perform musical theatre. TikTok gives these artists a venue to perform, draw an audience, grow a following, and, ultimately, build a brand. In the case of *A Chorus Line* TikTok, dancers performing "I Hope I Get It" embody both literal and metaphorical interpretations of Hamlisch's song. The "it" takes on several meanings: fame, followers, virality, stress relief, and, of course, the chance to dance. Arguably the show's most iconic song, dance, and moment, "I Hope I Get It" encompasses what so many of us desire—to belong. Hoffman affirms that the musical is a "comment on what it means to be human: the desire to be picked, the desire to be loved, the desire to 'make it' in the world."[9] In essence, *A Chorus Line* TikTokers mirror the musical's central struggle, that of retaining individuality while also being one with the chorus line, blending in in such a way as to lose individualism altogether.[10] Although speaking directly to the musical, Hoffman's analysis is relevant to the politics of TikTok. He writes, "Being part of a chorus line means conforming to the group, blending in, not drawing attention to oneself. It's the opposite of what it means to be the star of the show, to be an individual."[11] US popular performance scholar Brian

Eugenio Herrera adds that the musical's opening number enables us to see "both the audition as physical reality and also the audition as emotional reality," another aspect that plays out in the TikTok archive as dancers reveal their physical and emotional connections to the musical.[12] That is, *A Chorus Line* TikTokers, by recreating the show's choreography in a digital community, reimagine the show's politics.

Even as these dancers work to integrate into the TikTok archive, the platform facilitates individuality in a way that the musical doesn't allow. Zach cuts dancers throughout *A Chorus Line*, but TikTok does the opposite, constantly bringing more people into the fold. As the archive of *A Chorus Line* TikToks has grown, so, too, has a community of dancers who have done something most musical theatre fans only dream of doing—dancing the entirety of *A Chorus Line*. Yet, this TikTok repertoire is not limited to the performers themselves. Like with other social media platforms, the community is defined as much by creators as it is by the fans who interact with their creations. The community of *A Chorus Line* TikTok fully embodies this. As the archive expands, musical theatre fans—many of them aspiring young performers—perform the dance, essentially auditioning for their followers in the hopes of landing on the app's coveted For You Page (FYP) and, maybe one day, attaining a role in a production of *A Chorus Line*.[13] *A Chorus Line* TikTok reveals how the pandemic has pushed musical theatre's mobility into a digital realm. Something new was happening in spring 2020, something harmonizing the tremendous growth that TikTok was experiencing and highlighting the need for the musical theatre community to get its musical fix during the pandemic.

The repertoire of *A Chorus Line* TikToks forms part of a much larger community, one that I call TikTok Broadway. From *Beetlejuice* and *Six* to *Wicked* and *Ratatouille: The TikTok Musical*, this book tells the story of TikTok Broadway, the Great Digital Way, which has transformed musical theatre fandom in the digital age.

TikTok Broadway explores the phenomenon of musical theatre fandom as it has materialized on TikTok, a social media app that, despite only being available to US audiences since August 2018, has become one of the dominant social media platforms, only rivaled by mainstays Facebook, Twitter, and Instagram. Given the critical mass of TikTok and the app's cultural influence across nearly every industry, it is time to unpack different TikTok subcultures such as its thriving musical theatre community. I argue that TikTok democratizes musical theatre fan cultures and spaces, creating a new canon of popular musicals thanks to the way virality works on the app. This new TikTok canon is not a substitute for the old, analog canon of musicals that have appeared on Broadway and reached a certain level of success. Rather, it expands musical theatre into a purely digital realm, which then spills into other, nondigital aspects of US popular culture. Even so, TikTok is not *just* for musical theatre; its virality spans across many cultural communities. Its centrality and digital accessibility make it easy and attractive. TikTok is also free to use, whether one is posting or viewing videos. This makes it significantly more economically accessible than Broadway theatre, with its astronomical ticket prices, allowing more audiences to engage with this digital work.

TikTok Broadway is a cultural history of the recent past, documenting the first phase in the development of TikTok as a vehicle for musical theatre. This book offers an account of musical theatre fandom at the height of TikTok's ubiquity, while providing a substantive glimpse into what changed over time from 2018 to 2022, a time span defined not only by the COVID-19 pandemic but also by shifting discussions around conflict, crisis, care, and community. As a book of social documentation and cultural history, *TikTok Broadway* explicates not only the social dimensions of a booming digital subculture but also the operational particulars of how users engage a hugely popular social media app's features in service of following their own interests and finding their fellow nerds (their musical theatre fandom). As a piece of scholarly musical theatre criticism, this book offers generative insights into how the musical—as an artistic form, as a theatrical commodity, and as a constellation of cultural practices—is evolving and changing in the twenty-first century, in no small part because of this changing fandom.

TikTok's musical theatre community has energized fan practices, leading to innovative digital fandom aesthetics and a democratized approach to fan community formation. In this democratized mode of creation, fans and audiences dictate trending content and, subsequently, canon formation. Fans have the agency to make shows popular (*Six*, *Heathers: The Musical*),[14] make them commercially successful (*Beetlejuice*), and develop new shows (*Ratatouille: The TikTok Musical*, *Bridgerton: The Musical*). The power lies in the fans, who have a far greater reach than on Tumblr, Facebook, Twitter, or Instagram. Just like TikTok has the capacity to dictate what music trends on the Billboard Hot 100, TikTok can also canonize musical theatre, something it achieves through virality and the repetitions that coincide with becoming a TikTok trend.[15] As the case studies in this book convey, canonization on TikTok is at times a byproduct and at times an explicit goal.

Whether derivative or purposeful, TikTok canonization transpires *through* democratization.

The origins of TikTok Broadway predate the COVID-19 pandemic. Even so, much of the work that follows transpired after Broadway's shutdown began, and much of the analysis is informed by how fans engaged with musicals at a time when every theatre in the United States was dark. The pandemic shifted how US audiences got their entertainment fix. Musical theatre was no different. As the *A Chorus Line* archive conveys, musical theatre activity exploded on TikTok in 2020, after musicals stopped face-to-face performances, and it shows no signs of lagging even three years later. Of course, live-streaming theatre boomed during this same time period, and digital musical performances from full-scale musical productions to benefit concerts were weekly occurrences.[16] But the TikTok boom is distinct in that it has occurred far from the capitalist constraints that dictate commercial theatre in the United States. This is an organic movement from the people for the people. The goal is not to make money or to keep a theatre company running. Rather, musical theatre on TikTok is, at its core, about making art and building community. Of course, TikTok Broadway did not emerge from a vacuum. Musicals and fannish creations have routinely thrived in any number of digital spaces. Message board All That Chat has been a home for musical theatre fans for decades. Bootlegs have been popular on YouTube. Twitter has been used to draw audiences and expand on musicals' narratives. Facebook groups have been critical for connecting fan communities. As I later explain, TikTok extends what these vital internet spaces have done for musical theatre fandom.

As teenagers learned during the summer of 2019 (the Golden Age of TikTok, as Gen Z lovingly refers to the time period) and the rest of the world would realize the next year, against the backdrop of COVID-19, TikTok has transformed the way we live our day-to-day lives.[17] In addition to its role as an entertainment hub, the app also features content tailored to each user. TikTokers can watch cooking lessons, view crafting tutorials, take microdance lessons, learn a language, discover little-known facts about their most obscure interests, watch makeup tutorials, get updates on current events, view cute cat videos, and keep up with their favorite celebrities. TikTokers follow accounts based on their interests. The TikTok algorithm then sends users a constant feed of content tailored to those interests, giving each TikToker an individual experience and enabling cultural identification and community formation. The app has shifted the way digital communities assemble, develop, and thrive. TikTok musicals are no exception. Like its digital predecessors, TikTok has "altered the way musicals are marketed, admired, reviewed, researched, taught, and even cast."[18] As this book attests, the digital revolution has also transformed how fans interact with musical theatre, something that has been continually morphing from the early days of the internet to the present. In fact, while the focus of this book is on TikTok, I am aware that a new platform may have emerged by the time this book is published. This doesn't diminish TikTok's cultural role from 2018 to 2022.

This book's subtitle, *Musical Theatre Fandom in the Digital Age*, pays homage to musical theatre scholar Jessica Hillman-McCord's landmark edited collection *iBroadway: Musical Theatre in the Digital Age* (2017). Hillman-McCord's volume makes the case for a deeper exploration of the role of digital technology in all facets of musical theatre, from development and performance to marketing and fandom. The chapters in *iBroadway*, which focus on social media's relationship to musical theatre, could never have predicted how digital platforms would transform the musical theatre world just a few years later.

Accordingly, *TikTok Broadway* picks up where *iBroadway* left off, and shares with it many project goals—namely, exploring fan practices, digital marketing, and social media creativity. I propose that musical theatre fan practices began to shift in the lead-up to the COVID-19 pandemic, cultural work that was being realized by Zoomers, or so-called members of Gen Z. By the time Broadway shut down in March 2020, musical fans were ready to migrate their fandoms to TikTok, creating democratized fan practices in the process. Although Zoomers had a significant role in this work—after all, TikTok is a largely Gen Z space—Millennials also flocked to TikTok. Zoomers and Millennials bolstered TikTok's numbers, enabling it to flourish. So, too, did musical theatre fandom blossom on the platform. Hillman-McCord states, "As a highly popular art form, musical theatre has always acted as a mirror to society. Unsurprisingly, then, the form also reflects the ways we react to sweeping technological change."[19] We are in the middle of a shift into the TikTok Age. As TikTok becomes more embedded in US popular culture, now is the time to understand its relationship to theatre at large.

TikTok Broadway intervenes into our collective understanding of how social media reimagines musical theatre fan practices. The TikTok revolution is already on us. The archive of TikTok Broadway has grown in the time it has taken me to write this sentence. Musical theatre fans have uploaded videos recreating Andy Blankenbuehler's *Hamilton* choreography to "The Schuyler

Sisters," doing Anne Boleyn *Six* cosplay, belting "Don't Rain on My Parade" as high as they can in the bathroom, and telling us little-known facts about *Into the Woods* (1987). The archive is already in motion. Welcome to the Great Digital Way.

"There's a (Digital) Place for Us": Musical Theatre Fandom in the Digital Age

"There's a place for us / somewhere a place for us," Tony sings at the top of "Somewhere," part of the Somewhere Ballet from *West Side Story*, the 1957 musical from Leonard Bernstein, Arthur Laurents, Jerome Robbins, and Stephen Sondheim. In the stage musical, as Tony and Maria sing about an imagined future, the walls to her bedroom dissolve, revealing a dreamlike space where they can "find a new way of living." Theatre scholars, queer folks, and musical fans have taken to Sondheim's lyrics since the musical's debut, using "a place for us" as a metaphor for an imaginary future free of oppression, one in which communities can "find a new way of living." Everyone wants to feel part of a group culture. We want to find community with like-minded people. We want to grow with them. We want to belong. "A place for us" imagines that future.

Since the dawn of the internet, musical theatre fans have taken to cyberspace to find that special place, one where they can perform their fandom in concert with others.[20] One free of critical siblings and high school bullies. One where it's okay—and expected—to love musicals. Although the culture around musicals has changed in the twenty-first century, musicals weren't always "cool," despite being commercial and middle-brow pop-culture entertainment. Take, for instance, my own coming-of-age experiences, loving musicals but keeping that hidden because I didn't want the social stigma that came with it. As I grew up, I became keenly aware that musicals were something I wanted to hide. Even after I graduated from college and began teaching high school, I'd stand in front of my classroom, preaching to my students about embracing their identities. I'd finish my sermon and go check the Broadway chat boards on my school computer. A student would interrupt me, asking me what my favorite type of music was. I'd tell a half-truth. "Hip-hop . . . Pop . . . Anything but country," I'd tell them. But when I got in my car after school, I rarely listened to hip-hop or pop (and *never* country), even if I did enjoy those genres. I listened to Stephen Sondheim. But I couldn't tell them that Stephen Sondheim was my favorite artist. That would have been cringe. Or so I thought.

Like many musical fans, it took me far too long to embrace my inner fanboy. My story isn't unique. In *Place for Us*, D. A. Miller describes his own ritual of finding solace in his parents' basement to secretly listen to showtunes, singing along to scores from musicals of the so-called Golden Age. Miller knew that to be outed as a musical theatre fan was to be outed as gay (even if not).[21] And, from Miller's basement to my AOL chatrooms, from the fifties to the nineties and early aughts, being queer was "social suicide," to quote *Mean Girls*' Janice Ian. Being queer was marked by panic, fear, and internalized homophobia. Thus, being a musical theatre fan meant expressing it in secrecy for many years. But for many, digital technologies have altered the way that musical theatre fandom can exist, allowing it to transpire even in public-facing ways. Because musicals have gone mainstream on social media, being a musical fanboy doesn't carry the same negative valence that it might have carried when I was growing up in the 1990s. Moreover, cultural attitudes about sexuality and queerness have shifted during the same period. For the young Miller in his parents' basement, the way we engage with musicals today would be unfathomable.

My earliest memories of Broadway and the internet are of watching press reels of *Rent* (1996) on Broadway.com. They would take far too long to load, buffering along the way. But I was patient. I knew it was worth the wait. After watching a *Rent* video a few times on repeat, I'd move on to other shows. Even ones that didn't really capture my interest, did. Of course they did. I was a teen growing up far from the bright lights of Broadway, and all I wanted to do was watch a musical on a Broadway stage. But that wasn't feasible. Engaging with musicals on the internet was. From pixelated videos, I soon found chat rooms—All That Chat and Broadway World. Although I rarely posted, I was an avid reader, obsessed with learning what complete strangers thought about the musicals I had only listened to or seen performed on the Tony Awards. I may have often felt alone in my fandom, but as the penultimate number of *Into the Woods* proclaims, "No one is alone."

My fan practices growing up mirrored a robust fan culture that roots itself in all things musical theatre to shape individual and communal identities. Although our identities are complex, we are, in a word, fans.[22] In the foundational *Fan Cultures*, fan studies scholar Matt Hills defines fans as people who are "obsessed with a particular star, celebrity, film, TV programme, band; somebody who can produce reams of information on their object of fandom, and can quote their favoured lines or lyrics, chapter and verse." Hills continues, "Fans interpret media texts in a variety of interesting and perhaps unexpected ways," which often take place in community with other like-minded fans.[23] In the case of musical theatre fans, fan practices have frequently included seeing shows multiple times, memorizing cast albums, and collecting theatre memorabilia from buttons and magnets to window cards and playbills.

Like other fan cultures, the musical theatre fandom has adapted well to changing technologies. In the twenty-first century alone, musical lovers have taken to message boards, LiveJournal, Sirius XM On Broadway, YouTube, Instagram, Tumblr, and Clubhouse to perform fandom (not to mention engaging in traditional fan practices like listening to cast albums, seeing shows, and performing in high school productions). These only represent a small corner of digital spaces where musical theatre fandom flourishes. Stacy Wolf proposes that online platforms have made Broadway "universally accessible," with technology serving as "a source of information, cultural acquisition, and knowledge."[24] Although the notion of the internet as "universally" accessible disregards accessibility politics for some disabled communities (Blind, Deaf, and Hard-of-Hearing folks, for example), the internet *has* expanded accessibility at large for musical theatre fans, who use digital spaces to "perform cultural work." Fan spaces enable a communal culture to materialize, and, accordingly, they give fans the opportunity to embrace fan identities. Hills proposes that many fan identities are "improper" identities in that they are baked in celebrating something that the mainstream deems insignificant.[25] For musical fans, this mirrors how the public disregards musicals as a serious form of culture. Such critiques only see the stereotype—a land of jazz hands and kick lines. To be a musical theatre fan, then, is to embrace the stigma. Finding a community of other theatre nerds who love something so incredibly mainstream and yet that is also often represented according to the stereotype is a powerful act of resistance, one that claims musical theatre fandom as a viable identity.

As digital technologies have expanded, so, too, have the ways that musical fans perform their fandom. Musical theatre scholars, in addition to theatre and performance scholars in general, have recognized this phenomenon. Aya Esther Hayashi, Jessica Hillman-McCord, Kelly Kessler, Laura MacDonald, Holley Replogle-Wong, Kirsty Sedgman, and Stacy Wolf have forged a viable subfield within musical theatre studies that unpacks this phenomenon. MacDonald's work, for example, speaks to the breadth of musical fan practices, from digital engagement and *Hamilton* audience development to tourists as audiences at Shanghai Disneyland and university students performing *In the Heights* in China.[26] In *Changed for Good*, Wolf introduces us to the world of *Wicked* message boards, where young girls debate all things Oz, and in *Beyond Broadway*, we meet musical theatre lovers across the United States performing in amateur and educational theatre.[27] Kessler proposes that musicals have always been quick to embrace emerging digital platforms, with interventions such as *Dr. Horrible's Sing-Along Blog* and *Buffy and Firefly* facilitating an increasingly participatory culture.[28] Replogle-Wong advocates for a deeper understanding of how musical fandom shifts between the personal and the communal, two ends of the fan spectrum that are linked through the act of performance.[29] This extant scholarship demonstrates a need to both recognize and acknowledge the growing body of spaces where musical theatre lovers perform their fandom. And, as the intersections between musical theatre and mediated cultures continue to grow, so, too, will the ways that musical fans digitally express their fandom.[30]

TikTok Broadway adds to a significant body of work exploring how the internet has revolutionized all aspects of live performance and theatre-making, including the fan experience. Studies by Gabriella Giannachi, Matthew Causey, Michael Kustow, Rosemary Klich and Edward Scheer, Bill Blake, Amy Petersen Jensen, and Valerie M. Fazel and Louise Geddes have demonstrated the nuanced ways that digital media is shifting theatre practices.[31] Social media is often central to this work. Patrick Lonergan's *Theatre and Social Media* understands social media as a performance space. As such, Lonergan's work considers the various implications social media has for the way that audiences interact with professional theatre productions. Lonergan proposes that viewing social media through a performance lens encourages "new ways of thinking about authenticity, creative proprietorship, authorial intention, and the relationship between artist and audience."[32] Of particular relevance to *TikTok Broadway*, Lonergan touches on how theatre fans use social media to extend the world of theatrical productions into the digital realm. Although he is speaking of a pre-TikTok era, many of these fan practices have become normalized on social media. For example, fans use social media "to cover songs from musicals, to link moments in our own lives with events from plays that we have seen, to post photos of ourselves in costumes from favourite productions, to write messages that might appear onstage and online simultaneously, and so on." Ultimately, Lonergan questions whether the aforementioned digital fan practices empower audiences, or whether they instead enable theatre producers to exploit fan practices as free marketing.[33] As *TikTok Broadway* attests, the answer lies somewhere in the middle. TikTok fan practices bask in the gray area where the borders of creation and exploitation are muddled. Musical theatre TikTokers opt in to this community, knowing that their work contributes to the dramaturgical—and commercial—world of the musical in question. As I suggest throughout this book, to perform musical fandom is to intentionally engage in fan marketing. Musical TikTokers want to promote certain shows even if they are aware that they are performing unpaid labor to do so.

Despite the scholarly interventions from Lonergan and so many others into digital-media and theatre practices, there has yet to be an in-depth book-length study examining the relationship among digital cultures, musical theatre, and fandom as it materializes on *one* platform. But if, as Wolf writes, digital fan spaces "can reveal some clear patterns of use, engagement, and utterances of feeling," then a platform such as TikTok—with a global presence and broad impact on popular culture—merits our critical attention.[34] That is where this book comes in.

Tik, Tok . . . BOOM!

"Dr. Boffone, do you want to make a Musical.ly?" My student Luke, a theatre technician, had recently told me about Musical.ly, an app that the theatre kids at our school had been using to make short-form music videos. "Do they have any ABBA?" I replied. Of course they had ABBA. I then proceeded to do a short song and dance number in the hallway, set to "Take a Chance on Me" from the *Mamma Mia!* (2008) film soundtrack. Making short videos like this was the norm for me and my students. Musical.ly was one of a number of apps that would become part of our everyday vernacular.[35] By this point, in fall 2018, Musical.ly had already been purchased by its foreign competitor TikTok, which had used the merger to enter the US market earlier in the year. Musical.ly would soon phase out, and TikTok would phase in, becoming the most popular app among Gen Z before becoming one of the most downloaded apps in the world across all generations. The TikTok Boom was upon us.[36]

It took TikTok around eighteen months to become the dominant social media app in US culture. Owned by Chinese conglomerate ByteDance, TikTok became available to US iPhone and Android users in August 2018.[37]

It was adopted as *the* most critical site for Zoomers to spend time online, creating silly videos and memes, interacting with one another, growing their followings, and building a fervent sense of generational culture and identity in the process. As digital natives, Zoomers have only known a digital world.[38] Whereas Millennials like myself had to adjust to digital technologies as we came of age, Zoomers, largely born between 1996 and 2013, have never had to adapt. Generations before might have had soda fountains, drive-in joints, roller rinks, arcades, and malls to visit in their leisure time, but, for Zoomers, engaging with friends, popular trends, and culture formation simply requires access to a cell phone, where a host of apps dominate the social scene. Mainstays such as Instagram, Snapchat, and Twitter, along with flash-in-the-pan apps such as Among Us, Yik Yak, Kik, ooVoo, Houseparty, and BeReal, have all served as valuable spaces for Gen Z at some point.[39] But one app has ruled the roost—TikTok. In fact, over 60 percent of TikTok users are Zoomers.[40] TikTok trends have become the memes that dominate high school hallways. TikTok sound bites are today's soundtrack; trending songs on the app command the radio airwaves. TikTok popularity has led to Fleetwood Mac experiencing a renaissance, Ocean Spray cranberry juice selling out, Lady Gaga Chromatica Oreos flying off shelves, feta-cheese pasta recipes becoming kitchen staples, and a bunch of soccer moms being one of the most talked about friend groups of 2020.

This raises the question: why TikTok? If a host of other digital platforms—such as social media sites, and, of course, message boards—have served as critical sites of musical theatre fandom, why does TikTok (and not its predecessors or competitors) merit a book-length study? Of course, I do believe that other digital platforms merit more in-depth studies, but I find that TikTok's import stands alone. In 2020, as entertainment and social media practices were in flux, TikTok exploded, becoming the most downloaded app in the United States and one of the most downloaded apps of the decade. October 2020 data reveals that users open the app eight times per day, spending on average fifty-two minutes per day scrolling TikTok.[41] The app generated over $500 million in revenue in the United States in 2020 alone.[42] Having surpassed two million global downloads since its launch in China in 2016 (as of the first quarter of 2020), TikTok has achieved something even its predecessors could never have dreamed of—instant market dominance. Given TikTok's relationship with Zoomers, *TikTok Broadway* privileges young creators. Even so, this book goes beyond Gen Z. The chapters that follow explore musical theatre fandom across a span of generations, not just Gen Z but also Millennials and, every so often, Gen X and Baby Boomers.

TikTok has revolutionized fan practices. As a democratized space, TikTok shrinks the distance between fans and their potential audiences, privileges authenticity, and enables anyone to gain a following and do what everyone wants to do: go viral. In this regard, TikTok boosts content creators and facilitates community engagement around subcultures on the app. Hip-hop studies scholar Kyesha Jennings proposes that digital spaces "offer the necessary tools to create meaning that is far more visible and accessible than other [nondigital] spaces allow."[43] Indeed, digital spaces such as TikTok enable what cultural studies scholar Raymond Williams calls "formal innovation," or the process whereby new cultural forms, practices, and spaces destabilize mainstream culture. Williams proposes that it is easy to miss or dismiss this "innovation as it is happening; innovation in process."[44] In the case of TikTok, a key aspect of this cultural innovation lies in its being a democratized space, or a space that privileges open access, individuality, inclusivity, community-building, and responsiveness.

Aside from its notorious algorithm, TikTok's most successful attribute is that it combines the best parts of other Gen Z faves: "Vine's video snippets for copious amounts of content consumption; Instagram's user feeds for easily following influencers; Twitter's trending hashtags for keeping up with what's going viral."[45] Yet, to explore TikTok through these lenses would be to miss the nuance that makes the app so popular with Zoomers. Journalist Sejla Rizvic explains how the internet that came to define the Millennial experience "had grown stale, populated by overly posed pictures, inane hashtags, and SEO-friendly self-branding. TikTok promised something different: a space where a younger generation of users embraced idiosyncrasy and irreverence over conformity and overwrought styling."[46] TikTok became a place to push against trademarks of Instagram and Facebook culture, which are fashioned around presenting a certain, more idealized version of reality. TikTok content isn't as polished (read: filtered) as Instagram. It isn't as political and self-righteous as Facebook. It's not as wordy as Twitter. Rather, Rizvic suggests that TikTok is "an unruly playground" that presents us with "a new way of imagining our online lives," one that feels "extemporaneous, genuine, and convincingly human."[47] Cultural studies scholar Melanie Kennedy notes, "TikTok's particular aesthetic" is "goofiness and relatability."[48] TikTok is "a place for teens and tweens to come to be silly, unashamed, unfiltered."[49] The result is a platform that privileges authenticity; what you see is what you get. And, it should be noted that teens flock to TikTok due to the increased likelihood of going viral on the platform, compared to its social media competitors.[50]

Fan studies scholar Louisa Ellen Stein recognizes that each digital platform "develops and maintains its own community norms, expectations, and limits of code and culture."[51] TikTok is no different. Zoomers use TikTok to express ethics, aesthetics, and attitudes that become ingrained in generational culture through repetition and virality.[52] As such, Zoomer culture dictates TikTok. Even if Millennials, for example, engage with TikTok trends or create their own trending content, they inevitably engage with the culture that Zoomers have forged on the app. As always, teenagers are the trendsetters.

Gen Z has embraced the internet as a critical site for the coming-of-age experience; nowadays, in fact, TikTok users intentionally attempt virality. This is a far cry from the digital world that I grew up in, at a time when social practices on the internet were largely cloaked in anonymity. When my friends and I were coming of age in the 1990s, our parents warned us Millennials of the dark corners of the internet. We were told not to trust anyone. And, never, and I mean never, post anything about ourselves, much less give someone information about where we lived, went to school, or spent time with friends. Of course, like generations before us, we didn't listen. We became more comfortable with cyberspace as its capabilities expanded beyond our wildest imaginations. As my generation moved into social media practices that showcased our lives, we remained dedicated to producing a certain type of content that kept up appearances. We wanted our lives to seem aspirational. We wanted people to like pictures of us traveling to exotic destinations or seeing the hottest concert. We wanted them to see how picture perfect our new relationship was. At every turn, we wanted to highlight the positives in our lives, while aggressively suppressing the negatives on social media. Zoomers shifted this culture entirely. No longer is the internet a place to promote a heightened identity performance. Rather, Zoomer-influenced culture rejects superficiality and filtered depictions of reality. Zoomer aesthetics offer a constant stream of selfies and vlogs, where teens' physical appearances and personalities are on full display.

Accordingly, TikTok is a space to build community in a way that other popular apps don't necessarily allow. This is how TikTok operates as a democratized space. The algorithm helps users find the community, rather than necessitating that users seek it out. The algorithm knows. That is, because of the algorithm, users are fed a constant stream of content tailored to their specific interests, geographic location, and interactions with videos on their FYP. For example, as soon as I watched the initial *A Chorus Line* TikTok of Christopher Rice dancing "I Hope I Get It," I began teaching the algorithm about my interests in musical theatre and, more specifically, *A Chorus Line*. The algorithm studied how many times I viewed the video, how much time I spent on the video, and what I did with the video: favoriting it, sharing it, liking it, and commenting on it. It didn't take TikTok long to recognize that this was content I wanted to engage with. My experience is common. TikTokers have stories of how shockingly accurate the content on their FYPs is, from geographic location to niche interests that even their best friends don't know about; nearly every journalist acknowledges this in the growing body of TikTok journalism. What this does is begin the process of situating TikTok as a community space. And what every community needs is a clear sense of who belongs. Rizvic suggests that TikTok creates "the feeling of intimacy and immediacy between users."[53] Intimacy and immediacy enable the sense that niche communities such as musical theatre TikTok are indeed a "place for us." These communities do fundamental work to foster a collective sense of generational culture and identity. In the case of TikTok Broadway, Zoomer and Millennial musical theatre fans use the app to find like-minded theatre nerds, disseminate fandom, geek out, and strengthen their sense of identity. In Rodgers and Hammerstein's *Cinderella*, the title character longs for a space of her own. She sings, "In my own little corner / In my own little chair / I can be whatever I want to be." While Cinderella imagines the different worlds she can escape to and the different identities she can embody, musical theatre fans need not long for this imagined future. With TikTok, they can become a "thief in Calcutta," a "queen in Peru," a "mermaid dancing upon the sea," and a "huntress on an African safari."[54] All they need is a cell phone, TikTok, and their imagination.

But just as productions of *Cinderella* face criticism—the cultural stereotypes in the lyrics certainly don't help—TikTok has its critics. And I am no stranger to these critiques.[55] In *Renegades*, I argued that TikTok is a White space.[56] It's not just that the majority of the app's most followed accounts belong to White Zoomers who fit into conventional Western beauty standards; the app's internal politics also reflect systems of White supremacy that try to suppress communities of color in addition to other marginalized peoples. That is, as much as TikTok operates as a democratized space, it is not utopian. Democratization is indeed a fraught issue. While progress and inclusion are characteristics of the app, which perhaps casts a wider net than its predecessors, it is still a space that has been problematic in its supposedly egalitarian playing field. Leaked internal documents from March 2020 reveal that TikTok encouraged app moderators to suppress, or shadowban, any content that wasn't aspirational.[57] Aspirational, in the case of TikTok, is to be White, young, attractive, and wealthy. Anyone who doesn't fit the bill faces extra challenges on the app. In a similar vein, TikTok banned the hashtag #Intersex in February 2021, shutting off the ability of the Intersex community to engage with the app's full potential as an affinity space. Media studies scholar Jessica Sage Rauchberg sees TikTok's shadowbanning practices of disabled creators as "digital eugenics."[58] Indeed, TikTok's imbalanced power issues parallel the ways new technologies can bolster Whiteness and further social inequality. This is supported by landmark studies from Safiya Umoja Noble and Ruha Benjamin, who advocate for a deeper understanding of the intersections between race and technology. In *Algorithms of Oppression*, Noble demonstrates how search algorithms "reflect the values and norms" of those who create them.[59] In this case, systems such as White supremacy can become baked into algorithms. In *Race after Technology*, Benjamin uses the term "New Jim Code" to encompass "the employment of new technologies that reflect and reproduce existing inequalities but are promoted and perceived as more objective or progressive than the discriminatory systems of a previous era."[60] Fan studies scholar Elizabeth Ellcessor affirms that we must be aware of the power imbalances when discussing fan platforms, as well, since digital platforms "often build in particular forms of behavior and expression while making others difficult, and they are often constructed in accordance with dominant cultural ideologies, technological practices, and economic structures."[61]

Despite how rampant Whiteness runs on TikTok, the app has still been a critical site for activist work to take place.[62] The app played a key role in helping Black Lives Matter protesters organize during the summer of 2020. People on the ground uploaded video content of police brutality, quickly circulating it and raising awareness of the issues as they were happening. Moreover, teenagers used TikTok to book over one million tickets to Donald Trump's Tulsa rally on June 20, 2020, leading event organizers to believe the rally would need an overflow space. When only a couple thousand Trump supporters showed up in Tulsa, it became clear that Gen Z had found a hole in the Trump campaign. This energy continued with the Black TikTok Strike in June 2021. When Megan Thee Stallion's "Thot Shit" hit the radio airwaves, Black creators collectively sat this one out, forgoing the usually Black choreographic TikTok culture and conveying just how much White TikTokers rely on the creativity of Black TikTokers to go viral.[63] These digital activist efforts collectively reveal how TikTok can serve as an activist space to spur critical conversations on social justice, conversations that have analog effects.

Given these points, I ask: what does it mean for TikTok to be a space that reinforces problematic power dynamics while also being a welcoming home to musical theatre fans? It's not lost on me that much of the archive of TikTok Broadway focuses on White content creators and, by extension, Whiteness. This mirrors how the Broadway musical has historically been a vector for Whiteness. As Hoffman proves in *The Great White Way*, even musicals without any discussion of race are inevitably about Whiteness. Whether it is *The Music Man*, *Next to Normal*, or *Dear Evan Hansen*, much of the Broadway canon that claims to be race neutral is anything but neutral when it comes to race. When race isn't explicitly mentioned, White is the default, reinforcing Whiteness as the norm and consequently White supremacy as the prevailing power structure.

Welcome to TikTok Broadway

As TikTok has taken over the global social media market, musical theatre, too, has grown on the platform. While *Beetlejuice*, *Heathers: The Musical*, and *Six* were mainstays in the early days of TikTok in the United States, musicals such as *Hamilton*, *Newsies* (2012), *Mamma Mia!* (1999), *The Lightning Thief*, *Wicked* (2003), *Frozen* (2018), and the collectively generated *Ratatouille* have all become integral parts of musical theatre TikTok. This cohort of musicals make up their own digital theatre community, TikTok Broadway, in a way that is reminiscent of (if not fully comparable to) how the Richard Rodgers, the Belasco, the Gershwin, and the St. James Theatres constitute the Broadway theatre district in New York City. TikTok Broadway is a collection of trends on TikTok that riff off musical theatre, sometimes within the context of the show, but other times in a way devoid of the show's original context. The app is home to a growing community of adept, young social media users who use the platform to engage with musical theatre fandom, at times even doing so unconsciously. As a democratized fan space, TikTok Broadway eschews several core tenets of commercial Broadway theatre, such as competition, rejections, and expensive tickets. In this digital world, musical theatre isn't cost prohibitive. It's accessible to everyone. There are no barriers.

TikTok Broadway privileges creativity, while helping fans find their fandoms and embrace their fan identities. Within this space, the archive of TikTok Broadway is a complex collection of musical theatre fandom and, as an extension, can "reveal some clear patterns of use, engagement, and utterances of feeling."[64] As media studies scholar Andreas Schellewald proposes, TikTok videos, although ephemeral, "present themselves not as random and short-lived entertainment but as complex, cultural artifacts."[65] Using this lens, we can begin to consider what musical theatre content on the platform reveals about fan identity formation and musical theatre engagement in the TikTok Age. This archive of cultural artifacts is expansive. Popular TikTok Broadway trends can facilitate hundreds of thousands of videos. Hashtags such as #MammaMia, #Wicked, #Hamilton, and #TheLionKing can lead to archives with hundreds of millions of video views (*Mamma Mia!* and *Wicked*) and even billions of views (*Hamilton* and *The Lion King*). Even smaller, more niche trends such as the *Newsies* "Seize the Day" Challenge (#NewsiesDanceChallenge) have garnered over thirty thousand videos. Although this is a blip on the radar in the world of TikTok, this is a considerable number of musical theatre fans recreating, viewing, and interacting with Christopher Gattelli's Tony Award–winning choreography. And it's just the tip of the TikTok Broadway archive.

It should not be surprising, then, that TikTok would become a home for musical theatre fandom. TikTok Broadway facilitates what Amy Petersen Jensen refers to as a "participatory spectator," who, "influenced by interactions with media forms, has learned to advance theatrical narratives beyond the threshold of the theatre space into their own private space."[66] In *Changed for Good*, Wolf confirms that digital spaces enable the self-expression of theatre fans, serving as "valuable sources to understand reception."[67] Wolf acknowledges the overwhelming nature of Broadway fan platforms, and TikTok is no exception. As Hillman-McCord notes, "Attending a live musical is now only a fraction of the experience a fan may have with a musical."[68] According to journalist Zachary Pincus-Roth, in the TikTok Age, "the most exciting theater is a figment of our imagination." In this "new ecosystem of musical theater fan fiction," "creativity flourishes in unpredictable ways."[69] By the same token, multimedia director and designer Jared Mezzocchi posits that TikTok performances have deeply affected the theatre industry, adding, "Theater is thriving when you step outside of the definition that it must be a certain length and in a venue."[70] Musicologist Elizabeth L. Wollman notes, "musical theater has by necessity repeatedly reinvented itself to fit the needs of its ever-changing audience," which has helped musicals grow in popularity across the globe, no doubt in part thanks to the capabilities of digital platforms.[71] Indeed, as Wolf proposes, "the Broadway musical truly lives beyond Broadway."[72]

TikTok Broadway makes musical theatre popular and mainstream again, much like musicals were in the 1940s and 1950s with popular stage titles such as *Guys and Dolls* (1950), *West Side Story*, and *The Music Man* (1957), not to mention films such as *An American in Paris* (1951), *Singing in the Rain* (1952), and *Gentlemen Prefer Blondes* (1953). This phenomenon sees musicals and musical theatre sound bites cement themselves into the Gen Z lexicon and Zoomer meme culture. As such, this movement makes TikTok Broadway part of cultural literacies. This cultural effect shouldn't be surprising. Musical theatre scholar Barrie Gelles demonstrates how musicals are "imbedded in media culture," something exacerbated in recent years with an explosion of movie musicals and television series that engage in musicalness.[73] As such, TikTok exemplifies how musical theatre intersects with popular culture. It is noteworthy that TikTok makes musical theatre accessible to demographics that wouldn't necessarily have access to theatre in a traditional way. To engage with TikTok Broadway, a fan doesn't need to spend hundreds of dollars on tickets. They just need a cell phone, internet, and TikTok to have access to the world of digital fandom. And, making musical theatre TikToks is fun (to say the least), allowing fans a form of escapism.

TikTok Broadway content covers much aesthetic and thematic ground. While some content creators use the platform to perform musical theatre cosplay and drag, other creators recreate their favorite Broadway choreography from the comfort of their living rooms. Some savvy creators marry popular TikTok trends with the musical theatre canon, enabling TikTok Broadway content to extend far beyond the TikTok Broadway subcommunity. Other creators showcase their musical theatre knowledge: Broadway Bob flexes his Sondheim trivia muscles; composer Pablo David Laucerica plays the piano while teaching about the composition of some of our favorite showtunes.[74] Or take JJ Nieman (see Figure I.3 and Figure I.4), for instance, who spills the tea about the backstage practices of Broadway chorus members.[75] Shoebox Musicals recreates well-known scenic designs from *Beetlejuice* and *Wicked*, offering a nightly live performance that includes sound effects, fog machines, and lighting design on scenic design models.[76] Alexa Chalnick plays

Figures I.3 and I.4 Niemann pokes fun at the backstage practices of musical ensembles. Posted on September 23, 2021.

showtunes on her piano, encouraging her followers to duet the video and sing along.[77] She even holds auditions for nonexistent musical productions, soliciting videos, choosing the best, and posting the cast list. Katie Johantgen uses TikTok to post musical spoof videos. Installments such as "How to run offstage if you're a guy in a musical," "How to write a letter if you're in a musical," and "How to open a door if you're in a musical" have been popular, opening up a robust conversation on TikTok about musical theatre stereotypes.[78] As these examples convey, the possibilities of fan expression on TikTok are endless.

As the spectrum of TikTok Broadway content continues to expand, an emerging group of theatre "critics" have taken to using TikTok as a vlogging platform to discuss musical theatre press releases, reviews of new shows, advice about seeing different musicals, and, of course, hot takes. This #TheatreTok cohort features something for every musical theatre lover on TikTok. There's Bryan the Business Analyst, who unpacks the weekly Broadway grosses and the oftentimes confusing financials of commercial theatre.[79] Ashley Hufford, Kate Reinking, and Katherine Quinn use TikTok to vlog about their experiences seeing (a lot) of musical theatre across the United States and abroad.[80] Being the theatre lovers they are, this trio often peels back the curtain into their fandom, showing audiences intense spreadsheets about theatre trips, show openings and closings, and Sondheim bucket-list shows. Much like former theatre critic Broadway Bob, Brandon Powers takes a more dramaturgical approach, using his TikTok as a virtual classroom from which to educate his followers about musical theatre history, choreography, direction, and larger trends in the TikTok Broadway community.[81] And, speaking of dramaturgy, look no further than dramaturg Grace Walker, whose TikTok account is perhaps the most effective example of what possibilities TikTok facilitates for digital dramaturgy.[82] Given TikTok's sizable user base, it should be no surprise that these theatre vloggers are a mere fraction of the theatre fans who use TikTok as a launching pad for digital theatre criticism and conversation starters.[83]

TikTokian fan expressions are not limited to explicit engagements with musical theatre content. Rather, for every obvious video engaging with *Wicked* or *Beetlejuice*, there is a counterarchive of undercover musical theatre fandom taking place on TikTok. I use the term *stealth musicals* to underscore how some musicals penetrate TikTok's mainstream culture in a way that is entirely divorced from the dramaturgy of the musical itself. *Heathers* and *Six*, the two musicals I discuss in this context, create pop culture divorced from the musical, thus expanding the ways that TikTokers engage with musical theatre. When sound bites from these musicals go viral, users from far outside of musical theatre fandoms engage with them, oftentimes without recognizing their source material. Even these "unknowing" engagements with musical theatre still lead to the canonization of particular musicals. Although these TikTokers would hardly claim musical theatre as one of their fandoms or TikTok communities, by mimicking or engaging with a popular stealth musical TikTok trend, they nevertheless contribute to the growing community of TikTok Broadway.

And, of course, TikTok is home to a growing number of musical theatre stars, who use the app to extend their brand and fan interactions. Although this book doesn't focus on Broadway icons such as Laura Benanti, Kristin Chenoweth, Idina Menzel, or Mandy Patinkin, the ways they have used TikTok have been integral to this conversation and, accordingly, merit our critical attention. In a similar vein, TikTok is now an essential part of a Broadway musical's social media marketing plan; it's no longer just an option. Before Broadway's shutdown, *Beetlejuice, Hamilton, The Lightning Thief*, and *Six* were successful in using TikTok to promote their brand and interact with fans. When the Broadway shutdown ended in August 2021, the culture had shifted, with nearly every Broadway musical having an official TikTok account.

The explosion of TikTok Broadway has had reverberations far beyond the theatre community. Per usual on TikTok, as TikTok Broadway grew in popularity, so too did its reach into TikTok's mainstream, and later into general popular culture in the United States. In many ways, this mirrors *Hamilton*'s crossover success beginning in 2015. Not surprisingly, some see this as another opportunity to make fun of the expressiveness of musical theatre fans. In June 2020, well before musical theatre exploded on TikTok, the *Onion* published a satirical article in which TikTok apologizes for accidentally giving theatre kids a new platform:

> Expressing their sincerest regret for the massive oversight, video-sharing app TikTok issued an apology Monday after inadvertently giving a platform to thousands of theater kids. "Rumors that users are exploiting our service to perform *A Star Is Born* covers are deeply disturbing, and we're very sorry we've allowed this to happen," said CEO Kevin A. Mayer, who explained the company never intended their app to fall into clutches of individuals who spend their entire weekend memorizing the soundtrack and choreography of *Dear Evan Hansen*. "TikTok was devised as a harmless way for hot, popular teens to have fun. Elaborate harmonies and costuming have no home on TikTok. TikTok is no place for using a split screen to sing a duet with yourself in full *Wicked* makeup. Honestly, it's sickening that these videos are circulating, and we're going to do everything in our power to crack down on the users responsible." At press time, Mayer added that the app's moderators would begin flagging all videos that feature dancing.[84]

Given that the *Onion* is the country's most well-known satirical news site, this article reveals much about musical theatre reception on TikTok and beyond. This musical theatre fan culture isn't relegated to the dark corners of Broadway discussion boards or Tumblr. Rather, TikTok Broadway lives within the mainstream in a way that most musical fan communities do not. The *Onion*'s satire demonstrates how this TikTok subculture can't be contained to *just* its digital white way. It goes much further.

Personalization, Virality, Afterlife

TikTok Broadway is possible because of how TikTok divides the app into subcultures. There's DracoTok, which focuses on all things Draco Malfoy from *Harry Potter*. There's CottageCore, which romanticizes farm life. There's WitchTok, BookTok, ASMR TikTok, Willy Wonka TikTok, and FrogTok.[85] There's a TikTok subculture for everything. These TikTok communities are typically self-aware that they belong to a nonnormative space on the app. Matt Hills claims, "Fans are fans because fan communities exist and can be entered."[86] Labeling subcategories on TikTok helps personalization take place, giving fans an entry point into emerging fan cultures. App users will often comment on a video, "commenting so I can stay on *Wicked* TikTok," both to declare to their fellow TikTokers that this is a space for them and to tell the algorithm that they want similar content on their FYP. These users want a more specific TikTok experience that better matches their identity.[87] Social media scholar Crystal Abidin refers to this type of behavior as "algorithmic practices," in which TikTokers engage "in patterned and routine behaviour in the belief that their repeated actions will persuade and trigger the platform's algorithm to work in their favour."[88] Accordingly, the more a TikToker wants to "stay" in (i.e., belong to) one of the app's subcultures, the more they will engage with posts belonging to that community.

In *Making It Personal*, Tanya Kant proposes that digital spaces privilege personalization as a way for platforms to grant users an online experience catered to them. Kant adds that social media platforms collect users' data in various ways, and, as such, "your needs and interests can be algorithmically inferred and your experience 'conveniently'—and computationally—personalized on your behalf."[89] TikTok does this through its powerful algorithm and the FYP, the app's default landing page, which is "one of the most addictive scrolling experiences on the Internet."[90] Whereas the landing page for other social media sites like Instagram and Twitter is a collection of content the user has chosen to follow, the TikTok FYP gives users content specifically targeted to them based on their engagement with the algorithm.

As users begin a TikTok session, they are met with auto-play content that the algorithm assumes they will enjoy and interact with. TikTok content appears endless. Schellewald affirms that TikTok videos "are, in fact, looping by default. Once they have been watched, they automatically start over again."[91] As the loop continues, the algorithm homes in on the personalization process, feeding audiences a stream of content increasingly tailored to their various interests. Media studies scholar Andrea Ruehlicke proposes that TikTok "represents a new development in how we think and talk about personalization in virtual spaces."[92] The level of personalization separates TikTok from its competitors and fosters a proliferation of subcultures.

Personalization enables subcultures such as TikTok Broadway to exist in such a way that fans *know* they are a part of the community. On the one hand, TikTokers follow accounts they enjoy. On the other hand, the algorithm feeds users an endless stream of videos it knows they will enjoy, cementing the community in the process. This is how TikTok organizes subcultures and, in turn, institutionalizes them. As an organized fandom, TikTok Broadway is, to quote fan scholar Henry Jenkins, "an institution of theory and criticism, a semi-structured space where competing interpretations and evaluations of common texts are proposed, debated, and negotiated and where readers speculate about the nature of the mass media and their own relationship to it."[93] As TikTok spectators engage in this process, they unconsciously contribute to the virality of a particular video. Once TikTokers upload content, the algorithm tests it out with small pods. Based on this performance with its given focus group, the video either fizzles down or expands its reach. With each share, comment, like, favorite, and view, TikTokers teach the algorithm about what they're interested in and about what videos *should* see more life on the app.

Although other social media sites—in particular, Instagram and Twitter—are known for virality, TikTok is distinct because of how the algorithm enables content to remain viral far after what would otherwise be its expiration date.[94] The process of virality mirrors how fandoms, according to Hills, create fandom rules that attempt "to build up different types of fan skill, knowledge, and distinction."[95] In this case, engaging in musical theatre TikTok challenges makes them trend. Trending content, in turn, accumulates various forms of engagement (likes, comments, views, etc.). As this process continues and the (supposed) cream rises to the top, musical theatre is canonized on the platform and the videos go viral, penetrating the app's mainstream before "spill[ing] over into other social platforms and mainstream media."[96] This viral content then becomes memes, which form cultural literacies.[97] To recognize these memes and partake in "meme speak" is to engage with the phenomenon of virality. All told, then, musical theatre content holds the potential to leave TikTok and enter mainstream meme culture as experienced on other social media apps as well as in offline spaces. This is the power of TikTok virality.

Throughout the case studies in this book, I unpack how virality factors into the TikTok Broadway archive. As the following chapters reveal, virality has worked differently for *Beetlejuice* than it has for *Ratatouille: The TikTok Musical*. *Wicked* follows a different pattern than *Heathers: The Musical* and *Six*. In these cases, virality depends on the content leaving its subculture and enter the app's mainstream, where any casual TikToker regardless of their (lack of) interest in musicals will see it. Although these videos can be narrow in focus, oftentimes they are videos with crossover appeal. That is, content that plays with *Hamilton*, *Wicked*, *Mamma Mia!*, or *Rent* has a higher likelihood of going viral on TikTok than do videos living in the world of *Follies* (1971), *The Band's Visit* (2017), *Passing Strange*, or *Fun Home*. At the end of the day, the music of ABBA and the imagery of the Wicked Witch of the West are thoroughly embedded in popular culture. Sally Durant Plummer and Phyllis Rogers Stone (both from *Follies*) are not. While any musical theatre content can thrive within the confines of TikTok Broadway, its potential to cross over into the mainstream and achieve true virality depends on brand appeal and name recognition. Here, TikTok isn't too far from Broadway's commercialism: regardless of comparative quality, *Wicked* has a brand that extends far beyond the stage show in a way that musicals such as *Passing Strange* will likely never experience.

TikTok virality enables musical theatre sound bites and, by extension, musicals to enter what theatre scholar Jonathan Miller calls the "afterlife."[98] Although Miller is referring here to how Shakespeare's plays are canonized, I find his analysis helpful in unpacking the ways that a viral trend not only goes viral but *stays* viral and, as such, becomes a canonical piece of internet culture, especially youth cultures. Each subsequent video performance builds a body of work that accounts for a digital musical theatre challenge's afterlife. The larger this body of work becomes, the more likely it is that the challenge's afterlife will lead to canonization, extending the musical's cultural capital and public life. The case studies that follow speak to this to varying degrees. For example, as *Heathers: The Musical* (Chapter 2) demonstrates, its prolific afterlife and sustained collection of repetitions on TikTok have meant that cultural capital continues to accrue. As a result, sound bites such as "Martha Dumptruck in the flesh" enter into a public life extending beyond the musical itself. Indeed, quoting "Martha Dumptruck in the flesh" is as synonymous with Gen Z as it is with the musical *Heathers*: it signifies normality and coolness. It elicits cultural capital that shapes a sense of generational belonging and community. In the same way, as *Ratatouille* the TikTok experiment became *Ratatouille: The TikTok Musical* (Chapter 4), its public life left TikTok entirely, becoming ingrained in the cultural zeitgeist. *Ratatouille* was featured on countless media outlets in the United States in the lead-up to its famed benefit concert. It circulated across all social media platforms. As these repetitions accumulated, *Ratatouille* developed afterlives that canonized it. The case studies of *Heathers: The Musical* and *Ratatouille: The TikTok Musical* are just the starting point. Each musical within the larger TikTok Broadway archive has its own unique afterlife.

Given the expansiveness of TikTok, musical theatre's afterlife can seem endless. According to theatre scholar Alicia Corts, this mirrors the unique capabilities of virtual performance spaces: "we experience ways of performing that step outside the boundaries of the physical world, giving the illusion that virtual performance is unlimited."[99] TikTok is unlimited. Repetition and virality "give the illusion" that there is no end to TikTok Broadway. In fact, you can scroll with no end in sight. You are only limited by your phone's battery and your attention span. As such, musical afterlives offer new possibilities to connect with musicals, something especially true for young Zoomer fans, who aren't limited by analog in a way that previous generations were. By prioritizing musical theatre as an integral part of identity formation, young musical fans demonstrate how musical theatre can become canonized in a digital space. Although musicals such as *Beetlejuice*, *Heathers: The Musical*, *The Lightning Thief*, and *Be More Chill* (2019) might not have achieved critical success (when they premiered in New York, at least), their digital afterlives have changed the narrative, cementing these shows in the musical theatre canon.

Chapter Organization

In the introduction to *The Routledge Companion to the Contemporary Musical*, Jessica Sternfeld and Elizabeth L. Wollman propose, "Like virtually all popular entertainment forms, musicals don't merely reflect the world; they can help shape it, change it, and make it a happier, move livable place for fans worldwide."[100] The case studies in *TikTok Broadway* reveal the nuances of how musical theatre engagement on TikTok has shifted the musical theatre industry at large. As much as this book is about musical theatre, it's also about how Gen Z is reshaping US popular culture, the result of which has been a thriving fan community for musical lovers.

Each chapter highlights a broad category of TikTok Broadway. Additionally, four interludes emphasize manifestations of the TikTok Broadway archive that, while not as robust as the case studies in the four chapters, further speak to the ways that TikTok hosts fan practices. A comprehensive overview of the TikTok Broadway archive would be impossible to achieve due to the expanses (and perpetual expansions) of the TikTok universe. Even so, clear patterns emerge. Throughout this book, I understand these categories and corresponding trends as identity blueprints. That is, when TikTokers mimic, recreate, and riff off musical theatre trends, they are engaging with existing identity blueprints and, thus, performing identity.[101] This approach is informed by media studies scholars Howard Gardner and Katie Davis, who propose that social media apps are "identity templates and also opportunities to create a more unique, stronger identity."[102] TikTok, therefore, forges new spaces for musical theatre fans to be creative and mold their identity around this creativity. This is especially true for teenagers, who are still in the throes of coming of age. For these young musical fans, TikTok Broadway serves a critical purpose.

Chapter 1, "Marketing Musicals the TikTok Way: The Unexpected Case of *Beetlejuice*," begins where TikTok Broadway first began—*Beetlejuice*. This chapter explores how the internet and social media have helped drive Broadway and its fan engagement. The chapter questions how the norms of Gen Z culture and the TikTok interface and aesthetic changed that game. And, how does the ultimate rise of *Beetlejuice* reflect this? The musical's journey from critical failure to commercial success is closely tied to its rise and perseverance as a TikTok commodity. Indeed, even as the musical opened to lukewarm reviews and a tepid box-office advance, a legion of musical theatre fans began engaging with the musical's dramaturgy on TikTok, facilitating the musical's rise to the top of the app's FYP, creating a robust body of *Beetlejuice* afterlives, and, ultimately, rendering the musical's Broadway production a commercial success. *Beetlejuice* as a case study facilitates a discussion of how fans can claim agency through TikTok, even holding the power to make a musical turn a profit and perhaps become a long-running show. As such, this chapter unpacks the relationship among digital fan performances, the dramaturgical world of a musical on TikTok, and the thing that makes Broadway tick—turning a profit.

Extending the ways that *Beetlejuice* revolutionized Broadway marketing practices, the book's first interlude reveals how musical theatre TikTokers use the platform as a digital stage door to peel back the curtain and bring fans backstage into the world of musical theatre. I focus on popular TikToker Amber Ardolino, whose interactive, fan-centered TikTok account positioned her as one of *Hamilton*'s most approachable stars when Broadway reopened in fall 2021.

In Chapter 2, "Stealth Musicals: The TikTok Broadway Archive from *Heathers* to *Six*," I question how musicals become memes, a practice that solidifies musicals as central to popular culture. This chapter explores two popular trends from TikTok's Golden Age that make use of sound bites from original cast recordings of Broadway musicals. Contrary to *Beetlejuice* TikTok trends, which lived within the dramaturgical world of the musical, the "Martha Dumptruck in the flesh" challenge from *Heathers: The Musical* and the "Yeah that didn't work out" challenge from *Six* were, by and large, detached from the musicals. These musicals became what I term *stealth musicals*, or undercover musicals that proliferate on TikTok in ways that are removed from their dramaturgy. With viral canonization, *Heathers: The Musical* and *Six* demonstrate how cultural capital accrues in digital spaces, and, as a result, how sound bites such as "Martha Dumptruck in the flesh" enter a public life that extends beyond the musical itself.

The second interlude explores how the dance call for the Muny's summer 2022 production of *Legally Blonde* went viral, becoming a micro trend among musical theatre fans on TikTok before spilling over into Facebook and Twitter and becoming the talk of the theatre community. The *Legally Blonde* dance call's unexpected virality speaks to how video dance auditions align with TikTok's dance-challenge culture. As such, the Muny dance call blurred lines between TikTok challenges and actual auditions, with many dancers even commenting that they weren't sure whether they were actually auditioning for the production (spoiler alert: they weren't).

Chapter 3, "DIY Diva Drag: *Wicked*'s Elphaba on the TikTok Stage," explores TikTok's DIY drag culture as it intersects with the mega musical *Wicked*. Specifically, this chapter questions how TikTok facilitates identity performances that extend offline queer fan practices. Although *Wicked*

TikTok content runs the gamut, there is a noticeable trend of queer men performing Elphaba drag to the musical's rousing act 1 finale, "Defying Gravity." These TikTokers engage in what I call *DIY drag*, or TikTokian drag performances that make use of quotidian objects to achieve a fully fledged drag performance. In the case of Elphaba drag, a towel, bed sheet, and a Swiffer WetJet achieve the same results as an extensive drag costume and makeup routine. As this chapter conveys, drag is native to TikTok, having been a core aesthetic of the app since its debut in the United States. TikTok normalizes drag culture, thus forging spaces in which queer men can engage in drag performances as part of the mainstream, normalized, and expected culture.

The third interlude shifts the focus to another role-playing culture—cosplay, or the fan practice of dressing in character costumes. Using my own cosplay experiences as a point of departure, I explore how the *Mamma Mia!* fandom uses TikTok as a virtual playground to display their love for all things ABBA. As a silly place to cosplay, TikTok is a virtual answer to traditional cosplay sites like Comic-Con (or, in the case of musical theatre, BroadwayCon). Accordingly, TikTok expands the breadth of opportunities that musical theatre fans have to cosplay and imagine themselves as their favorite musical characters.

The book's final chapter, "Anyone Can Cook, Anyone Can Create: *Ratatouille: The TikTok Musical*," unpacks how TikTok enables fans to crowdsource new musicals, which can, in turn, extend the life of TikTok Broadway far beyond the platform. By means of the algorithm, TikTok allows anyone to create. Aspiring musical theatre artists from composers and designers to actors and dancers joined the #RatatouilleMusical community by creating TikTok videos, using the appropriate hashtags, dueting one another, commenting on one another's videos, and the like. The typical process of building a musical was flipped on its head. This was of the people by the people for the people. This was something new, something different, and throughout the lead-up to the benefit concert, the musical theatre community took notice. What was this recipe that was changing musical theatre creation at a time when musical theatre development had all but ceased? Ultimately, as *Ratatouille: The TikTok Musical* illustrates, the question is not *can* a TikTok meme-musical become a fully fledged Broadway musical, but, *how* does TikTok make this form of fandom a reality?

The last interlude talks about the one thing we aren't supposed to talk about—Bruno. Following the Disney+ release of *Encanto* in December

2021, the film's soundtrack became TikTok's latest sonic playground. The soundtrack's signature song, "We Don't Talk about Bruno," rode TikTok popularity to the coveted spot on the Billboard Hot 100. The popularity of "We Don't Talk about Bruno" on TikTok crystalizes many of the themes explored throughout *TikTok Broadway*. That is, "We Don't Talk about Bruno" became a critical site for musical fans to engage in a variety of digital practices that cemented their fannish identities, facilitated *Encanto*'s commercial success, and expanded the ways in which musicals can be a source of creativity.

The book's conclusion explores how the musical *KPOP* engaged with TikTok as the musical became one of the biggest commercial flops of the twenty-first century (despite its artistic merit). Although *KPOP* began its TikTok journey with limited buzz, the production shifted gears, even as the show was struggling to sell tickets. Under the direction of TikToker Brandon Powers, *KPOP*'s TikTok account began to create authentic TikTok content that highlighted many of the styles, aesthetics, and genres explored throughout *TikTok Broadway*. As *KPOP* leaned in to TikTok trends, dance challenges, digital stage doors, DIY aesthetics, behind-the-scenes development footage, and the like, the show began to amass a digital following. The experiment was short lived: the production closed after just sixteen performances. But *KPOP* ended its run with a TikTok Boom—the musical live streamed the show's final fifteen minutes on TikTok. The TikTok live stream was perhaps *KPOP*'s most significant mark on Broadway, igniting industry conversations about the potential of social media live streaming to bring musical theatre directly to its fans' cell phones.

Indeed, as musicals like *KPOP* reveal, TikTok isn't just a fun way for fans to engage with musical theatre. TikTok can be the revolution. TikTok can be a radical space for musical theatre fandom in the digital age.

1
Marketing Musicals the TikTok Way

The Unexpected Case of *Beetlejuice*

On March 30, 1988, director Tim Burton's career skyrocketed with one of the unlikeliest of hit films. It had all the makings of a flop: script development issues, dark subject matter, comedy where it couldn't possibly work, and an off-putting title character. The film in question? *Beetlejuice*. *Beetlejuice* flips the horror genre on its head, questioning what it would be like for the ghosts to be good and the humans to be bad.[1] What does a ghost story look like when audiences undoubtedly root for the ghosts? Well, evidently it looks like success. *Beetlejuice* has become ingrained in US popular culture. Even those who haven't seen the film can inevitably identify the film's repulsive-yet-charismatic title character. Just say his name three times in succession, and there's no turning back.

Beetlejuice.
Beetlejuice.
Beetlejuice.

Beetlejuice tells the story of Adam and Barbara Maitland, a recently deceased couple who just want to live in peace in their quaint Victorian home in Winter River, Connecticut. When tacky yuppies Charles and Delia Deetz and their goth daughter, Lydia, move in, Adam and Barbara's afterlives are upended as they try to save their home from Delia's tasteless renovations. To their rescue? None other than Betelgeuse, a mischievous poltergeist who lives in a miniature model of Winter River in the attic.[2] All Adam and Barbara must do is say his name three times in a row to unleash mayhem on the Deetz family and return to their picture-perfect afterlife. The result is a comedic, sleezy, weird, and shockingly charming film that has been canonized as not just a cult classic, but a *classic* classic. Jacob Stolworthy affirms, "*Beetlejuice* takes the subject of death and turns it on its head, presenting not only an alternative version of the haunted house film, but also the afterlife. In the film, it's presented as . . . well, not too dissimilar from reality. Just far dustier."[3] Tim Burton adds,

"The movie's view is that when you die, your problems aren't taken care of. We tried to portray the afterlife as a cheap science fiction movie; not as clouds in a beautiful sky but an IRS office." The film was an unexpected commercial and critical success, grossing $73.7 million in North America against a budget of $15 million—only $1 million of which went to visual effects.[4] Much like TikTok aesthetics, the effects in *Beetlejuice* were, according to Burton, intended to appear "cheap and purposely fake-looking," much like the B movies he grew up watching. The film makes use of obvious practical effects such as stop-motion, puppetry, prosthetic makeup, and replacement animation.[5]

Although *Beetlejuice* might not sound particularly kid friendly, the film was in fact a substantial hit with young people. The film led to an animated series and a popular stage show at Universal Studios Theme Parks.[6] Just over three decades later, *Beetlejuice* would once again prove popular with young people—but not by design. Riding the wave of hit films turned into musicals, *Beetlejuice* was adapted for the stage as a Broadway musical with music and lyrics by Eddie Perfect and book by Scott Brown and Anthony King. *Beetlejuice* the musical made its way from development to an out-of-town tryout at the National Theatre in Washington, DC, in October 2018, to a Broadway opening on April 25, 2019. Throughout this journey, the musical was not heavily marketed toward families or young people in the way that shows such as *The Lion King* (1997), *Aladdin* (2014), *Be More Chill*, and *The Lightning Thief* have been. Sure, *Beetlejuice* as a commercial property has proven family friendly time and again, but this musical wasn't supposed to be the next Broadway show riding on the success of ticket sales to adolescent theatregoers. And then the TikTok revolution happened. In late 2019, as TikTok was experiencing exponential growth in the US market, *Beetlejuice* landed on the app. Regardless of what subculture of TikTok users belonged to, they soon found videos from *Beetlejuice* on their For You Page (FYP). TikTok—and Broadway—would never be the same.

In this chapter, I focus on the origins of TikTok Broadway—*Beetlejuice*. The musical's journey from critical failure to commercial success is closely tied to its rise and perseverance as a TikTok commodity. Indeed, as the musical opened to lukewarm reviews (at best) and a tepid box-office advance, a legion of musical theatre fans began engaging with the musical's dramaturgy on TikTok, facilitating the musical's rise to the top of the app's FYP, creating a robust body of *Beetlejuice* afterlives, and, ultimately, driving ticket sales for the Broadway production. Laura MacDonald suggests that social media and web platforms "have expanded the potential reach of musical theatre marketing."[7] The case of *Beetlejuice* and TikTok is no exception. *Beetlejuice* as a case study facilitates a discussion of how fans can claim agency through TikTok, even holding the power to make a musical turn a profit and perhaps become a long-running show. Speaking of social media marketing in musical theatre, musicologist Elizabeth Titrington Craft suggests, "this collaborative offstage aspect of theatrical production is nevertheless a crucial part of the art/commerce we call Broadway. Examining this oft-neglected area sheds light not only on the process of staging a Broadway show, but also on how that show comes to be understood and discussed."[8] With this in mind, I closely read the *Beetlejuice* TikTok archive alongside the rise of TikTok Broadway, highlighting how musical theatre was ingrained in the platform from its origins, thus normalizing musicals as mainstream on the platform. Teenage TikTokers enabled this phenomenon to emerge. In *Fan Cultures*, Matt Hills recognizes that fans "claim agency through their later 'performances' of fan identity" rather than their stories of how they became fans.[9] This is precisely how TikTok Broadway began. Fans claimed agency.

TikTok is not simply a place to share fandom: it's a place to perform fandom. Fan performances on TikTok are what enabled *Beetlejuice* to defy the odds and become a commercial success at the Winter Garden Theatre. In doing so, they proved TikTok to be an essential (not just viable) marketing tool for Broadway musicals. Simultaneously, they showed Broadway how TikTok can be used to foster a community of dedicated fans, giving these fans a digital space to begin their fandom before realizing their dream of attending the musical in person. As such, this chapter unpacks the relationship between digital fan performances, the dramaturgical world of a musical on TikTok, and the thing that makes Broadway tick—turning a profit. I question: How have the internet and social media helped drive Broadway and fan engagement with Broadway? How have the norms of Gen Z culture and the TikTok interface and aesthetic changed the game? What is the marketing potential of TikTok? How has TikTok changed marketing musicals on Broadway? And, how do musical theatre fans factor into this conversation? How does the ultimate rise of *Beetlejuice* reflect this?

Marketing Broadway the Digital Way

Every social media platform has led to its own phenomenon regarding musical theatre. In most cases, social media initiatives are rooted in selling tickets, blurring the line between generosity and commercialism. Social media holds the potential to bring musical theatre to fans in an accessible way that removes barriers typically associated with commercial theatre. Jessica Hillman-McCord acknowledges, "Now producers and marketers manipulate the web and social media in order to reach and develop audiences in constantly shifting ways."[10] In previous work, I have argued that musical theatre social media performance creates "a feeling of accessibility in a space—Broadway—that isn't known for being accessible."[11] The most successful musicals on social media have been those that create content that is both tailored to the platform in question and targeted at authentic fan engagement. This latter element of authentic engagement, in particular, can help drive sales even as it obfuscates the goal of selling tickets and turning a profit. While Broadway marketing teams were already looking at social media and the internet at large as viable spaces to publicize and sell musicals, in the early aughts, YouTube largely changed the game. Broadway productions of *Spring Awakening, [title of show], In the Heights, Xanadu,* and *Rock of Ages* used YouTube "from an early point to provide fans with free and accessible content."[12]

Spring Awakening helped spearhead this development. In late 2006, the year after YouTube launched, *Spring Awakening* uploaded a music video for "'The Bitch of Living," which became the central focus of the production's digital marketing campaign. The production was able to attract hordes of young fans, both to its online offerings and to performances at the Eugene O'Neill Theatre. MacDonald credits much of the production's success with young people to the youthfulness of the cast itself. Because the stars of *Spring Awakening* were young, teens easily connected with them; they saw themselves in the performers.[13] YouTube facilitated this recognition among teenagers in much the same way that TikTok would later do for *Beetlejuice*.

Like *Spring Awakening*, *[title of show]* was an early adoptee of YouTube, producing *the [title of show] show* in 2007–9. This video series followed Hunter Bell, Jeff Bowen, Heidi Blickenstaff, and Susan Blackwell as they developed the musical toward a triumphant—and unexpected—Broadway bow and Tony Award run. Ultimately, however, YouTube did not help the production find an audience. The show opened in July 2008 but ran for only 13 previews and 102 regular performances at the Lyceum Theatre on Broadway before closing.

In the Heights (which opened on Broadway in March 2008) made initial waves in Fall 2007 on its road to Broadway with a series of YouTube videos uploaded to Lin-Manuel Miranda's YouTube account (@usnavi, bearing the name of his theatrical doppelgänger from the musical). In these videos, musical fans got up close and personal with Lin-Manuel Miranda and the cast and creatives of what was becoming one of Broadway's hottest shows. According to Hillman-McCord, Miranda is a "digital diva," and the YouTube content he spearheaded reveals how even in his early days of Broadway, Miranda understood the potential in social media to market a new musical and to engage with fans.[14] Miranda's *In the Heights* YouTube content isn't polished; when viewed now, nearly fifteen years later, the videos are quite gritty and DIY (albeit exciting in their encounter with pre-celebrity Miranda). But they dropped the walls around Broadway, giving fans of the show a chance to get to know Miranda and his *In the Heights* playmates—Andy Blankenbuehler, Chris Jackson, and Karen Olivo, among others. Craft sees *In the Heights*'s social media use as revolutionary: "The show's marketing team has run a pioneering campaign in its extensive use of social networking, viral marketing and online advertising."[15] This would later continue with other Lin-Manuel Miranda–headed projects, such as *Hamilton*, which promoted digital accessibility as a core value of the production.[16]

In the Heights's initial YouTube content was somewhat scattered, offering fans a glimpse into the world of the show and life backstage with Miranda and company (and, occasionally, Jonathan Groff). This would change in September 2008, when the musical formally entered the YouTube webseries community with *Legally Brown: The Search for the Next Piragua Guy*. *Legally Brown* used the format of the MTV show *Legally Blonde: The Search for the Next Elle Woods* (2008) to fictionalize a reality show in which Broadway vets such as Allison Janney and Matthew Morrison competed to become the coveted Piragua Guy in (the now Tony-awarded) *In the Heights*.[17] The series relied on reality show tropes and the comedic talents of its cast, and it concluded with a twist ending (and tongue-in-cheek wink to its fans) when *The Search for the Next Elle Woods* winner Bailey Hanks was named the new Piragua Guy.

While *In the Heights* was up to typical Miranda-inspired shenanigans, the Broadway production of *Xanadu* (which opened in July 2007) used YouTube to disseminate its Tony campaign webseries, titled *Cubby Bernstein*. The popular webseries featured a ten-year-old Adam Riegler as the title character, a wicked-smart and incredibly savvy Tony-campaign manager who was going to help *Xanadu* defy the odds and win the coveted Tony Award for Best Musical in 2008 (spoiler: nope. *In the Heights* won). The webseries introduced Cubby Bernstein—who riffed off decades of stereotypes about Jewish Broadway musical producers—as "the mini mogul behind Broadway's biggest Tony success stories. Silent for years, here he steps out from the shadows to establish himself as a public figure of epic proportions. Broadway may never be the same again."[18] The series featured three- to five-minute videos of Bernstein using various strategies to get *Xanadu* the votes it needed, with appearances from the cast of *Xanadu* in addition to Broadway heavyweights such as Nathan Lane, Patti LuPone, and Cynthia Nixon.

Building on the successes of *In the Heights* and *Xanadu*, *Rock of Ages* soon joined the fray. The *Rock of Ages* webseries focused on the highly dramatized backstage life of the musical (which opened Off-Broadway at New World Stages in late 2008 before opening on Broadway at the Brooks Atkinson Theatre in April 2009) from March to September 2009. While some webisodes were informed by reality, such as when Will Swenson left the show, other webisodes (like the horror-inspired installment "The Haunting of the Brooks Atkinson") were purely fictional. From *In the Heights* to *Xanadu* and *Rock of Ages*, one thing remained standard. YouTube had quickly become a legitimate digital space to expand the dramaturgical world of musical theatre. Naturally, musical fans relished the opportunity to view more content revolving around their favorite musicals and, ultimately, gain agency in their fan performances. Fans would soon embrace YouTube to publicize their own fannish creations. Now, in the third decade of the 2000s, YouTube is not just an accessory to fan behavior and performance. Rather, it is a core component of the musical theatre fan's social media tool kit.

With YouTube off to the races, Twitter was next.[19] As a platform that privileges the written word, however, Twitter did not allow Broadway productions to simply replicate YouTube or other video content on the platform. Marketing content would have to be tailored to Twitter if it were to land with audiences. *Next to Normal*, which opened on Broadway in April 2009, saw Twitter as a unique opportunity to create a show within a show.[20] Over the course of thirty-five days in spring 2009, *Next to Normal* performed a Twitter version of the musical, which saw brief updates (up to 140 characters) offering a glimpse into the characters' actions and emotions during the musical as well as their off-stage actions and thoughts. *Next to Normal*'s Twitter performance created what MacDonald refers to as a "digital musical theatre hypertext."[21] Each tweet added to the dramaturgical world of *Next to Normal* and gave fans on Twitter a unique experience that complemented traditional methods of fan engagement such as seeing the show, stagedooring it, and listening to the cast album. The Twitter play gave fans a wholly new and innovative way to interact with one of the surprise hits of 2009.

The 2011 revival of *Godspell* tried to capitalize on the emerging power of Twitter, holding special social media–friendly performances in which select audience members were encouraged to live-tweet the production. Of course, this was met with resistance by many musical lovers, who saw the Broadway theatre as a sacred place, free of cell phones and audience distractions. Although not speaking directly to the *Godspell* live-tweeting experiment, musical theatre scholar Kathryn Edney proposes in her article "Let's Misbehave" that cell-phone interactions question "what it means to be present at a live performance as an audience member."[22] Perhaps the *Godspell* Twitter experiment was ahead of its time, or perhaps it exemplified musical theatre overreach into the world of social media. In any case, this experiment reveals that musical theatre productions are keenly aware of the power of social media. Although *Godspell* was not able to capitalize on Twitter (it ultimately closed at a financial loss), the production's willingness to embrace new social media foreshadows how Broadway musical productions would later fully embrace a wide range of social media platforms, TikTok among them.

Twitter proved to be a game changer in the world of musical theatre fan engagement, operating as a digital stage door. Theatre fans suddenly had access to their favorite musical theatre creatives. The Twitter shift has been marked by accessibility. No longer must fans travel to New York, see a show, and wait at the stage door for the coveted chance at a few seconds of in-person interaction with musical theatre actors. Neither must fans mail Broadway paraphernalia to theatres in the hopes that actors will sign and return their playbills, pictures, and cast-recording booklets. Twitter facilitates public conversations and authentic interactions between fans and musical talent. Although many Broadway figures have found Twitter success, there is perhaps no better example than Lin-Manuel Miranda. As Elena Machado Sáez notes, Miranda's much-publicized Twitter activity is marked by a high percentage of tweets directed at fans.[23] MacDonald echoes these thoughts, demonstrating how Miranda's Twitter presence (in tandem with that of *Hamilton*) fostered a culture of generosity that radically reimagined the type of access fans have had with musical theatre productions, casts, and creatives.[24] This culture of generosity is directly linked to an aesthetics of accessibility, which drives forward Latinx theatre-making.[25]

In the case of Miranda and *Hamilton* (which opened on Broadway in August 2015), the early days of the Broadway production were marked by

Ham4Ham, five-minute street performances that took place during the lottery before every preview performance and then sporadically once the show opened.[26] While Ham4Ham was an in-person event, it had a robust digital life that extended the reach of the performances far beyond the Richard Rodgers Theatre. Each performance was archived on YouTube, where hundreds of thousands of views racked up, enabling more people to view Ham4Ham than *Hamilton* itself at the time. Hamilfans then took to Twitter, using the hashtag #Ham4Ham, to circulate and discuss Ham4Ham videos. These videos would later make their way to TikTok, extending Ham4Ham's afterlife in a digital way that continually adapted to distinct, emerging social media platforms.

As social media has become ingrained in US culture in more ways than we could have ever imagined just decades prior, its relationship to musical theatre and, specifically, Broadway productions has continued to evolve, expanding from an optional way to grow interest in a show to a necessity for every Broadway production. Although several social media platforms remain critical to marketing musicals, TikTok—in the wake of its 2018 US launch—quickly emerged as a leading player in this ecosystem. As TikTok has grown in global import, so too have the nuanced ways that the platform is changing social media marketing. CEO and cofounder of social media marketing agency Movers + Shakers Evan Horowitz claims, "What TikTok got right is they really understand what consumers are looking for right now, and consumers have been looking for something as an alternative to the big incumbent platforms like Facebook, Instagram, YouTube."[27] Whereas previous generations leaned in to the polished, filtered aesthetics of Instagram marketing, for example, teenagers today want something that feels less refined and less edited, and that doesn't necessarily meet a certain standard of quality. TikTok aesthetics make marketing with great authenticity not just a possibility, but, more importantly, a priority.

Compared to its social media competitors, TikTok makes it easier for musicals to reach new audiences given how trending content works on TikTok. For example, a musical can engage with popular TikTok trends, marrying the show's aesthetics, score, characters, and dramaturgy with trending content on TikTok. *Wicked* might feature the actors playing Elphaba and Glinda in their iconic show looks, TikToking to the "Wow, you can really dance" sound bite. *The Lion King* might showcase Simba and Nala in their costumes, perfectly executing the Renegade dance challenge. Or, *Chicago* might have the entire cast do the infamous "Rich Man's Frug" dance from *Sweet Charity*.[28] Or, take for instance the new musical *Shucked*'s wildly successful TikTok marketing strategy leading up to its April 2023 opening; *Shucked* leaned into TikTok's silly aesthetics and bizarre culture to digitally sell the musical about corn (seriously, it's just about corn). The possibilities for authentic Broadway TikTok engagement are endless. Crucially, in all of this, TikTok enables musicals to expand their audience reach far beyond their own dedicated fan communities as well as Broadway's most coveted ticket buyers (real: older White women). By way of comparison: whereas *Heathers: The Musical* content found a robust fan community on Tumblr, for example, that did not lead to an expanded afterlife for the musical. This is because the dynamics of the Tumblr platform largely keep fan communities insular, separated from one another and sheltered from the hyper-public presence that marks TikTok. (Of course, Tumblr posts always have the potential to circulate beyond Tumblr, most notably as memes on Instagram and Twitter, but such static, often text-based images are still of more limited interest.) Or, take the previously mentioned YouTube engagements: these were largely confined to in-the-know musical theatre fans. They didn't penetrate mainstream pop culture. On TikTok, fan cultures can live an incredibly visible life. To put it simply, TikTok virality is a game changer; going viral, becoming "TikTok famous," and spilling into other digital and analog spaces can extend a musical's reach and, accordingly, make cultivating new fans a viable reality.

Musical theatre productions use TikTok for various marketing purposes, many of which continue to expand as TikTok grows in global import. Much of this marketing power lies in the consumers, who, on TikTok, skew heavily in the Gen Z and Millennial demographic. Journalist Zoe Paskett acknowledges, "It's almost as though TikTok was created for young musical theatre fans."[29] But how do Broadway productions market to these young fans? According to journalist Alexander Vuocolo, teenage TikTokers "are more discerning and skeptical about traditional forms of advertising, which forces brands to think more creatively about outreach."[30] Ads that are "trying" to be ads don't do as well as content that feels organic to the platform, and ads that work on Instagram, Facebook, or YouTube won't necessarily work on TikTok, where the content may seem foreign. Journalist Maria Sibirtseva writes of two key advertising strategies that do work on TikTok: "You can create your brand's account and invest in the production of original content. You can also advertise on TikTok using its tools or partner with influencers to achieve your goals."[31] Of course, the approaches that musical productions take vary according to target audience and other factors such as budget, time, and knowledge of the platform. But the bottom line is that on TikTok, authenticity is the name of the game. Content that grabs attention and goes viral on TikTok fits aesthetically into the platform. It doesn't *feel* like marketing. As I will explain later in this chapter, this is precisely where *Beetlejuice* found success. The content created in and around the musical production never felt like marketing. It just felt like TikTok.

Beetlejuice: From Flop to Commercial Success

When *Beetlejuice* opened on Broadway in April 2019, the mixture of lackluster word of mouth, unenthusiastic reviews, and low box-office advance all signaled that the musical would be headed back to the graveyard. As with so many Broadway musicals, *Beetlejuice*'s critical reception did not match its lofty expectations. And, of course, with tepid critical response, Broadway musicals face an even greater challenge to draw an audience and eventually turn a profit. There are notable exceptions to this rule (e.g., *Wicked*, *Memphis*, and *Frozen*), but how a musical performs upon opening largely dictates the life of the show on Broadway and beyond. In the case of *Beetlejuice*, it was dead on arrival.

Writing for the *New York Times*, critic Ben Brantley noted how the show was far from invisible: "overcompensating from the fear that it might lose an audience with a limited attention span . . . this show so overstuffs itself with gags, one-liners and visual diversions that you shut down from sensory overload."[32] The *Washington Post* theatre critic Peter Marks found the show greatly improved from its out-of-town tryout, which was "suffocating under the weight of sophomoric, phallic gags." Even so, Marks's review frequently signaled how the show "pumps up" and "amps up" its ghoulish antics "a bit too frantically." Marks wrote, "This may be of more concern to overly entertained theater analysts than to those musical-theater enthusiasts who thrive on the supercharged exertions of an ensemble on hyperdrive. On a measurement scale of energy-output-per-minute, high-octane *Beetlejuice* would now be the safest ticket in town."[33] *Variety*'s Frank Rizzo echoed some of these thoughts, noting that despite the production's flaws, "Keeping things entertaining enough are the off-the-wall humor, endless visuals and aural delights, tuneful music and wicked lyrics of Perfect."[34] In the same vein, *Vulture*'s Sara Holdren called the production "theme park-y," noting, "it's loud, it's cheeky, and it's all about excess." While these adjectives could easily be considered a rebuke in the realm of Broadway, Holdren admitted that the show was "a pretty fun time."[35] Summing up the production's reviews, Eddie Perfect conceded to EJ Dickson of *Rolling Stone*, "Things had not exactly been all beer and skittles on the critical front, let's just say that." Dickson observed as well that "the musical was roasted by many establishment theater critics."[36] By all accounts, *Beetlejuice* was between a rock and a hard place.

Although these reviews are hardly the type of reviews that producers dream of, they do reveal much about how the production would eventually become a hit. That is, the way that Brantley, Marks, Holdren, and the like discussed *Beetlejuice* is reminiscent of how critics discuss TikTok aesthetics and cultures. TikTok's critics (both positive and negative) use similar language. TikTok is loud, cheeky, excessive, frantic, always in hyperdrive, and filled with off-the-wall humor. But, all in all, it's a pretty fun time. And, just like on TikTok, *Beetlejuice* eventually attracted a much younger audience than do typical Broadway shows, an audience that reveled in the idiosyncratic and self-deprecating nature of the dramaturgical world of *Beetlejuice*.

With largely negative and lukewarm reviews from nearly every major media outlet, *Beetlejuice* seemed like it would be a flash in the pan, losing nearly all of its $21 million investment and fizzling out much like other film-to-stage adaptations, such as *The Wedding Singer* (2006), *Honeymoon in Vegas* (2015), *Pretty Woman* (2018), and *Tootsie* (2019). The collective Broadway imagination would quickly forget about the production, perhaps only occasionally remembering David Korins's eye-popping fun-house scenic design and Alex Brightman's zany turn as the show's title character. But then suddenly everything changed. *Beetlejuice* had found TikTok.

To trace this history, though, we need to first take a step back, from stage to screen. When the *Beetlejuice* film opened in 1988 to critical and commercial success, it shocked many. This was a film that, by most accounts, shouldn't have worked, but it was, in fact, firing on all cylinders. Naturally, think pieces began to pop up, explaining how a grotesque poltergeist had captured the hearts across the United States. Writing for *Rolling Stone* in June 1988, David Edelstein recognized the film's appeal to misfits, outcasts, and weirdos:

> If you've ever felt out of place, you'll plug into the ghosts' awkwardness—and into Burton's dopey, matter-of-fact surrealism. Aside from Betelgeuse (the spelling has been simplified for the title), no one quite fits in. The afterlife isn't grand and Spielbergian but a mangy series of typing pools and waiting rooms, in which you must take a number to see your caseworker.

Next to you sit horribly mutilated people in the state they were in when they bit the big one, but used to it now [sic], so they're blasé, as if they weren't charred or squashed.[37]

Take, for instance, one of the film's breakout characters—a man with a tiny coconut-sized head and a full-sized human body. By any account, this undisputed oddball is a misfit, but, in the netherworld of *Beetlejuice*, he is at home. Regardless of your identity or place in society, we have all felt like him before. This is precisely the energy that would take *Beetlejuice* from Broadway flop to TikTok hit.

When *Beetlejuice* began previews at the Winter Garden Theatre, it had one thing that most Broadway shows didn't have—teenagers in the cast. Even in properties that are largely *about* teenagers, such as *Fun Home*, *Mean Girls* (2018), *Be More Chill*, and *The Lightning Thief*, these roles are rarely played by teenagers. They are played by twenty-something-year-olds who can pass for sixteen-year-olds. (Or, take *Wicked*: Kristin Chenoweth and Idina Menzel were in their thirties when they played teenagers.) Of course, there are exceptions to the rule of teenagers on the Broadway stage (hello, *Spring Awakening*). But in spring 2019, they were largely absent—except backstage at *Beetlejuice*, that is, where Presley Ryan, the Lydia understudy, was a "veteran" TikToker ready to introduce Broadway to the TikTok revolution.

The journey began in June 2019, when Ryan started telling cast members about this wild, new place where teens were flocking to—TikTok.[38] Bolstered by Ryan's energy, the cast began making TikToks backstage in full *Beetlejuice* costumes, hair, and makeup. Ryan's (@prezryan) first video with the cast conveys how musical productions can merge with trending TikTok audio memes. In this June 15, 2019, video (Figure 1.1 and Figure 1.2), Ryan, Alex Brightman, Leslie Kritzer, and Dana Steingold dance to Billie Eilish's "Bad Guy," one of TikTok's most popular sound bites in 2019. This sound bite was unavoidable on the app, with many TikTok videos at the time mimicking the style of popular influencers like Charli D'Amelio and Addison Rae. The *Beetlejuice* cast video departs from the aesthetics typically seen on the platform: Brightman dons the signature Beetlejuice look, while the others wear purple robes from the "Fright of Their Lives" scene. The short video isn't necessarily innovative or creative, but it showcases backstage life at *Beetlejuice* and the way the cast began to use TikTok as a form of community-building and audience engagement. It also reflects what Shauna Pomerantz and Miriam Field call "radical media engagement," in which intergenerational bonding

Figures 1.1 and 1.2 Alex Brightman, Presley Ryan, Dana Steingold, and Leslie Kritzer dance to "Bad Guy" by Billie Eilish. Posted on June 15, 2019.

takes place on TikTok.[39] For this and subsequent *Beetlejuice* cast TikToks, a Zoomer (Ryan) invited Millennials (Brightman and Rob McClure) and Gen Xers (Kritzer and Kerry Butler), among others, to engage with a definitively teenager platform and culture, something they did in conversation with thousands of musical theatre fans online. These viral *Beetlejuice* cast TikToks became "interactive multimedia texts," to quote Craft, texts that circulate "within an online cultural sphere governed by its own ethics and aesthetics," thus blurring "the boundaries between advertising and art."[40] While the cast may have initially engaged with TikTok as a fun way to pass the time and build intergenerational cast relationships, the virality of their TikToks soon became a form of free advertising for the *Beetlejuice* marketing team, an indirect result of the cast's engagement with TikTok's silly, off-the-wall aesthetics.

From the very beginning, *Beetlejuice* distinguished itself from its peers because its cast was creating these TikToks alongside fans, often in conversation with fans. That is, alongside Ryan, Broadway vets Brightman, Butler, and Kritzer were continually in conversation with teenagers in the United States who wanted their digital *Beetlejuice* fix. The cast stood out. And TikTok audiences wanted more, commenting that they loved this content, clicking on Ryan's videos to see more, and ultimately engaging with the sound bite. While Eilish's "Bad Guy" didn't need *Beetlejuice* to thrive, it offered a blueprint for the *Beetlejuice* musical to further replicate and find harmony between Broadway and TikTok. Riding the wave of their first video's success, the cast continued to engage with popular TikTok trends, many of them marked by sound memes. For example, in a July 23, 2019, video uploaded by Ryan, the cast celebrated a milestone performance by hitting the Woah, the signature Gen Z dance move.[41] In the video, Ryan travels backstage at the Winter Garden, prompting Brightman, Butler, and Kritzer to hit the Woah for their hundredth show (notice the rhyme?). At the end of the video, Ryan stares into the mirror and lifts up her arm in celebration of forcing these adults to perform not-so-successful-but-nevertheless-spirited iterations of the Woah. One comment (@jessthemess7) noted, "Presley..... your power ... iconic." Iconic perhaps, but Presley Ryan was just getting started.

At Ryan's artistic direction, the *Beetlejuice* cast continued to make on-trend backstage TikTok content. Ryan and the cast performed dance challenges such as "Shake It" by Metro Station and "Spooky Scary Skeletons." In the videos, the cast separated themselves from the TikTok masses by wearing their costumes and makeup. In one video, Brightman stands with the shrunken-head guy offstage while the action onstage happens just feet from them. The cast's videos even included intertextual interventions into the TikTok Broadway canon; on September 5, 2019, for example, Ryan uploaded a video in which she, Brightman, and Goldstein do the Martha Dumptruck Challenge, inspired by the song "Big Fun" from *Heathers: The Musical*. Indeed, in the digital theatre district of TikTok Broadway, musical casts engage with other musicals, further cementing the feeling of community that digital spaces can engender.

Comments on early Presley Ryan TikToks began asking for one thing—for the cast to make TikToks using sound bites from *Beetlejuice*. Perhaps taking the bait, Ryan and the cast began to do precisely this, making videos using Perfect's score. On September 28, 2019, Ryan and Brightman

48   TIKTOK BROADWAY

Figures 1.3 and 1.4 Alex Brightman and Presley Ryan lip sync to "Say My Name" from *Beetlejuice*. Posted on September 28, 2019.

introduced the TikTok world to "Say My Name" (Figure 1.3 and Figure 1.4). Clad in their costumes, the duo lip-syncs the sound bite, recreating their onstage characterizations, while in a dressing room at the Winter Garden. The video exploded, accumulating over 5.5 million views and catapulting *Beetlejuice: The Musical* into TikTok fame. The video's comments reveal much about *Beetlejuice* fan engagement. One user (@jessthemess7) wrote, "They win, this is the only video that exists now." This comment gained 34,500 likes. Others noted: "You two are freaking royalty" (@distortedcorvid, 37,000 likes), "THIS IS THE ONLY WAY THIS SOUND SHOULD BE USED!! THANK YOU FOR BLESSING MY LIFE" (@_sarahdarling_, 22,000 likes), and "if y'all don't know who they are ... bye" (@jappomutt, 3,000 likes).

Beetlejuice benefited from TikTok's challenge culture. The "Say My Name" challenge accumulated thousands of videos in which TikTokers attempted to mimic Brightman's hand and hip movements from the song in which Beetlejuice tries to get Lydia to say his name three times. The song is one of the score's catchier numbers, and the quick lyrics offer physical cues that play into how TikTok dance is often literal. Writing about *Beetlejuice* TikTok, journalist Brendan Wetmore noted, "this sensibility is a must for the stage, but also part of the implicitly designed secret formula for TikTok fame."[42] In the case of "Say My Name," Beetlejuice and Lydia's playful onstage interactions with each other offer much inspiration for TikTokers who wish to mimic Alex Timbers's staging and Connor Gallagher's choreography, as well as those who choose to riff off how the scene plays out onstage, offering their own spin to the archive. The "Say My Name" TikTok archive also features a robust collection of videos in which users duet each other, playing off each other's characterizations of Beetlejuice and/or Lydia, giving a new meaning to scene work. With each subsequent duet, the archive grows, of course, but something else happens—fans begin to interact with one another in a more nuanced way than simply viewing, sharing, and commenting on videos. In these instances, fans form a relationship centered on their fan identities. As videos go viral, fans go viral together, which strengthens their relationship. TikTok virality is addicting. Part of TikTok's success lies in how the algorithm gives users a taste of virality before ultimately taking it away. Inevitably, TikTokers continue creating new content with the hopes of going viral again and having that feeling of success and TikTok fame. When a duet or a collab goes viral, TikTokers experience this together, forming more intrinsic communal fan bonds.

Prompted by Ryan's success on TikTok, the *Beetlejuice* marketing team created an official TikTok account for the production—@beetlejuicebway—in November 2019. The account quickly achieved success. It became an extension of the success and type of content that the cast had already been creating on Ryan's TikTok. That said, @beetlejuicebway made a more concerted effort to disseminate the musical's score, which then became adopted by TikTokers at large (some songs to more success than others). As the cast's videos to the cast recording began to achieve popularity and go viral, the archive quickly grew. Soon, audios from *Beetlejuice* songs such as "The Whole Being Dead Thing," "Say My Name," "Dead Mom," and "What I Know Now" became TikTok standards. "Say My Name," for example," had over six hundred thousand unique videos on the platform. Perfect reflected on this growth: "TikTok started to vibe with it, that's when things got insane."[43]

Not surprisingly, the production account's follower metrics skewed heavily into the Gen Z demographic, with women between the ages of eighteen and twenty-four (not too far off from *Beetlejuice*'s Lydia herself) accounting for its highest percentage of followers.[44] All in all, TikTok content featuring *Beetlejuice*-related hashtags (#Beetlejuice, #BeetlejuiceMusical, #BeetlejuiceCosplay, and #BeetlejuiceBway, for example) had been viewed over one trillion times by early 2023. One *trillion* times. That's not a typo, folks.

While the reasons are varied, perhaps the clearest explanation for *Beetlejuice*'s sudden success lies in the source material itself, which appeals to Gen Z in much the same way that it appealed to young people in 1988. Beetlejuice is a rebel: antiestablishment and sexually fluid. He rejects labels as much as he is horny for everything. Even the song "Say My Name" (and the corresponding TikTok trend) is undeniably, well, horny. Meanwhile, the property's other breakout character, Lydia, is a cynical teenager who continually rolls her eyes at the behavior of the adults around. Lydia is "Ok, Boomer" personified. "Positivity is a luxury few can afford," she even tells Delia, an eccentric life coach. Perhaps there is no better example of this in the TikTok archive than Foxberri (@foxberri.cosplay), one of the more successful *Beetlejuice* TikTokers, who was nineteen when her *Beetlejuice* cosplay TikToks began to rack up millions of views.[45] Speaking to a reporter, Foxberri admitted, "A lot of people in my generation can relate to the character because they feel out of place and not normal. And I've always felt like that too."[46] Foxberri's thoughts convey how *Beetlejuice* TikTok became a place for misfits, weirdos, and outsiders.

Lydia Deetz is the musical's human embodiment of being an outcast, yet the *Beetlejuice* phenomenon goes far beyond simply Lydia. Although Lydia is a highly "relatable" character for Zoomers, Perfect believes the show's TikTok success is also tied to the camp aesthetic, zaniness, and off-the-wall humor of both musical and film. These aesthetics match TikTok's silly aesthetics; it's not a reach to find the similarities. Take, for example, the cast's TikToks for trends such as the Renegade Challenge, the "Say So" dance, and the #OutWest Challenge, all of them performed in the cast's macabre *Beetlejuice* costumes. The juxtaposition makes for good entertainment. But behind the kookiness of *Beetlejuice* lie themes that resonate deeply with Gen Z, a generation that is coming of age at a time of great economic unrest. Naturally,

Zoomers, just like Millennials, harbor collective resentment toward adults who have allowed them to graduate high school and college into an economy that can quite literally not support them. Perfect observed, "It's about the very real stress of trying to discover for yourself how and why you should live, and how to hold onto the people who matter in your life. We just happen to address it in a very macabre and irreverent way."[47] These themes mirror TikTok themes. Teens frequently take to TikTok to give their hot takes on any number of issues: political, social, or anything in between.

TikTok has given Gen Z *Beetlejuice* fans a platform to find like-minded musical theatre fans, to discuss the show, and to find agency in their fan identities. *Beetlejuice* collectively contributed to a fan-driven digital marketing campaign (and it's not alone here: *Dear Evan Hansen*'s (2016) case is similar).[48] Jennifer Graessle, *Beetlejuice*'s social media manager, admitted, "This community has been extremely vocal, and TikTok has amplified their voices into the millions."[49] Although *Beetlejuice* fannish practices are varied, in many cases, fans engage in cosplay on TikTok, even bringing this practice to the Winter Garden Theatre in much the same way that HedHeads would dress as Hedwig and Yitzhak when attending performances of the Broadway revival of *Hedwig and the Angry Inch* (2014–15). The stage door has long been a critical site to express fan agency. Musicologist James Deaville explains the practice of stagedooring a show: "spectators wait at the stage door after the performance of a show to express their appreciation for the actors' efforts, get cast members' autographs or photos as memorabilia, and engage with an actor regarding their performance that night."[50] Stagedooring is the pinnacle of musical theatre fan performance. Yet, in an analog world it's only viable for those with access to New York City. In a digital world such as TikTok, productions such as *Beetlejuice* have been able to create a digital stage door that replicates audience/artist interactions in a familiar, yet entirely innovative, way. As the archive of *Beetlejuice*-generated TikToks grew, so too did interactions between fans and the musical, primarily in the comment sections and through the use of duets. Surprisingly (or perhaps not), these digital stagedooring practices translated to live, in-person stagedooring practices after TikTok fans finally saw *Beetlejuice* at the Winter Garden Theatre. At every turn, *Beetlejuice* rode the TikTok wave, leaning in to how the platform was cultivating new fans, and leading to box-office success. As scholar Aya Esther Hayashi discusses in her work on YouTube musicals, "Perhaps, one key to diversifying audiences lies in developing active ones, thus in cultivating theatrical fandom."[51] That is, rather than viewing teenager

TikTok activity as ancillary to the world of *Beetlejuice*, the production and marketing teams saw these fannish behaviors as an opportunity to lean in to the unknown, supporting Gen Z social media creativity.

Mimicking Instagram takeovers—in which actors post frequent updates on a production's stories and give live updates to fans throughout their day—*Beetlejuice*'s TikTok content offered fans a glimpse behind the curtain, into the off-stage life of the actors in was quickly becoming one of their favorite musicals. The marketing team may have had a say in things, but in terms of the creation and curation of content for TikTok, *Beetlejuice*'s actors did the heavy lifting. The result was a more organic form of digital marketing, one that never really felt like marketing at all. This is not unique to *Beetlejuice* or even the world of musical theatre. Business reporter Caitlin Mullen affirms, "Brands are increasingly looking to their employees to be the source of TikTok content that does the heavy lifting for them with Gen Z."[52] Mainstream examples of this are endless. Cold Stone Creamery, Walmart, Dunkin' Donuts, and Wendy's have all made use of "TikTok famous" employees to create new content, engage potential buyers, and accumulate high follower counts. In fact, some brands' TikTok personae are entirely hinged on one personality. Such is the case with the *Washington Post*'s TikTok account (@washingtonpost), which features daily original content from Dave Jorgenson, a journalist who creates timely and often hilarious videos marrying current headlines with TikTok aesthetics and trends. TikTok personalities have even spurred brands to join TikTok, as was the case with Doggface (Nathan Apodaca, @420doggface208). After a video of him skating on a longboard, drinking Ocean Spray cranberry juice, and singing along to "Dreams" by Fleetwood Mac went mega viral (89 million views), Doggface became the unofficial face of Ocean Spray, prompting the brand to engage with him, TikTok, and a growing legion of fans who ensured that grocery stores couldn't keep their cranberry juice on the shelves in October 2020. These examples encompass a wide range of stories, goals, and successes, but there is one commonality: their TikTok marketing practices engage with fans in a way that doesn't feel like marketing. Fans and potential buyers don't feel like brands are trying to gain their purchases. Rather, fans feel like they are simply engaging in TikTok culture, even if fans are showing allegiance to brands.

On the account @oompa_loompa_dobadibo, *Beetlejuice* TikTok commentary reveals much about fan behavior. For example, a video from October 11, 2020, well past *Beetlejuice*'s heyday on the app, features a production clip from "Say My Name." The video, which had over 10 million views by the end of 2020, has a robust comments section that speaks to how *Beetlejuice* has consistently moved within TikTok's most mainstream circles. One comment (@jacksonparagraph) with 63,500 likes noted, "bruh this musical RULED this app in its prime." Another TikToker's (@jessx_5) comment garnered 22,700 likes: "I miss tiktok when we were all obsessed with this musical." Replies to these comments echoed the same thoughts, recognizing that only elite TikTokers—those who were on TikTok in 2019, pre-pandemic—will recognize the import of *Beetlejuice*. Other comments bragged about having seen the show, with replies conveying how seeing *Beetlejuice* on Broadway leads to TikTok clout. Of course, many comments were from folks who were completely unaware that a *Beetlejuice* musical even exists. Replies to such comments questioned how a teenager could possibly *not* know about *Beetlejuice*, given its popularity on TikTok and especially with Gen Z. Throughout the comment section on this video, TikTokers corresponded with the dramaturgical world of *Beetlejuice*, showing how, as the archive grew in 2019, musical theatre became more thoroughly ingrained in the Golden Age of TikTok.[53]

And this growth had repercussions far beyond TikTok, influencing how musical productions on Broadway understood the possibilities of social media to grow a different kind of audience, one that has historically been far outside the purview of the typical Broadway ticket buyer. Graessle acknowledged, "TikTok was a game changer for *Beetlejuice* because it allowed our original cast recording to reach millions more young people than Broadway marketing campaigns usually allow."[54] Graessle credited the show's TikTok success to its fast-paced, off-the-wall lyrics. The three- to sixty-second song clips are easily digestible, offering fans a lot of freedom to put their own spin on trending songs. Moreover, the lyrics allow for literal interpretations, which have become a hallmark of successful songs on TikTok. Users encounter sound bites on TikTok, favorite the sound, use it in their own video, and, in the process, are fed by the algorithm an endless stream of other videos using the same sound. The sound bite then becomes an earworm: the only logical thing to do at this point is to look up the song on Spotify, Apple Music, or YouTube, to hear it in its entirety. Once the song is over, autoplay will likely feed fans another song from the same source. Driven by this phenomenon, the original *Beetlejuice* cast recording hit a hundred million streams within twenty-one weeks of its debut, the second-fastest trajectory for any musical cast recording, only behind *Hamilton*.[55] And those listens appear to translate to increased revenue in other ways, as Graessle noted: "its [*Beetlejuice*'s] popularity, both on TikTok and beyond, has had a residual effect on the show's social media presence and ticket sales."[56]

Of course, engaging with fans on social media does not always lead to box-office success. TikTok is globally based and free to access; many TikTokers will never make it to New York or the Winter Garden. This became the production team's challenge. In Graessle's words, "the challenge set out for us on TikTok is how to turn those eyes back towards the Broadway show."[57] Yet, *Beetlejuice* did it. According to journalist Chris Stokel-Walker, the TikTok effect "seems to be working—seven in 10 *Beetlejuice* audience members are aged between 19 and 54 . . . 20 percentage points higher than the average Broadway show."[58] Moreover, data reveals that *Beetlejuice* audience members were not just young adults, but, in many cases, first-time theatregoers. Fifty-five percent of audience members had never purchased tickets on Telecharge, the platform used by *Beetlejuice* and many Broadway productions (the rival being Ticketmaster).[59] By any account, this data demonstrates how *Beetlejuice* was drawing a new, different audience (at least until the Broadway shutdown in March 2020).

While *Beetlejuice* saw weekly grosses hover around $600,000 and $900,000 per week in April and May 2019, respectively, the TikTok explosion of fall 2019 saw the musical not only begin to turn a profit but also shatter box-office records at the Winter Garden Theatre, no small feat for a theatre that has played home to landmark productions such as *Follies*, *Cats*, and *Mamma Mia!*. Of course, we can largely credit the inflation of Broadway ticket prices in the twenty-first century, but even so, this data reveals that the musical became an undisputed financial success. For example, the musical grossed $1.48 million the week of November 10, 2019.[60] Box office success proved contagious, and the musical continued to turn a profit every week until the Broadway shutdown of March 2020. From November 2019 to March 2020, the musical played to between 90 and 102 percent capacity, averaging well over a million dollars per week and playing between 75 and 148 percent of its gross potential.[61] This data, in tandem with the momentum generated from TikTok, indicated that the show would soon return its investment and turn a profit. That *Beetlejuice* did this during the notoriously slow winter months is laudatory. Unfortunately, although *Beetlejuice* returned to Broadway on April 8, 2022, at the Marquis Theatre, the production struggled to match its previous financial success, much like most Broadway productions following the COVID-19 shutdown. *Beetlejuice* closed on January 8, 2023, having played 679 performances and 27 previews.

Once on the brink of closing early and becoming a massive financial failure, *Beetlejuice* caught the TikTok bug and became a hit, all because of how teenage fans interacted with the musical. The young audience demographics defied the traditional Broadway scripts that dictate that a show must be family-friendly fare (à la *The Lion King*, *The Little Mermaid*, *Aladdin*, and *Mary Poppins*) to have audience demographics that skew so young. The TikTok effect caught many people (creatives, critics, and audiences alike) by surprise when it spun *Beetlejuice* to success—but perhaps, as Craft explores in her work on *In the Heights*, this phenomenon could have been anticipated. After all, marketing teams have known since the early days of YouTube that "the easiest, most affordable way to reach younger and more diverse groups was [is] through the Internet, with the increasing potential for market segmentation and free visibility offered by online targeting, social networking and viral marketing."[62] Although the landscape for social media marketing and fan engagement has radically shifted since *In the Heights* debuted in 2008, Craft's analysis still rings true, explaining how social media can be a game changer when it comes to attracting new audiences to Broadway musicals.

Throughout the experiment, *Beetlejuice*'s TikTok content was organic and authentic to the platform. Accordingly, teens never felt like they were being advertised to, which made *Beetlejuice* an unexpected success with teenagers, something the show never imagined would have happened. Although some Broadway shows have included teenagers in their marketing plans (musicals about teens such as *Be More Chill*, for example, and popular teen film adaptations such as *Mean Girls*), Broadway marketing strategies are not typically geared toward teenage ticket buyers. In most cases, teenagers are simply *not* buying tickets. Of course, this conversation largely excludes family-geared entertainment such as *The Lion King*, *Aladdin*, *Newsies*, and *SpongeBob SquarePants: The Broadway Musical* (2017), which rely on broad appeal that enables the entire family to enjoy a night out on Broadway. But, even so, in most cases, the parents are the ticket buyers and, thus, hold great power over their family's Broadway theatregoing activity. In this case, parents bought tickets for their families to see *Beetlejuice*—but we could say that it was Zoomers that were holding the power.

Conclusion

TikTok is no longer just an option for Broadway musicals. Eddie Perfect admitted that the *Beetlejuice* success could mean more work for later shows: "I imagine that Broadway shows will now have incredibly annoying mandatory social media experts advising them on how to inject their shows into TikTok."[63] And Perfect would be correct in that assumption. For Jim Glaub, founder of the Broadway marketing agency Super Awesome Friends, part of this shift toward TikTok lies in the platform's discoverability: "Discovery is really happening in the world of TikTok, which is great for new musicals and new shows that are trying to organically reach audiences that might not have heard of them before."[64] In this case, shows like *Beetlejuice*, *Six*, and *Heathers: The Musical* can build audiences through virality (entering the mainstream social media culture) and thereby become part of a new musical theatre canon. Whereas name-brand Broadway shows such as *West Side Story*, *A Chorus Line*, *Rent*, and *Hamilton* have all relied on critical success, *Beetlejuice* TikTok suggests a different path. Even tepid reviews and lukewarm (at best) word of mouth don't necessarily force a show to close and wither away into oblivion, as long as there is a considerable social media movement built around the show. This hasn't been lost on Broadway producers or, specifically, marketing firms.

In March 2020, Glaub was working on six Broadway shows' marketing campaigns, all of which were leaning in to TikTok. "Right before the shutdown, I think a lot of shows were really shifting their strategies towards TikTok," Glaub stated, adding, "you cannot really get that type of discovery on Facebook, Instagram, or Twitter right now."[65] As always, all roads lead back to TikTok's powerful algorithm, which holds a far greater likelihood for virality than its competitors. For Broadway, this means that not only can productions hop on trends and build a sense of community through digital stage doors, but musicals can go viral through short snippets of their cast recordings as these become audio memes on TikTok. And other shows took notice of the *Beetlejuice* effect, with *Hamilton*, *Dear Evan Hansen*, *Hadestown*, and *Six*, for example, all turning to TikTok as another tool in their social media arsenal in 2019 and early 2020.[66]

Of course, TikTok success does not necessarily translate to ticket sales—and the curious case of *The Lightning Thief* (which opened in October 2019) offers a useful counterpoint to *Beetlejuice* in this regard. The musical's masterful social media campaign jumped on the TikTok bandwagon in August 2019, seeking to create authentic content to correspond with its robust Twitter presence. Like Presley Ryan and the cast of *Beetlejuice*, *The Lightning Thief* (@tltmusical) found success on the app by marrying the musical's dramaturgy with TikTok trends. Its initial video, of August 14, 2019, recreates a recipe challenge in which users add water representing different ingredients to a mixing pot. In this case, the recipe depicts "the gods creating chris mccarrell," the actor playing Percy Jackson. In the video clip, set to the show's score, ingredients are added: hot, cute, dork, photographer, Percy Jackson. The result is Chris McCarrell, who would become one of the faces of *The Lightning Thief*'s TikTok campaign. McCarrell is a Millennial, but he was an ideal choice to engage with TikTok aesthetics since he fits the Gen Z e-boy aesthetics, which have resurrected nineties skaterboy looks. McCarrell's aesthetic reads as authentic on TikTok, where the platform's upper echelon—Chase "Lil Huddy" Hudson, Ondreaz Lopez, Tony Lopez, and other members of the Hype House—all sport the e-boy lewk. This marriage of e-boy aesthetics, Gen Z culture, Percy Jackson, and TikTok culture is apparent throughout *The Lightning Thief* archive. For instance, an August 20, 2019, video posted by the production account recreates the "New Flesh" challenge, in which TikTokers get ready to go out for a night on the town dressed in stereotypical eighties fashions, makeup, and hairstyles (all to a sound bite from the band Current Joys). This video, captioned "pov it's 2019 you're getting ready to be the son of poseidon on broadway," shows McCarrell getting the perfect e-boy-meets-eighties-meets-Percy Jackson look. While the video successfully recreated the trend, offering a dramaturgically sound intervention into the archive, the comments section, as always, had much to reveal about TikTok's potential to radically engage Zoomer musical fans. In this case, the comments section was filled with young people focused on McCarrell rolling his jeans to expose just the right amount of ankle, which is largely considered bisexual canon in Zoomer and Millennial social media culture. Comments such as "Did he just confirm Percy Jackson is Bi?" (@justjill62001), "percy is bi. this video confirmed it" (@pallasalfaro), "percy jackson the big bi ocean boi" (@artistry_avenue), and "the bi energy in this video" (@puthybandit) stoked the flames of the popular fan theory that Percy Jackson is bisexual. The musical's TikTok team did little to squelch the theory, instead opting to let fans use this space to engage with one another, theorize Percy's sexuality, and, ultimately, celebrate the musical and extend its afterlife into a definitively fan-focused space.

In the end, *The Lightning Thief* was a commercial and critical flop on Broadway. The musical opened to negative reviews and was never able to find a paying audience, even if the production did have a legion of supportive fans who engaged with the musical on social media. Thus, while *The Lightning Thief* TikTok, in tandem with *Beetlejuice*, does convey authentic ways to engage with Zoomer musical fans and potential ticket buyers, TikTok alone can't make or break a musical. Rather, TikTok is part of an ecosystem that can market a musical and foster fan engagement. TikTok is just one piece of the puzzle.

Interlude

All the Way from TikTok?! Damn! Amber Ardolino's Digital Stage Door

Midway through act 2 of *Hamilton*, the shit hits the fan. The musical introduces audiences to the United States' first major sex scandal and, boy, oh boy, is it popcorn worthy. Our protagonist, Alexander Hamilton, has just done the dirty with Maria Reynolds. When Reynolds's husband, James, learns of the affair, he blackmails Hamilton (extortion!). To keep Reynolds quiet, Hamilton pays him off. Everything is gravy until Aaron Burr (Hamilton's nemesis) and Thomas Jefferson find out about the payments and believe that Hamilton is siphoning money from the Treasury Department to pay Reynolds. To protect his name—and legacy—Hamilton publishes the "Reynolds Pamphlet," which leaves his dirty laundry out to dry. Hamilton writes, "The charge against me is a connection with one James Reynolds for purposes of improper pecuniary speculation. My real crime is an amorous connection with his wife, for a considerable time with his privity and connivance."[1] To match the real-life brouhaha around *le scandale*, the staging of the musical number "The Reynolds Pamphlet" erupts into chaos. While Lin-Manuel Miranda's book and score, Thomas Kail's direction, Alex Lacamoire's orchestrations, and Andy Blankenbuehler's choreography are meticulously tight throughout the nearly three-hour show (which opened on Broadway in August 2015), in this moment, all hell breaks loose. Blankenbuehler's Tony Award–winning choreography transitions from razor-sharp movements to a rare moment of improvisation. The ensemble has creative liberty to add in their own dance moves for a few bars. Blankenbuehler could never have imagined that this climactic moment would become a vehicle for viral dances from a social media platform.

Enter Amber Ardolino. Broadway veteran. *Hamilton* swing. TikTok star.[2] During a fall 2021 performance of *Hamilton*, Ardolino used this fun improv moment during "The Reynolds Pamphlet" to do the viral dance challenge to "WAP," Cardi B featuring Megan Thee Stallion's hit song celebrating "wet-ass pussy." The dance, originally choreographed by Brian Esperon in summer 2020, includes a dramatic mixture of kicking, crawling on the floor, humping the floor, and twerking in a split.[3] While the song gave Cardi B her fourth number-one single on the Billboard Hot 100 in the United States, Esperon's dance remains one of the most well-known and widespread TikTok dance challenges.[4] To put it simply, there is no masking "WAP." When you see it, you know it. And, to make sure that audiences outside the Richard Rodgers knew that Ardolino did the WAP challenge onstage during an actual performance of *Hamilton*, she posted the video proof on her TikTok (@ambernicoleardolino), amassing millions of views.

Ardolino's TikTok is a digital stage door. While Ardolino posts a wide assortment of TikTok content, fan interactions are the through line of her account. At every turn, whether it's leading backstage tours at *Moulin Rouge!* (2019), doing the WAP challenge onstage at *Hamilton*, or inviting fans to partake in the 2022 revival of *Funny Girl*'s first "Saturday Night on Broadway," Ardolino conveys how TikTok can revolutionize stage-door practices by rendering digital spaces an extension of and a new frontier in organic, personality-driven fan interaction.[5] Of course, Ardolino isn't the only theatre-maker who approaches TikTok as a digital stage door. Broadway ensemble stalwarts like Max Clayton (@maxmclayton), JJ Niemann (@jjniemann), Ian Paget (@ianpaget_), Christopher Rice (@chrisriceny), and Alex Wong (@alexdwong) all experienced similar pandemic isolation–induced rises to TikTok fame. This is not to mention the bona fide Broadway stars like Kristin Chenoweth and Mandy Patinkin who regularly use the platform to stay present and interact with fans. But Patinkin isn't twerking onstage. At least not yet.

Ardolino's journey with TikTok began with another Broadway stalwart—*Moulin Rouge! The Musical*. In February 2020, the *Moulin Rouge!* marketing team started an official show TikTok account (@moulinrougebway), following the blueprint that *Beetlejuice* had created. Ardolino became *Moulin Rouge!*'s answer to *Beetlejuice*'s Presley Ryan, running the account and becoming the musical's connection to the untapped market of Gen Z TikTokers. Ardolino's tenure at the TikTok helm was short lived, however, because a month later in March 2020 COVID-19 swept through the cast of *Moulin Rouge!*—including Ardolino—and the show shut down for what would turn out to be eighteen months. With *Moulin Rouge!* on hiatus, Ardolino moved back home to Zelienople, Pennsylvania, near Pittsburgh. She could no longer make *Moulin Rouge!* TikToks at the Al Hirschfeld Theatre, so she started her own account to be able to continue this creative—and addicting—practice at home. Like with other musical theatre performers, Ardolino's early TikTok days reflected the isolation felt in being sequestered at home, with minimal face-to-face social interaction. TikTok became a respite and a place to find joy. As Ardolino continued to post original content to her personal account, her TikTok identity shifted from *Moulin Rouge!* to Amber Ardolino. Although TikTok virality is largely based on individual posts as opposed to personality, Ardolino's success conveys how personalities can grow a sizable following on TikTok, especially with musical theatre as the through line of their content.

When *Moulin Rouge!* returned, Ardolino did not, instead moving one block down the street to *Hamilton*, where she worked as a swing, understudying a handful of roles. Now, in arguably the most famous Broadway show of all time, Ardolino could capitalize not just on her personality but also on the attention the show inevitably receives. *Hamilton*'s relationship with social media has been a pillar of its success and parallels Miranda's engagement with Twitter as a high-yield marketing tool.[6] *Hamilton* has been able to leverage nearly every major social media platform—Facebook, Twitter, YouTube, Tumblr, you name it—as lucrative sites to drive up fan engagement, saturate US pop culture with the show, and, ultimately, sell tickets. Although Ardolino did not run the official *Hamilton* account as she did with *Moulin Rouge!* (and would later do with the *Funny Girl* revival), she was able to capitalize on the *Hamilton* machine. And, this isn't to say that Ardolino used *Hamilton* or even created hyper *Hamilton*-specific content. At the end of the day, her TikTok account prominently features *her* and peels back the curtain on what it is like to be a swing on Broadway. Yet, even a simple act like wearing costume designer Paul Tazewell's iconic *Hamilton* ensemble costumes gives Ardolino clout and credibility—what she needs to have to answer Eliza Hamilton's question from the end of the musical, "who will tell your story?" In the TikTok age, it isn't necessarily Broadway stars like Miranda, Renée Elise Goldsberry, Christopher Jackson, or Phillipa Soo who will tell *Hamilton*'s TikTok story. It is the ensemble members, the swings, the dancers, like Amber Ardolino, Jennifer Geller (@itsjennifergeller), and Preston Mui (@prestonmui) who will tell this story, peeling back the curtain and bringing Hamilfans backstage at the Richard Rodgers Theatre.

Ardolino's account is built around fan interactions, many of which are dictated by fans' TikToking choices. That is, Ardolino is the account's personality, but the fans dictate the type of content that Ardolino creates. She brings fans behind the scenes, helping them become a part of something they may not have had access to previously. The timing of Ardolino's rise to TikTok fame should not be lost. She rose to prominence in late 2021, at a time when Broadway was "back" but many theatre fans no longer felt connected to the New York theatre community. Productions were running again, but many people outside of the New York area were hesitant to travel for theatre. A number of factors limited fan engagement at this time: travel costs, high ticket prices, sudden cancellations, and, of course, the lingering reality that COVID-19 was (and still is) out there. Fewer people were seeing shows, something evidenced by low gross numbers and general social media conversations. Everyone was longing for connection and the chance to be a part of something.

Ardolino's bread and butter is fostering this sense of connectedness and belonging. For instance, in a March 20, 2022, video, Ardolino welcomes fans to the sitzprobe for the much-anticipated Broadway revival of *Funny Girl*. In the video, Ardolino explains how excited she is to finally hear the full *Funny Girl* orchestra, after only hearing the show's score on a rehearsal piano and a set of drums throughout the rehearsal process so far. The video brings fans into a room that they typically aren't invited into, revealing the absolute joy and excitement—tears even—that these artists experience in intimate moments such as a sitzprobe. The video creates a digital intimacy that typically doesn't exist.

Ardolino uses TikTok not just to invite fans behind the scenes but also to meet fans where they're at, with surprise face-to-face interactions at the theatre. For example, in a January 23, 2022, TikTok (Figure 1.5 and Figure 1.6), Ardolino begins her video by replying to a comment on-screen from @torifromhr: "I'm at the show right now and a bunch of people are pointing at your picture in the playbill saying I follow her on TikTok." Ardolino sadly reveals that she is not on that night, so these Ardolino fans won't get to see their fave onstage. "Fuck it. I'm gonna go surprise her," exclaims Ardolino. And before these unexpecting Ardolino fans turned Hamilfans can even realize it, Ardolino is surprising them in the mezzanine at the Richard Rodgers. A fan's tears of joy convey how Ardolino's digital presence translates into real-life fans, who will continue to support her career as she "careers from career to career."[7] Whether it's revealing aspects of the musical-making process that fans rarely see or surprising unsuspecting fans in the audience, Ardolino illustrates how a TikTokian digital stage door can create access to the world of musical theatre, in some ways that extend other social media platforms and in other ways that are wholly new.

ALL THE WAY FROM TIKTOK?! DAMN! 63

Figures 1.5 and 1.6 Amber Ardolino surprises a fan during a performance of *Hamilton* at the Richard Rodgers Theatre. Posted on January 23, 2022.

But that brings us back to our question. Why was Ardolino doing the WAP dance challenge onstage at the Richard Rodgers in fall 2021? How did a viral TikTok dance choreographed in 2020 make it into the choreography of *Hamilton*, a show that had opened in 2015, well before TikTok was even a thing? What the hell was happening?

A key aspect of Ardolino's TikTokian digital stage is how she uses the space to ask fans for suggestions on what type of content they want to see. This is a common TikTok practice, in which one's followers will request the TikToker to hit certain dance challenges or to create videos in specific locations or with other well-known TikTokers. The TikToker will then create a video reply that displays the comment on the video, so casual viewers will know that this is a fan request. This is the hallmark of TikTokers like Brian Esperon (@besperon), Austin and Marideth Telenko (@cost_n_mayor), and Gage Williams (@gwillikers), who regularly create viral dances and trends and perform the dances in different ways to appease their fans. In Ardolino's case, she asked her followers what dances she should perform during "The Reynolds Pamphlet" improv section and then proceeded to not only do the dances, but upload video proof. Fans were able to see her perform pre-TikTok dances like the Itsy Bitsy Spider hand movements and Disney's *Camp Rock* march as well as TikTok challenges like "WAP" and "Best Friends." With each new iteration of the series, Ardolino's following grew, and even folks offline became aware of how she was incorporating TikTok dances into *Hamilton*. As her videos racked up millions of views, musical lovers flocked to Ardolino's comments section, effectively transforming it into a robust and interactive FAQ as well as a site to take requests for more dances to perform during *Hamilton*. As fans were keenly aware, anyone could offer the winning suggestion, thus influencing Ardolino's performance *and* appearing in Ardolino's video by means of the on-screen comment and the caption. With this wave of support, Ardolino continued the experiment. The proof was in the video pudding. Ardolino's experiment represents a rare instance when TikTok dance and culture have infiltrated the actual onstage performance of a Broadway musical, a phenomenon a step further than using TikTok to make backstage videos or to create marketing materials.

Despite the success of Ardolino's "The Reynolds Pamphlet" video series, she eventually deleted the videos, seemingly attempting to wipe them from the internet. Of course, thousands of people saved these videos to their phones (and surely some were uploaded elsewhere), but they are now incredibly difficult or nearly impossible to find, conveying how TikTok can be an ephemeral space. One day a video is available for millions of people to engage with, and the next day it's gone.[8] But why would Ardolino delete videos that had amassed millions of followers and had become her calling card on TikTok? Although *Hamilton* is one of the most saturated shows within the TikTok Broadway archive, the videos in this archive are decidedly *backstage*: capturing moments behind the curtain or in front of the theatre's doors. Ardolino's video series was onstage, during a performance, thus becoming an incidental bootleg of twenty seconds of "The Reynolds Pamphlet." This may seem inconsequential, but taking videos—much less posting them online— of performances of *Hamilton* breaks company rules. Noticeably, those with power at *Hamilton* turned a blind eye throughout Ardolino's rise to fame, perhaps due to the undeniable fact that Ardolino was attracting many potential ticket buyers to the Broadway production of *Hamilton*. At the end of the day, her playful fun on TikTok doubled as unpaid marketing labor for the production.

The fun and games came to a screeching halt, however, after John Devereaux (@thejohndevereaux), who was in the ensemble of one of the *Hamilton* national touring troupes (the Angelica tour) at the time, posted a TikTok criticizing an unnamed *Hamilton* actor who was breaking company policy by posting videos of the performance itself. In the video, which Devereaux has since deleted, he stated, "When management says you can't record any of the show but you see a cast member blowing up on TikTok for doing exactly that."[9] While Devereaux never named Ardolino, it was abundantly obvious to many viewers that she was meant, and his comments section was flooded with support for her. Yet, Devereaux's video did raise questions about the ethics and legality of Broadway bootleg recordings, even when the videos are so short and so focused on one performer that they don't reveal much of the production itself. Even when a much-lauded pro-shot of the production lives on Disney+ and has been seen by hundreds of millions of people. Ardolino's videos were still bootlegs. They were still illegal.

But most Broadway fans aren't concerned with legality, especially when it comes to bootlegs. "Slime tutorials" and other cleverly named videos of Broadway productions have circulated on YouTube for years.[10] These bootlegs may be hard to find in some cases, but that doesn't mean they don't exist. And fans find them. Scholars find them, too. Bootlegs are hella popular.[11] For many fans, the popularity of bootlegs lies in accessibility. That is, because Broadway can be prohibitive—from travel to New York City to ticket prices—fans more easily overlook the ethics of bootlegs. At the end of the day, this is often the only way they will be able to see Broadway productions. These sentiments appeared in Devereaux's comments section. TikTok user @rosatheswiftie wrote, "It's giving . . . broadway is reserved for the elite and the poors shouldn't get to see a clip." Another TikTokian, @melissabecraft, added, "Not here for the drama. She makes Broadway feel relatable and fun to people who can't experience it!"

Whether it's asking fans to curate her improv for "The Reynolds Pamphlet" or taking them backstage at a Broadway musical, Amber Ardolino conveys how TikTok can foster a feeling of belonging. Ardolino's TikTok reveals how the platform can blend, in effect, Instagram stories and lives with Twitter's immediacy and interactivity to create a digital stage door that can find musical theatre fans by way of TikTok's algorithm and For *You* Page. Although Ardolino is far from the only musical theatre performer to use TikTok in this way, her TikTokian experiments in stage-door creations have helped point the way toward future directions that fan engagement can take on social media. As Adolino's digital stage door conveys, any type of fan engagement is possible on TikTok.

2
Stealth Musicals

The TikTok Broadway Archive from *Heathers* to *Six*

On October 16, 2019, social media personality Dominic DiTanna (@dominicditanna) posted the first in a series of videos on TikTok.[1] In the video series, DiTanna is standing in Times Square wearing a TikTok hoodie and wielding a microphone. As pedestrians pass him on the street, he flags them down and, although they are surely expecting him to ask them a question, he instead quotes a lyric from *Heathers: The Musical*: "Martha Dumptruck in the flesh." DiTanna then points the microphone toward his interviewee, asking them to finish the lyric. The comedy of the video, which had 11.5 million views as of December 2019, lies in the responses and confused looks that the majority of the interviewees provide. "Is that a question?" asks one confused middle-aged man. One older woman tells him in perfect English, "I don't speak English." In the second part in the series, posted November 1, 2019, responses include "Applesauce," "Blackjack pepperoni," and "eats lots of ice cream." The experiment continues. DiTanna is met with laughter and bewilderment. But he soon finds someone in the know—a White teenage boy wearing a Duke basketball jersey and holding a large Dunkin' Donuts iced coffee immediately responds "here comes the cootie squad," to which DiTanna pumps his fist in celebration. DiTanna's *Billy on the Street*-style interviews may seem irrelevant, pure Gen Z nonsense, but there is much more to these informal interviews.[2] In using a popular TikTok sound bite as his prompt, he tests who is in the know about trends in popular culture, especially as they pertain to Gen Z. As the results of the videos illuminate, respondents either immediately answer by finishing the song or have absolutely no clue what is happening. There is no in-between. People either know exactly what this piece of pop culture is or they have already been left behind.

By October 2019, TikTok was already reaching the end of what many teenage TikTok users lovingly refer to as the Golden Age of TikTok. The further we have moved away from this so-called Golden Age, the more nostalgia that Zoomers harbor for this period, in which the app was still predominantly a place for young people. It was before Millennials migrated to the platform en masse, and it was well before the COVID-19 pandemic, which, after its March 2020 onset, would transform the platform from a Gen Z virtual playground to a global force with nearly one billion active users representing almost every walk of life and spanning all generations. This Golden Age of TikTok was marked by a dominant set of extremely popular trends that were mimicked, remixed, and remastered until they achieved widespread virality and became thoroughly ingrained in generational culture. Trends such as Mariah Carey's "Obsessed," "Spooky Scary Skeletons," Blanco Brown's "The Git Up," and the Woah were inescapable. And, surprisingly, musical theatre played a significant role in TikTok's early days. During this time, musicals began to achieve TikTok canonization as their songs were performed over and over again, both within and outside of their original musical theatre contexts. Musicals such as *Beetlejuice: The Musical*, *Heathers: The Musical*, and *Six* were as ubiquitous on TikTok as Lil Nas X's "Old Town Road," the Microwave Challenge to the soundtrack of Joji's "Slow Dancing in the Dark," and the Renegade Dance Challenge to K-Camp's "Lottery." If you're doubting musical theatre's role in TikTok pop culture, look no further than Dominic DiTanna's interview series. To recognize lyrics from *Heathers: The Musical* is to belong. It's to be a part of mainstream pop culture. It's to sit at the cool kids' table in the cafeteria. It's to be a Heather and to have all of the social media clout that comes along with it.

In this chapter, I question how musicals become memes, a practice that solidifies musicals as central to popular culture. I explore two popular trends from TikTok's golden age that make use of sound bites from musicals: the "Martha Dumptruck in the flesh" challenge from *Heathers: The Musical* and the "Yeah that didn't work out" challenge from *Six*. Contrary to *Beetlejuice* TikTok trends, which lived within the dramaturgical world of the musical, these two trends were, by and large, completely detached from the musicals themselves. TikTokers who engaged with these trends were highly likely to not even know that the sound bites came from musicals. These musicals, therefore, became what I term *stealth musicals*, undercover musicals that proliferate on TikTok in ways that are completely removed from their dramaturgy. As stealth musicals, *Heathers: The Musical* and *Six* didn't just go viral but *stayed* viral, spilling from TikTok into other digital and analog spaces and becoming canonical pieces of Gen Z culture. *Heathers: The Musical* and *Six* demonstrate how cultural capital accrues in digital spaces and how, as a result, sound bites such as "Martha Dumptruck in the flesh" enter into a public life that extends beyond the musical itself. Indeed, as I propose, quoting "Martha Dumptruck in the flesh" is as synonymous with Gen Z culture as it is with the musical *Heathers*.

With respect to stealth musicals on TikTok—specifically, *Heathers: The Musical* and *Six*—I illuminate what is happening in the musical song or in the scene of the sound bite in comparison to the different ways that the sound is used in TikTok trends. I pose the following questions: What is the role of stealth musicals in the TikTok Broadway archive? What are the contexts of *Heathers* and *Six* TikTok trends, and how do these contrast with the way the sounds are used in the musicals? What new contexts does the particular video add to the dramaturgy of the musical? How does the musical's dramaturgy complicate the viral trend? How does TikTok make musicals popular and, therefore, install them in generational Zoomer culture? And, how do teenage girls factor into this cultural work?

Stealth Musicals and the Making of TikTok Broadway

TikTok is filled with millions of sound bites. Some of these are incredibly obscure and have only been used once. Such was the case with "Hey Yo! Field Trip Check!," a sound bite that my student Katie and I created by stitching together Edith Piaf's "La vie en rose" with our "oohs" and "ahs" as we took a green-screen field trip to Paris. Our video is a blooper. We fail miserably. We laugh at our mishaps at attempting to record an original TikTok sound, and at one point I question, "Wait, what are we doing? How do we do this?" Although the video has been viewed a few thousand times, the sound bite has been used just once—by us. This is TikTok obscurity at its finest.

On the other end of the spectrum are sound bites whose popularity is so immense that we can call these TikTok Standards. TikTok Standards are ubiquitous on the app, and once they appear, they don't seem to go away. They remain on mainstream TikTok and become thoroughly ingrained in the TikTokian soundscape. Such is the case with "Another Day of Sun" from the *La La Land* soundtrack.[3] This song opens the 2016 film, setting the scene of Los Angeles freeway monotony-turned-musical playground and establishing the film's voice as a movie musical. "Another Day of Sun" is pervasive on TikTok.[4] Among the many ways the sound clip is used, one clear trend that has emerged is to set it as the backdrop in "pointing videos," or videos in which the creator faces the camera and points their fingers at different areas on the screen as text appears and tells a story. In this case, every time the vocalists sing "ba-ba-da-ba, da-ba-da-ba," new text appears, completing the TikTok's narrative. And yet, despite the popularity of this sound clip, *La La Land* itself only appears in the sound bites archive on rare occasions. On TikTok, there is almost no sign of the film: no movie clips or, say, cosplay creations. When most TikTokers interact with "Another Day of Sun" on TikTok, they do so in a way that has almost nothing to do with *La La Land*.

The "Another Day of Sun" phenomenon belongs to the subcategory of TikTok Broadway that I call *stealth musicals*. Riffing off Brian Eugenio Herrera's notion of the "stealth Latino" performer as theorized in *Latin Numbers*, I posit that stealth musicals are musicals that penetrate the TikTok mainstream in a way that is completely removed from the musical itself.[5] TikTokers engage with these stealth musical trends en masse but, by and large, remain unaware that the musical even exists. This is not the case with *A Chorus Line* fans recreating Michael Bennett's legendary choreography, *Beetlejuice* fans channeling the musical's titular character, or theatre nerds crowdsourcing content for a musical adaptation of *Ratatouille*. With regard to stealth musicals, TikTokers often don't know where the sound bite comes from. They aren't familiar with the musical. And they likely aren't musical theatre fans, even if they are engaging in a form of digital musical theatre fandom. They believe they are simply engaging with TikTok culture. But, as I propose, musical theatre culture *is* TikTok culture, so thoroughly embedded in TikTok culture that to engage with one is to engage with the other. These stealth musicals continue to operate in a clandestine way, and, as a result, the archive of TikTok Broadway grows, and musical theatre further cements itself in US popular culture.

Stealth musicals on TikTok follow a lineage of musical theatre songs that are better known than the musicals from which they came. While this phenomenon was far more common in the Tin Pan Alley era, plenty of recent musicals have featured songs that become popular independently from their productions.[6] "The Internet Is for Porn" from *Avenue Q*, for example, was made popular by World of Warcraft machinima on YouTube;[7] "One Night in Bangkok" was better known as a 1980s dance hit than it was in the musical flop *Chess*. TikTok continues this trend with a collection of musicals that appeal to teenage girls. As teen girls are TikTok's trendsetters, their creative choices inevitably influence the larger app's culture.[8] This dominance of teenage girls makes something like stealth musicals possible.

Stealth musicals defy the norms of musical theatre. Musical sound bites, quotes, and characters belong to the dramaturgical world of the particular show. Musical theatre is almost always grounded in context, be it narrative or place. Barrie Gelles affirms, "Musical theatre songs are not meant to be stand alone pieces of music. They are one component of an integrated piece of theatre." They form part of a large story, "not created to be complete in themselves, but . . . indeed part of a larger whole."[9] But when these songs are divorced from their original contexts, this sense of a larger whole is also disrupted, and the sound bites can develop lives well beyond that of the musical. Stealth musicals engage in what theatre scholar Henry Bial refers to as "double coding": the process through which pieces of popular culture develop different meanings for different groups, whether intentionally or not.[10] In the case of stealth musicals on TikTok, shows like *Heathers: The Musical* and *Six* have one set of meanings for fans of the musicals, and another set of meanings for those who aren't familiar with the musicals from which they originate.

When removed from their dramaturgy, stealth musicals are inevitably misread, adding new meanings to both the sound bite and the musical itself. To borrow an example from recent popular culture, the *Kinky Boots* line "Ladies, gentlemen, and those who have yet to make up your minds" is one of the most iconic moments of the 2012 musical: it's a line that's always quoted when people mention *Kinky Boots* (much like, say, *Hamilton*'s "Immigrants, we get the job done"). But this is a line that has to be situated within the dramaturgy of *Kinky Boots*. Within the context of the musical, drag queen Lola greets the workers at the Price and Son shoe factory during the rousing act 1 finale, "Everybody Say Yeah." Per usual, Lola's invocation is inclusive and fits within the personality and arc of that character, as collaboratively created by actor Billy Porter, book writer Harvey Fierstein, and composer and lyricist Cyndi Lauper. When the line is removed from *Kinky Boots*, however, context can get lost: this was the case when Billy Porter, reciting the line at the 2019 Emmy Awards, was interpreted as being transphobic, and met with a wave of criticism and backlash.

Perhaps not surprisingly, the way that musical theatre operates on TikTok is not unlike the way it worked on the television series *Glee* (2009–15). Gelles proposes that, in light of *Glee*'s popularity, "the way in which showtunes are used within the series will very likely have a lasting effect on the 'understanding' of these songs and how they are remembered. We must then consider the original context of the songs within their original piece of musical theatre and compare that with their recontextualised appearance in *Glee*."[11] Although *Glee* put musical theatre front and center, it often used showtunes in contexts that defied the dramaturgy of the original musical. The television series added new meanings to the songs, perhaps perplexing some viewers along the way. These out-of-context pieces of musical theatre engage in what Marvin Carlson calls "ghosting." In ghosting, spectators "encounter a new but distinctly different example of a type of artistic product they have encountered before," or "the identical thing they have encountered before, although now in a somewhat different context."[12] On TikTok, users may encounter showtunes in ways that are both familiar and unfamiliar. There is a certain level of recognition as much as there is a breakdown in context that can, at times, be baffling. By engaging in ghosting, then, stealth musicals not only distance themselves from but actively obscure their original dramaturgy.

"Martha Dumptruck in the Flesh": Here Comes *Heathers: The Musical*

The 1989 hit black comedy film *Heathers* would become one of the unlikeliest of Gen Z obsessions. Whereas Millennials fully embrace eighties culture and nostalgia, Gen Z is invested in resurrecting all things nineties, with a particular interest in music and fashion. The eighties are out; the nineties are in. *Heathers*, somehow, defies the typical pattern. The film, despite being fully grounded in the culture of its time period, is relatable today in theme and scope. Audiences love mean girls and all the drama they bring to the table. Depictions of mean girls and popular cliques are perennial in mass entertainment, and central to films like *Cruel Intentions*, *Jawbreaker*, *The Craft*, *Mean Girls*, *Easy A*, and *Do Revenge*. *Heathers*, which helped popularize such themes, features four teenage girls in Ohio, three of whom are named Heather and one of whom is named Veronica. Played by Winona Ryder (who also played Lydia Deetz in the *Beetlejuice* film), Veronica serves as the film's narrator and conscience. The girls' lives are thrown into disarray once popular students begin to die, seemingly of suicide; in fact, newcomer J. D., who becomes Veronica's boyfriend early in the film, is the killer.

Given its pop-culture status, *Heathers* was a natural choice for musicalization. With music, lyrics, and book by Laurence O'Keefe and

Kevin Murphy, *Heathers: The Musical* has enjoyed considerable cult status since its 2014 Off-Broadway debut, especially among teenagers.[13] The show, while no doubt dark, is energy filled as it touches on themes of bullying, suicide, sexual assault, and violence. These themes fit into a generational Zoomer culture that revels in dark, issue-driven television shows such as *13 Reasons Why* (2017–20), *On My Block* (2018–21), *Riverdale* (2017–23), *Euphoria* (2019–), and *Wednesday* (2022–), and young adult novels such as *I Am Not Your Perfect Mexican Daughter* (2017), *The Perks of Being a Wallflower* (1999), *They Both Die at the End* (2017), and *Gabi, A Girl in Pieces* (2014). These heightened and oftentimes unrealistic high school stories resonate with young people today.[14] Teens see their problems or experiences within the pages, screenshots, and characters of these stories. When viewers see glimmers of their own lives or experiences, they relate on a deeper level to the stories, therefore internalizing them more. This is precisely where *Heathers: The Musical* has found success. The musical has quickly achieved popularity with teens, joining the ranks of "cool" shows *Hamilton*, *Be More Chill*, *Hadestown*, and *Mean Girls*. In the years since its Off-Broadway premiere, *Heathers: The Musical* has achieved lasting popularity with teens, and found robust fandoms across social media, specifically on Tumblr and YouTube, before proliferating on TikTok in the summer of 2019.

Shortly after *Heathers: The Musical* became part of the TikTok lexicon by spawning the TikTok trend "Martha Dumptruck in the flesh," my partner's high school drama students began begging that the show be the all-school musical the following year. Another drama teacher I know across town had the same pressure from his students. Whenever I'd ask my high school students about musicals, *Heathers* always came up. As these teens knew, producing *Heathers: The Musical* at their high schools would lead to peak Gen Z street cred.[15] So, certainly, some TikTokers were well aware of and eager to participate in the dramaturgy of the musical. But these tended to be the musical theatre kids. Outside of these circles, *Heathers: The Musical* functioned as a stealth musical on TikTok, with the majority of *Heathers* TikToks being performed outside of, well, *Heathers: The Musical*. Considering the content of *Heathers: The Musical* and the film's status in pop culture, this raises the question: what happens when a musical sound bite is almost completely dissociated with the source's original context?

During that summer, TikTok users began uploading videos of themselves, often in groups of three, dancing and lip-syncing to a section of the musical's rousing act 1 number "Big Fun." The trend, which quickly became known as the Martha Dumptruck Challenge, features groups of teens, each of whom depicts one of the musical's Heathers. Similar to most viral TikTok trends that have clear sections, Martha Dumptruck is divided into two parts. During the first part, the trio bounces on one hip and lip-syncs "Martha Dumptruck in the flesh / here comes the cootie squad / we should / shut up, Heather / sorry, Heather / look who's with her / Oh my God."[16] Per usual, the more exaggerated and accurate the facial expressions are, the more likely a particular video will go viral.

During the second part, the "Heathers" continue bouncing on one hip, while lip-syncing "Dang-dang! Diggety-dang-a-dang" and vogueing with their right hand. The challenge has all the makings of a classic TikTok challenge. It's catchy, funny, and easy to execute. When the challenge went viral, it introduced a new generation of young people to the world of *Heathers*. Some TikTokers performed literal homages to the musical, using the cast-recording sound clip and, at times, even donning near replicas of Amy Clark's costumes from the Off-Broadway production. These TikTokers were keenly aware of the world of *Heathers: The Musical*. There are 4.4 million TikTok videos that use the cast recording sound bite with the voices of the original Heathers: Jessica Keenan Wynn, Elle McLemore, and Alice Lee. While this statistic is remarkable in its own right, it is just the tip of the iceberg. As of December 2020, there were nearly 400,000 TikTok videos using the hashtag #MarthaDumptruck.[17] And here is where the stealth comes in.

While a majority of these videos replicate the trend, a sizable number of them dispense with the tactic of lip-syncing to the cast recording. In many videos, members of the featured trio actually sing the lyrics, usually in very exaggerated ways. In other videos, creators of color put multicultural spins on the trend. For instance, a video from @kor915 posted on September 30, 2019, presents an Indian version in which the trio sings the lyrics in Punjabi while clapping and doing Bollywood-esque dance moves. In a similar vein, a video from @letmerobyoupls dated September 4, 2019, features the TikToker doing the classic version of the trend, lip-syncing, bouncing on her hip, and vogueing as she makes the trend her own by removing layers of hijabs from her head each time a new character sings their lyrics. These TikTok videos conjure *Heathers* as a stealth musical: they explicitly engage with the challenge's TikTok dramaturgy, but not with the musical's dramaturgy. In other words, many TikTokers are riffing off the Martha Dumptruck TikTok archive more than they are engaging in any way with *Heathers: The Musical* itself. But, as both iterations of the challenge grew, so too did the popularity of *Heathers* within Zoomer culture.

TikTokers began engaging with the dramaturgy of the *Heathers*-verse even when they were unaware of what the original content was, or what it meant. In the film and the musical, "Martha Dumptruck" is intrinsically tied to bullying; "Martha Dumptruck" is the moniker given to Martha Dunnstock, a fat girl at school who is taunted mercilessly by the Heathers and their friends as a result of her size. In the musical, the number "Candy Store" allows the Heathers to put a typically cruel encounter with Martha into motion. Ram Sweeney's parents are out of town, and he is throwing the hottest party of the school year (what else is he supposed to do?). For the Heathers, this is the perfect chance to bully Martha. They clandestinely invite her, encouraging her to believe that the uber-popular jock Ram has a crush on her and invited her to his party. At the party ("Big Fun"), the Heathers stumble across Martha with, of all people, Veronica. This is *Heathers*, and Martha soon learns that she was tricked by the Heathers. Ram doesn't like her, and she becomes the joke of the party. The scene is a microcosm of how the Heathers operate in addition to speaking to something large that many teenagers have experienced or executed. Their popularity hinges on girls like Martha *not* being popular. The mean girl trio relies on bullying and suppressing their classmates' hopes and dreams in order to retain the school's power structure that privileges pretty, rich White girls.

While the Martha Dumptruck Challenge might thus seem like it's wading into morally gray areas, trends on TikTok frequently use sound bites that are taken completely out of context from their source material. Thus, the majority of TikTok users rarely know—or likely care—where a sound bite comes from. What matters is the trend.

As this particular challenge's popularity grew, the connotations of "Martha Dumptruck" grew further apart from those of the musical. While the sound clip is deeply rooted in bullying, fatphobia, and high school power dynamics, all of these themes are comparatively absent from the *Heathers* TikTok archive. A Google search speaks to the power of algorithms to reveal popular thought and mainstream associations.[18] For example, a simple Google search for "Martha Dumptruck" reveals a mixture of TikTok content, the *Heathers* film soundtrack, and references to the stage musical. This is to say, TikTok is uniquely positioned in the group as the dominant outlier. The TikTok content may have nothing, if anything, to do with the musical or the film, but it is precisely what proliferates within Gen Z culture.

Not unlike in the world of *Heathers*, the most popular TikTokers are teen girls. They are "not only young, but female, normatively feminine, white and wealthy."[19] Michelle Santiago Cortés confirms that "teenage girls rule the internet right now."[20] Whether it's Charli D'Amelio, Addison Rae Easterling, Loren Gray, or Jojo Siwa, young White women help dictate what becomes popular on TikTok. Arguably, then, TikTok popularity can replicate the power structures that are baked into the US experience, whether it's in the halls of your local high school or in the fictional worlds of *Heathers* or *Mean Girls*. I have previously written about what I term the *D'Amelio Effect*, or the way that White teenage girls such as Charli D'Amelio influence trending content on TikTok and, as an extension, generational culture. Given these girls' high follower counts on TikTok, any dance challenge they execute or trend they engage with will inevitably proliferate on the app and beyond.[21]

Melanie Kennedy sees D'Amelio's meteoric rise to stardom as "a continuation and intensification of girl culture and the ideals of young female celebrity of the past two decades." The intense focus, on TikTok, on White teen girls overshadows "the dangers and impacts faced by girls around the world who are situated outside of the ideals embodied in TikTok stars like D'Amelio."[22] In this respect, if TikTok creates a certain ideal of what teenage girlhood should look like, then to perform TikTok Broadway trends such as Martha Dumptruck is to have clout. It's to be part of the popular crowd. It's to be a Heather.

Charli D'Amelio, Addison Rae Easterling, and Loren Gray may be nice, wholesome "girls next door," but they are TikTok's Heathers. We want what they have (i.e., what we lack)—clout, followers, beauty, fame, hot boyfriends, and supportive families, to name a few things. Even though the fictional Heathers are clearly bullies, TikTok stars are aspirational. They embody what Natalie Coulter calls the "esthetic of fun" of teenage visual culture, something that predominates on the app.[23] As Cyndi Lauper once sang, "girls just want to have fun," and in the digital age, they just want to have fun on TikTok. Yet, what does it mean to "have fun" by engaging in a piece of popular culture that is explicitly about being a mean girl? What does it mean for White TikTokers to cast themselves as privileged, obnoxious bullies?

It would be surprising if most teen TikTokers recognized the trend as a form of bullying or engaging in mean-girl culture. Regardless of the context of the original sound clip, TikTokers have remixed it into content that is purely silly and relatable. Even if the meanness of the source material remains, the trend enables a game of pretend, and the point is in the playing: TikTokers get to play at being mean girls, complete with eye-rolling and dismissive rudeness. TikTokers don't need to be familiar with *Heathers* to grasp the context.

Therein lies the power of stealth musicals: observers come across repetitions of a trend. At a certain point, the trend becomes immediately recognizable, which serves its viralness. Audiences spend more time watching trending content, which tells the algorithm to continue sending them similar content—whether it is more iterations of the trend or sibling trends. Thus, even in its stealth, the Martha Dumptruck Challenge may serve as a gateway into *Heathers: The Musical*, eventually leading digital audiences to stumble across repetitions of the trend that explicitly pay homage to the musical through characterizations, costume choices, or props (croquet sticks, for example). And so, with *Heathers*, the stealth musical takes us full circle, back to the dramaturgy of the musical itself.

"Yeah That Didn't Work Out": Becoming *Six*'s Katherine Howard

On June 18, 2019, TikTok celebrity Loren Gray (@lorengray) traded in her plaid skirt and croquet stick for a corset and choker, thereby seamlessly transitioning from a Heather into one of Henry VIII's six wives. Paying homage to Anne Boleyn from the musical *Six*, Gray spins into frame, flips her long blonde hair, and begins lip-syncing Boleyn's signature song, "Don't Lose Ur Head." In her TikTok video, Gray channels original West End actor Millie O'Connell's Anne Boleyn as she lip-syncs about becoming romantically and sexually involved with Henry VIII before being beheaded for infidelity. Gray does little to engage with the world of *Six* in this video, but as TikTok's most followed creator at the time, she helped the TikTok Broadway canon explode. Gray's video became one of the most watched, liked, and commented-on iterations of the song's nearly 1.4 million videos on TikTok. The trend became popular in April 2019 and maintained momentum through the end of the year.

While I coined the term *D'Amelio Effect* to specifically embody the viralness that Charli D'Amelio enables, Gray, too, has a tremendous level of influence, further exemplifying the effect. For nearly a year (from March 31, 2019, to March 25, 2020), she was the reigning "it" girl of TikTok, and she had 54 million followers as of March 2024. Her iteration of "Don't Lose Ur Head" amassed 19.2 million views, 1.8 million likes, and over 10,000 comments. Most commenters remarked on Gray's beauty, popularity, and supposed rivalry with D'Amelio (to riff off *Mean Girls*, the rivalry does not exist). Yet, several keen observers immediately recognized the sound bite, as comments on the video reveal. One user, @zoethellama, questioned, "Do you even listen to Six the musical." Another commenter, @zwiidz, lamented, "I'm mad that most ppl only know this from tik tok." By this point, "Don't Lose Ur Head," while clearly a showtune, was largely living in the world of stealth musicals.

This is not to say that *Six* was unknown in its own right. As TikTok was reaching the peak of its supposed golden age, *Six* was primed to become the next hit musical with teens. Well before it began previews on Broadway in February 2020, *Six* developed an enormous level of clout among teenage girls. With book, music, and lyrics by Toby Marlow and Lucy Moss, *Six* began its life at the Edinburgh Fringe Festival in 2017 before experiencing a meteoric rise. By the time the COVID-19 pandemic forced theatres across the world to go dark in March 2020, *Six* was arguably one—or at least becoming one—of the most popular new musicals. The show had simultaneous Broadway and West End productions, a UK/Ireland tour, an Australia/New Zealand tour, and three Norwegian Cruise Line productions. Because of the pandemic Broadway shutdown, the show ultimately opened on Broadway on October 3, 2021, to rave reviews and a consistently robust box office. Despite the pandemic throwing a wrench into *Six*'s path toward global domination, the musical is resilient and has retained its popularity, in large part due to the ways that the musical excels at "integrating with digital media."[24] The show is made and marketed for the social media age.[25]

Riding *Hamilton*'s wake, *Six* reimagines history by focusing on the lives of Henry VIII's six wives, who appear before audiences as performers in a pop concert modeled after the girl-power arena shows of the Spice Girls' heyday. During the wives' "Divorced, Beheaded, Live in Concert Tour," each performs a song that tells her story. Along the way, the audience helps decide who should be the group's lead singer, based on who suffered the most at the hands of Henry VIII. In what is treated as a feminist turn, Henry

VIII is relegated to the sidelines, leaving the focus on his six wives. Yet, as musical theatre scholar Grace Barnes proposes, the idea of *Six* as a feminist musical is shaky at best, given the "questionable depiction of women onstage."[26] *Six* "has at its core the abuse of women by men in positions of power": its entire premise revolves around the fact that when Henry's wives didn't comply with his demands of obedience and male heirs, he divorced them or had them beheaded. Barnes claims that despite how much fun *Six* is, "there is something unsettling about the reduction of the abuse and murder of women into a fun night out, particularly when dressed up as female power."[27] Theatre scholar Lindsey Barr concurs: "Though we hear more information about the personal lives of the queens in later songs, that their introductions are directly tied to their relationship with Henry VIII removes agency from the very narrative that the musical promises to rewrite as the Queens 'add the prefix' to the already existing archive."[28] In light of Barnes's and Barr's assertions, then, we must critically analyze the way that young women interact with the musical, especially questioning the brand of feminism that *Six* espouses.

Viewing *Six* as a contemporary iteration of the Spice Girls phenomenon makes sense: the six wives, modernized and live in concert, imply a message of collectivity and "girl power." That it is a female-focused musical makes it seem even more TikTok-ready, considering how many teenage girls are trendsetters on the platform. Given *Six*'s gender and sexuality politics, however, the way the show operates as a stealth musical facilitates an archive of TikToks that, when viewed within both the dramaturgy of the show and British history, are at times perplexing.

In addition to "Don't Lose Ur Head," two other *Six* trends emerged in November 2019, both of them from "All You Wanna Do," Katherine Howard's song about her nonconsensual sexual encounters with men from the age of thirteen until her inevitable marriage to Henry VIII and her eventual beheading. The sound bite "I guess you could all agree that I'm a ten amongst these threes" prompted many videos of friends comparing themselves to one another, and the other trend that emerged used Katherine's introduction to Henry VIII as a means to depict teenage girls meeting their new boyfriends: "Yeah that didn't work out."

Now, it is possible that some of these teenage girls *were* familiar with *Six*, even in the time before the musical had yet to truly reach the United States, when the musical's TikTok trends began and proliferated. It's additionally possible that these girls were fully aware and unbothered by the implications of their TikToking choices. But for most of these TikTokers and their audiences, it is abundantly clear that there is little to no knowledge of the musical. That is, the "Yeah that didn't work out" challenge is entirely detached from Katherine's number in the musical and, in many cases, perhaps even the historical figure Henry VIII. Inevitably, teenage girl TikTokers who engage with the trend are only unexpectedly engaging with the dramaturgy of *Six* and the history of Katherine Howard and her marriage to Henry VIII. On TikTok, "Yeah that didn't work out" more often than not lacks subtext, and is entirely disconnected from Katherine Howard's story.

In the challenge, girls begin the TikTok by showing pictures and videos of their ex-boyfriends. Katherine Howard tells us, "Yeah, that didn't work out / So I decided to have a break from boys / And you'll never guess who I met!"—and with that, the TikToker trades in her old boyfriend for the new and improved one.[29] In some videos the girls just show pictures of the ex, but in others the girls drag, dox (out), and expose their ex-boyfriends, leaving no stone unturned in telling viewers how their ex-boyfriends cheated on them and treated them as poorly as Henry VIII treated his wives (minus the beheadings, of course). With the tea spilled, the song continues, "Tall, large, Henry VIII / Supreme head of the Church of England." During this section, the video is filled with pictures or videos of the girl's new, "perfect" boyfriend. By TikTok standards, the trend was moderately popular, with 221,000 videos as of March 2020. So much for the sound bite, "All You Wanna Do" has a far darker meaning within *Six* itself.

Howard's "All You Wanna Do" is catchy, upbeat, and reminiscent of Ariana Grande's music.[30] Throughout the song, she details how she has enjoyed sex and has used her sexuality to improve her life since the age of thirteen. The song is "undeniably a highly enjoyable romp, until a feminist sensibility questions the ethics behind trivializing the issue of manipulative men grooming underage girls."[31] The only depiction of Howard that we see is as a "sexualized object whose desirability comes from her willingness to engage in sexual acts."[32]

"All You Wanna Do" is built on Howard "slowly realizing the objectification and sexualization she endured throughout her brief life, and designed to slowly put the audience on edge as the song progresses deeper into the assemblage of men who used her."[33] Howard details her relationship with her music teacher, Henry Manox. She sings, "He was twenty-three / And I was thirteen, going on thirty." Their relationship "went from major to minor /

C to D," leaving little doubt that Howard was a minor in a relationship with her teacher, which, by default, rendered the relationship nonconsensual.[34] Thus continues Howard's story until she is ultimately beheaded by Henry VIII for her infidelity. Her song is cute and funny at first, but audiences soon become implicit in her ruin for finding joy in Howard's trauma. By the time she details her relationship with Henry, it's too late. Despite her victimhood being clear throughout, "All You Wanna Do" points out the dissonance between the song style and the musical's message: we are all part of the problem.

Barnes proposes that in *Six*, Henry is "more clearly defined than the women of the title, and his abusive behaviour is dismissed in favour of jokes about beheading and sexual prowess, thus relegating his violence towards women to a passing footnote."[35] Throughout the seventy-five-minute musical, we learn about each wife, but while each woman gets a single song to state her case, Henry's presence pervades the show. The same power dynamics are at play in the "All You Wanna Do" TikTok archive, which sees teenage girls inevitably pitting their boyfriends against one another, proclaiming that their "Henry" is the tallest, largest, and most supreme of the TikTok boys. The girls compare their perfect boyfriends to the philandering and abusive Henry VIII, encouraging their followers to mimic the praise as evidenced in the comments. Just as the six wives are defined by Henry, these young women are defining themselves by the men in their lives. The trend of putting boyfriends on parade speaks to notions of attainment and jealousy, much like classic mean-girl films. It's about showing off what you have and telling everyone else what you want. The comedy of the TikTok and the gimmick of encouraging viewers to comment on the attractiveness of the new boyfriend, especially when compared to the basicness of the ex-boyfriend, mask the undoubtedly patriarchal forces at play in the videos. On the surface, these videos appear feminist in that they are entrenched in "girl power." These girls get what they want. They can always do better than the first guy. These women are always improving their lives by throwing one man over for another. Yet, the underlying message is that these women are defining themselves by how cute their boyfriends are. This blurs the supposed feminist message. In this case, there's no empowerment if the power comes from attaching yourself to a (better) man.

Not unlike "Martha Dumptruck in the flesh," to raise concerns around the problematic nature of a TikTok trend is to effectively ruin the joke. It's to think too hard. It's to make it something it isn't. And, as I write this, I'm fully aware that my high school students would tell me that I'm reading into something that isn't there. Scholar Kyra D. Gaunt argues that TikTok isn't meant to be a site in which cultural context is promoted; it's about entertainment. Although she is speaking about racism on the app, Gaunt's thoughts ring true across a number of power dynamics. She notes, "The whole system is about gamifying our humiliation, laughter, embarrassment, shame, crying. . . . It's all about monetizing and gaming that stuff for attention. But there is no critical reflection, downtime."[36]

As stealth musicals engage in Carlson's notion of ghosting, TikTok trends venture further and further beyond their original context. TikTokers engage in the viralness of these trends, despite not always having a shared understanding of the cultural elements that make up the sound, context, and dramaturgy of the challenge. The act of engaging with TikTok contributes to an entirely new cultural phenomenon. There is little to no critical reflection about making or engaging with the TikTok trend. Accordingly, teenage girls perform challenges such as "Martha Dumptruck" and "Yeah that didn't work out," without knowing the implications of what inserting themselves into this narrative entails. Even though their TikTok videos might be viewed as harmless social media activity, it is willfully naive for them to consider the comparison of a perfect boyfriend to the likes of Henry VIII. A teenage girl doing a silly TikTok video can still potentially internalize the message that having the cutest boyfriend makes you somehow better—a stronger woman, a more accomplished woman, a feminist. No art is without social context. To willfully ignore Katherine Howard's trauma, as these teenage girls seem intent on doing, is a context of its own.

Although videos of the "Yeah that didn't work out" trend are typically met with commentary focusing on the new boyfriend, some adept musical theatre fans have called attention to the trend's overall lack of subtext. On Madisen's (@madisensoccer14_) rendition of the trend—uploaded on November 22, 2019, to over 8.5 million views—the user @gaxh_pa.ge923 commented, "Please learn about what the sound is about before you use it. Not trying to hate." The comment, posted nearly a year after the video, on October 12, 2020, calls attention to the troubling gender and sexual politics of Howard's "All You Wanna Do." Similar comments pepper the trend's archive, but they are rare. TikTok is a place for teens to escape to, to be entertained. The girls making videos want to show off their new boyfriends. They may even want to get approval from their friends and strangers across the internet. But they, too, just might be implicated in the power dynamics at play in the feminism that *Six* claims to profess.

Conclusion

Although stealth musicals such as *Heathers* and *Six* penetrate the TikTok zeitgeist in ways that have little to do with the shows themselves, musical theatre fans will inevitably recognize these songs and immediately place them within the context of the shows. They will recall the character's arc and what is happening at that particular moment in the musical: the Heathers are bullying Martha; Katherine Howard is detailing how the men in her life have objectified and sexualized her. It is not easy to escape the original message for musical theatre fans on TikTok. Still, stealth musical videos also take on new contexts. As much as "All You Wanna Do" is about Katherine Howard, TikTokers remove her from her own narrative. The song, then, becomes about teenage girls who have left their "Henry VIII"-esque ex-boyfriends in the dust, trading them in for a new and improved model, one that recognizes their value. Willfully ignoring the song's context is an easy solution: it allows TikTok to remain a space to be silly and have fun. Even so, the archive of "All You Wanna Do" TikToks begin to create their own meanings. Although ignoring the context can result in the accidental antifeminist stance, the "All You Wanna Do" challenge allows young women some control.

Stealth musicals have changed the way Zoomers, and TikTokers at large, consume and interact with musical theatre. Showtunes join the TikTok playlist, adding nuance to the way that musical theatre has historically been consumed. As a result, many of these songs have become better known for their place on TikTok than from their role within the original musicals themselves. The sound bites, therefore, become more closely aligned with TikTok Gen Z culture than with musical theatre.

As such, the use of showtunes on TikTok complicates the musical theatre canon. Like with *Glee*, as Gelles writes, stealth musicals alter (and will continue to alter) how showtunes are received, "so the way the songs are appropriated will be ingrained in popular cultural memory." They are "reframing the consumption of musical theatre simply by suggesting that the songs can have a life away from their original story."[37] Just as songs on *Glee* can have a life of their own that lives well outside the dramaturgy of their musical theatre home, stealth musicals do the same on social media. And, in the world of TikTok, going viral can significantly alter a showtune's context and lead to the potential for that sound bite—and musical—to become an integral part of Gen Z culture. On TikTok, teenagers reshape musical theatre sound bites, working within and outside of the musical's dramaturgy, adding new contexts to musicals such as *Heathers* and *Six*, and demonstrating the potential of TikTok to further propel musical theatre fandom into the digital age.

Interlude

TikTok Self-Tapes: The Muny *Legally Blonde* Dance Call

One afternoon in late January 2022, I received a text from a fellow musical theatre nerd: "Please send me a link to The Muny dance call thing on TikTok. I need to know what everyone is talking about." I quickly spiraled into a scatterbrained overview of the thing that had become the latest hot topic in the musical theatre world: dancers posting self-tapes on TikTok of the dance call for the Muny's summer 2022 production of *Legally Blonde*, the hit 2007 musical by Nell Benjamin, Laurence O'Keefe, and Heather Hach based on the 2001 film of the same name. What had begun as a legitimate audition for the Saint Louis theatre had soon become a micro trend on TikTok. Widespread conversations among musical theatre fans erupted across social media; musical lovers couldn't stop talking about the dance call. While some TikTok Broadway trends are inexplicable and random (even bizarre at times), the Muny *Legally Blonde* dance call fit neatly into the tried-and-true formula for TikTok virality. That is, as Cienna Davis writes, "dance, as the de facto language of mainstream TikTok, has become a reliable method for virality on the app."[1] Unexpectedly following this formula—with snappy choreography set to a catchy snippet of music—the Muny *Legally Blonde* dance call had gone viral.

Set to act 2's "Legally Blonde (Remix)," the dance call caught the attention of TikTokers large and small, who were captivated by William Carlos Angulo's exciting, fast-paced choreography. One such TikToker was *The Book of Mormon*'s JJ Niemann, who has over 1 million followers on the platform (as of March 2024) and is known for his hilarious videos filled with musical theatre humor as well as energetic dance moves. Niemann was already planning to audition for the Muny, having worked there before and loving *Legally Blonde*. Niemann notes, "When I saw one person's post of the choreo, I was inspired to get off my couch that night and learn it in my living room! I filmed the next day with a few friends in a studio in NYC."[2] Like other iterations of the dance call, Niemann's video takes place in a rehearsal studio. As Niemann emerges from behind a red curtain—while Laura Bell Bundy's voice declares, "I said I'm never wearing that again . . . I'm wearing this!"—Niemann launches forward in a perfectly executed rendition of Angulo's complex choreography.

From Niemann's dance call submission (Figure 2.1 and Figure 2.2), it's easy to see how musical fans became obsessed with the dance. Like other viral TikTok dances, Angulo's choreography is difficult to do but simultaneously appears easy to reenact. Accordingly, the deceptiveness of the dance leads to a swelling collection of videos in which many dancers nail the challenge, some flounder in the complexity, and others sidestep the dance

Figures 2.1 and 2.2 Niemann performs the Muny *Legally Blonde* dance call. Posted on February 3, 2022.

altogether by building out the dramaturgical world of the dance (e.g., the person in the audience at the Muny, the casting director, the strong mover, the lead who shuffles off-stage during the dance break, the stage manager). As with other TikTok challenges, part of going viral is the way that a challenge can be executed at multiple levels; there are various entry points to participate.

According to Mike Isaacson, the Muny's artistic director and executive producer, the dance call's TikTok virality "caught us all by complete surprise."[3] The Muny was simply honoring the Actors' Equity Association requirement to not hold in-person auditions. The result? More than 1,400 people auditioned by the February 1, 2022, deadline, uploading a self-tape to YouTube or Google Drive and providing that link to the theatre. And then came TikTok. Over the February 4–6 weekend, Isaacson became keenly aware of how the *Legally Blonde* casting process had firmly left Saint Louis. He received emails and texts from colleagues saying, "Are you seeing this?" and "Wow, this is blowing up!" This included a message from Orfeh, who originated the role of Paulette in the original Broadway cast. Orfeh told him how much she was "LOVING THIS." Admittedly, Isaacson didn't know what "THIS" was at that point. He's not on TikTok, so his husband had to download the app to see what all the fuss was about. Isaacson adds, "It was amazing, a bit dizzying, and completely its own thing. People around the world were in on it."[4]

By February 17, 2022, the *Legally Blonde* dance call TikTok archive had swelled to around 1,000 videos, and popular videos had garnered between 30,000 and 50,000 views (Niemann is an exception, with 636,000 and 206,000 views on his two videos). On Twitter and Facebook—at least in the musical theatre world—the conversation about the dance call was so robust that it gave the illusion that the trend was far greater than the archive actually was. But while a thousand videos may seem expansive, if we compare the *Legally Blonde* dance call to other musical theatre trends detailed throughout this book, it's clear how TikTok fame works at varying levels. Take, for instance, the summer 2021 *In the Heights* challenge, which made use of Usnavi and Vanessa's argument during the film version of "Fireworks." There are over 1 million unique videos using the sound bite. Or, for example, the widespread popularity of *Encanto*'s "We Don't Talk about Bruno," which was able to ride TikTok popularity to the top of the coveted Billboard Hot 100. And, of course, few TikTok Broadway trends match the fire power that the *Heathers* "Martha Dumptruck in the flesh" challenge amassed, with over 4 million unique videos.

Much like 2021's musical theatre TikTok micro trend "Rich Man's Frug" from *Sweet Charity* and 2023's larger but still micro trend "The New Girl in Town" from *Hairspray*, the *Legally Blonde* dance call is far from this level of viral fame.[5] TikTok's upper echelon of dance challenges—Renegade, Savage, WAP, Corvette Corvette, Cuff It—are a beast of their own.[6] Yet, the *Legally Blonde* dance call is part of a larger trend of posting self-tapes and dance calls on TikTok. This has become standard practice for aspiring dancers hoping to book shows such as *Hamilton* and *Moulin Rouge!*.[7] This practice is multipronged—dancers are auditioning ("God, I hope I get it!") while also building a TikTok following. The more successful their video, the better chance they have of being cast. And, even if they aren't cast, the potential for a viral video is too enticing to dismiss. TikTok virality can lead to clout—blooming follower counts, paid promotions, collaborations, *and* casting opportunities based on TikTok celebrité.

Once you've landed on a TikTok subculture, it's very difficult to escape it. It consumes you. The Muny *Legally Blonde* dance call was no exception. Take, for instance, theatre-maker Ali Sousa's February 1, 2022, tweet: "why am i on muny 'legally blonde dance call self tape' tiktok and how do i leave."[8] The replies and quote tweets express similar feelings of being trapped in a pink Delta Nu explosion. And with that TikTokian explosion comes the confidence that you can also execute the complicated dance routine. Such was the case with dancer Julia Capizzi, who tweeted these sentiments on January 30, 2022: "The way I haven't been to a dance call since I embarrassed myself at a call for A Chorus Line three years ago and I still feel like I could do the MUNY Legally Blonde choreo this second from seeing so many TikTok's of people's self tapes."[9] This mimicked my own experiences of spiraling down the *Legally Blonde* self-tape rabbit hole. The more videos I consumed, the more I believed that I could not only do the dance, but maybe even make my Muny debut as Law Professor #3.

Of course, the issue of posting dance-call self-tapes on TikTok raises ethical concerns, particularly as it relates to dance copyright, something that mirrors larger conversations about TikTok and dance credit. The issue of credit and payment is precisely something on choreographer Angulo's mind: "The Stage Directors and Choreographers Society is my union, and they are responsible for protecting the work I do on plays and musicals. However, because their jurisdiction covers productions only, I am left to sift through the legal implications of 'going viral on TikTok' completely by myself. Because I have spent my entire choreography career being protected by my union, it never occurred to me to copyright my work until now."[10] With this in mind, Angulo began the long process of copyrighting the dance-call audition immediately after his choreography went viral.

Despite the muddy waters that TikTok dance copyright entails, Angulo recognizes the powerful culture-making that takes place on the platform. Both things can be true. Angulo acknowledges, "Learning dances in my living room by playing and rewinding tapes of old MGM musicals and award show performances brought me a lot of joy as a child. Seeing that reflected back to me through the thousands of videos of young people doing my choreography in their living rooms has brought me a new kind of joy that I cannot describe."[11] Since Angulo's initial choreographic goal was to spread joy via *Legally Blonde* and, by extension, the theatre community, he has been thrilled by the global response to his choreography. Of course, some TikTokers, namely its upper tier of influencers, can monetize TikTok in various ways, but for most musical theatre fans on the platform, engaging with TikTok Broadway trends is just another way to engage with their online community through dance and showtunes, much in the same way that we have historically used dance to build community in real life.

Yet, per usual on TikTok and beyond, the phenomenon is not without its complications or confusions. Is it a TikTok trend, or is it an actual audition? Several TikTokers posted videos saying that they weren't sure whether they were performing a TikTok trend or actually auditioning for the Muny. While this may sound absurd to a casual onlooker or TikTok denier, this absurdity aligns with TikTok's idiosyncratic, campy, and messy aesthetics and culture. That many of *Legally Blonde* dance call videos are self-deprecating adds to Gen Z aesthetics, which continue to set the tone on TikTok. Many of these dancers know they aren't going to book it. They know their skill is not going to lead to them seeing their name up there in lights. So, what do they do? They ham it up, finding the humor in the fast-paced dance.

But did people *actually* audition for *Legally Blonde* via TikTok? Nope. The Muny never asked anyone to post or share their audition submissions, nor does the Muny use TikTok as a source for auditioning. "The TikTok event is not changing our normal casting process, which takes in input from the director, the choreographer, the music director, myself and my associate artistic director," notes Isaacson, adding, "It's a long, rigorous process for each season, because we do 7 major productions basically back-to-back."[12]

Dance calls fit into TikTok's mainstream culture. Casually referred to as "Straight TikTok," mainstream TikTok is all about dance challenges, which content creators learn on repeat. As they learn these complicated dances, they boost the view count of the videos they're watching, making the videos more popular. Aspiring Delta Nu sorority sisters learn Angulo's complicated choreography while viewing videos of it on an endless loop. In doing so, TikTokers are telling the algorithm that this is content that should be pushed out to other similar TikTokers. Moreover, it teaches the algorithm about the type of content the TikToker themself wants to see. This explains why my TikTok FYP became an endless stream of *Legally Blonde* dance call videos after my first time engaging with the trend. And, as TikTokers spiral into the world of *Legally Blonde* dance-call self-tapes, they become privy to something that most audiences never even consider—the cattle call, or those massive open auditions that are exhausting for everyone involved, often leading to rejection and more heartbreak.

As has become customary with TikTok success, the Muny itself commented on videos via its official account (@themuny, 16,500 followers as of March 2024), something that does more than create good vibes. By engaging with fans, the Muny is building a following and demonstrating how TikTok has influenced theatre marketing. Indeed, when such engagement is done in an organic way, theatres and productions alike can harness TikTok in much the same way that they have previously used Twitter, Facebook, and Instagram.

By this point, February 2022, most folks in the theatre industry didn't need convincing as to the cultural power of TikTok. The platform had helped productions become commercial successes (*Beetlejuice*), made musical sound bites part of popular culture (*Heathers: The Musical, Six, In the Heights*), and even been a place to create new musicals (*Ratatouille: The TikTok Musical, Bridgerton: The Musical*). What next? The unexpected *Legally Blonde* dance-call phenomenon drew attention to the influence that TikTok has within the theatre industry. Niemann is no stranger to the benefits of TikTok. "Having a sizable following on TikTok has been wonderful and fruitful," remarks Niemann, who didn't try to get "TikTok famous" but went viral while making funny videos.[13] As a result, Niemann has been able to sign with a manager, secure brand details, and become one of Broadway's most recognizable TikTokers. Even so, for the most part, talent still rules the roost with regard to Broadway casting practices. Eight shows per week is not for the weak or timid. Neither is it for folks who simply went viral.

While the *Legally Blonde* micro trend is hardly a viral explosion by TikTok standards, it does convey how even a modest collection of videos can still move the needle in the musical theatre world. The unexpected sensation has been a success for the Muny's digital profile. "We do know this exposed so many to just the fact that we exist," admits Isaacson.[14] The hashtag #Muny on TikTok had a modest several hundred thousand views before the dance call; in its wake, the hashtag jumped to 17.8 million views.

Following the explosion of the *Legally Blonde* dance call, Isaacson and the Muny were optimistic that their newfound TikTok fame could translate to audience turnout to *Legally Blonde* and beyond. "Do I hope that 17.8 million people come to The Muny next summer? Sure, why not?" remarks Isaacson.[15] If we've learned anything from TikTok, it's to expect the unexpected.

3

DIY Diva Drag

Wicked's Elphaba on the TikTok Stage

I had never attended the Song, Stage and Screen Conference, so I didn't know what to expect. I had seen pictures of scholars presenting in ornate, old-school European university lecture halls at previous conferences. It didn't exactly seem like a venue in which things get silly, campy, and, to be honest, weird. But that balance between the ridiculousness of TikTok and the prestigious halls of academia is exactly where I found myself in June 2021 as I began preparing for my first Song, Stage and Screen Conference. I was set to present on a topic that had brought me immense joy over the past year: TikTok videos in which queer men perform lip-synced routines to "Defying Gravity" from the musical *Wicked*. Watching these videos on repeat as I wrote my presentation, and faced with the reality of doing yet another unexpected Zoom presentation (rather than traveling to Salzburg, Austria!), I had a lightbulb moment. What if I made a TikTok during my presentation? What if I became Elphaba? What if I defied gravity? I immediately texted my musical theatre confidantes Barrie Gelles and Bryan Vandevender to ask them whether it would be appropriate for me to do a mini, unannounced drag performance during my presentation. Being the supportive sounding board they are, Gelles and Vandevender responded with a resounding yes. The pressure was on. It was time for me to put up or shut up. It was time for me to bring TikTok to Song, Stage and Screen.

I began my presentation by asking attendees to imagine that they had just downloaded TikTok. After interacting with the platform for a few minutes, they were soon being fed musical theatre content by the algorithm. I tasked them with imagining their For You Page (FYP) filled with videos of *Beetlejuice* fans wearing Beetlejuice cosplay, teens lip-syncing the score from *Six*, and aspiring composers vying for a spot in the score for *Ratatouille* the musical. And, then, they came across something like *this* (Figure 3.1 and Figure 3.2). I immediately pushed back my chair, wrapped a white bedsheet around my neck to mimic a cape, clutched a Swiffer WetJet, crouched down low, and

 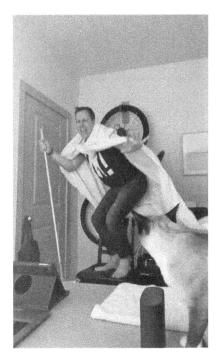

Figures 3.1 and 3.2 Author performs "Defying Gravity" in Elphaba DIY Drag during the Song, Stage, and Screen Conference in Salzburg, Austria by way of Zoom on July 1, 2021.

pressed play. As the crescendo of "Defying Gravity" began, I slowly stood up and lip-synced the lyrics. I moved the Swiffer WetJet around à la Elphaba with a broom, while my partner, Kayla, billowed the bedsheet off-screen. By any standard, I was just a dude standing on a chair in his guest bedroom acting a fool. But, by TikTokian standards, *I was Elphaba*. I didn't need a black cape. I didn't need the iconic pointy hat. I didn't need green makeup. I didn't need any of it. I already had everything I needed in my apartment: a chair, a bedsheet, and a Swiffer WetJet. On TikTok, that's all you need to become a character. Although I could have done more (added makeup and a proper costume, for instance), I didn't need to. On TikTok, DIY and camp aesthetics reign supreme. I became Elphaba, and everyone at Song, Stage and Screen knew it. *I* was defying gravity. All thanks to TikTok.

By this point, I had become incredibly familiar with the different ways that *Wicked* fans were using TikTok to remix, remaster, and reimagine the 2003 musical. I had seen the lip-syncs, restagings, cosplays, drag performances, inside jokes, and the like, the work of *Wicked* fans using TikTok to express and perform their fandom, extending the cultural imprint of earlier platforms like Tumblr. But until Song, Stage and Screen, I didn't really understand just how deep the digital *Wicked* fandom was. My research invited me to peel back the emerald curtain and tap into the empowering qualities of *Wicked*. Moreover, I hadn't fully understood the process of creating a *Wicked* TikTok. I didn't realize how empowering it would feel to become Elphaba, to fly high above the audience and embrace my queer musical theatre identity while belting Stephen Schwartz's now-iconic score. I had begun my journey into *Wicked* TikTok as a spectator and researcher, but, in the process, I became a fan. All of a sudden I was interested in *Wicked* again. I felt like a teenager listening to the original cast recording on repeat in my car.[1] I felt the joy that so many feel when watching the musical. But, more importantly, I felt the empowerment that so many people associate with *Wicked*. Here I was, stuck in my apartment for months on end as the COVID-19 pandemic kept us socially distanced and isolated, Broadway theatres sat dark, and we all collectively wondered when we would be able to see musical theatre, live, in-person again. TikTok gave me the fix I needed.

The process of making a *Wicked* TikTok in real time in co-presence with other musical theatre scholars not only brought me joy, but made me feel like my work mattered. It felt legitimized while lending a certain liveness to both platforms. It showed conference attendees that TikTok performance is more than what we see on our cell phone screens. And it brought TikTok into an academic space in which messy, chaotic, and, to be frank, ridiculous performances are few and far between. That is, this experiment in conference presenting extended TikTokian liveness and embodiment beyond the app itself, revealing how TikTok Broadway has become ingrained in analog musical theatre fan communities.

This chapter tackles the *Wicked* TikTok archive to explore how TikTok has expanded the musical's mobility into the digital realm. Specifically, I closely read what has become one of the signature TikTok trends pertaining to *Wicked*—videos of queer men doing Elphaba drag and "defying gravity." Throughout 2020 and 2021, as productions of *Wicked* lay dormant across the world, Elphaba drag exploded on TikTok. While my Elphaba drag performance may have been limited to those in my Zoom room at Song, Stage and Screen, drag TikTokers find a far larger audience on TikTok. These videos of queer men "defying gravity" have become common practice on the short-form video app and frequently rack up hundreds of thousands of views, and even millions of views in some cases. Yet, these TikTokian drag performances do not emerge from a vacuum. Rather, as I reveal, drag is a core TikTok aesthetic, having been baked into the app's culture in the United States since its early days in 2018. TikTok normalizes drag culture, thus forging spaces in which queer men can engage in drag performances as part of the mainstream, normalized, and expected culture. Indeed, as this chapter reveals, TikTok's knack for all things flexible, mobile, and outside-the-box enables *Wicked* to enter the cultural system of TikTok Broadway.

Something Queer Is Happening in Oz

Wicked as a TikTok commodity is layered. With music and lyrics by Stephen Schwartz and book by Winnie Holzman, the 2003 musical is based on Gregory Maguire's novel *Wicked: The Life and Times of the Wicked Witch of the West* (1995), which, of course, is a reenvisioning of L. Frank Baum's novel *The Wonderful Wizard of Oz* (1900) and the subsequent MGM film *The Wizard of Oz* (1939).[2] As Jane Barnette conveys, "Contemporary considerations of witches in American popular culture typically have two common reference points: the 1939 film *The Wizard of Oz*, and the Salem witch trials of the seventeenth century." As a cultural touchstone, *The Wizard of Oz* teaches viewers the "expectations of how both [a good witch and a wicked one] should look."[3] The film gave us the Wicked Witch of the West (Margaret Hamilton), with her iconic green skin, black clothing, and pointy hat. These are the basic elements that audiences inevitably associate with the iconic character, regardless of how they view her (that is, as good or evil). This questioning of the Wicked Witch of the West's intentions, ethics, and morality is precisely where *Wicked* intervenes.

Wicked imagines what happens *before* Dorothy arrives in Oz, questioning much of the *Oz* canon that audiences surely had considered standard beforehand. In this retelling, we bear witness to the friendship between Elphaba (the so-called Wicked Witch of the West) and Glinda (Glinda the Good Witch) as they struggle with personality clashes, opposing ideologies, a shared love interest, and disparate reactions to government corruption. While Glinda decides to be a "good witch" and maintain her squeaky-clean public image, Elphaba leans in to her wickedness, refusing to acquiesce to the Wizard's unethical demands. *Wicked* is informed by and inseparable from the expansive popularity of *The Wizard of Oz* franchise, which has been remixed and engaged with in a variety of ways. Since at least the 1970s, *The Wizard of Oz* has been adopted by queer men. Of course, this is in no small part due to gay icon Judy Garland's role as Dorothy.[4] In the film, Dorothy escapes the black-and-white small town in Kansas to go to the technicolor world of Oz, where she meets a host of quirky and gender-bending characters.[5] Dorothy immediately accepts other outsiders, such as the Lion, whose "cowardly" moniker is tightly linked to his stereotypical "gay" (read: effeminate) mannerisms. Early on, "Friend of Dorothy" became a way to identify other members of the LGBTQ+ community, giving queer men a coded language to speak about themselves, avoiding harm. In Oz, whether the fictional or metaphorical place, you can be your true self. Indeed, something queer is happening in Oz.[6]

Despite opening on Broadway to lukewarm reviews, *Wicked* was an instant hit with audiences, and it won three Tony Awards, proving yet again for stars Idina Menzel and Kristin Chenoweth that they belonged among the upper echelon of Broadway divas. *Wicked*'s Broadway success has spawned sit-down productions on the West End, in Chicago, in San Francisco, and in Los Angeles, as well as countless productions across the globe. The musical's characters and score have become as recognizable as those from *Chicago* (1975), *Les Misérables* (1985), *The Phantom of the Opera* (1986), and *Rent*. *Wicked* is a well-known commodity, and, accordingly, its various fandoms have extended the life of the musical well beyond what transpires at the Gershwin or the Apollo Victoria.

It should come as no surprise, then, that *Wicked* fans would extend their fandom onto TikTok, which is part of a continuum of *Wicked* fan spaces that have been crucial to the Ozian fandom since the show's debut in 2003. In *Changed for Good*, Stacy Wolf details just how far *Wicked* fans will go to perform their fandom, amid what began as a critical response that was as harsh in its judgment of the fans as it was of the musical. It didn't take long for the musical to develop a "cult status among tweens (preadolescent) and teenage girls," she notes, observing that some critics used this cult status as justification for not liking *Wicked*: they "[argued] that girls, who could not distinguish between good and bad theater, were the obvious audience of the silly show."[7] Of course, the practice of devaluing the nuanced ways that young girls began to engage with *Wicked* is baked in misogyny, given how *Wicked*'s critics paint these girls "as easily fooled, as unreliable, as possessing bad and fickle taste." Yet, as Wolf knows well—and I see every day as a high school teacher—to disregard the cultural capital of teenage girls would be foolish.

Tween and teen girls are not "cultural dupes," but rather cultural trendsetters in many ways.[8] And where did these young girls flock to? Message boards. When *Wicked* debuted, bona fide social media sites were few and far between. Myspace was just entering the conversation, and Facebook was waiting in the wings. The performance possibilities of sites like Instagram and Twitter would have been unthinkable. But message boards were ample, providing endless opportunities for *Wicked* fans to talk about the show and show just how much they loved the musical. Although some scholars may primarily focus on what happens onstage, the question of how musical fans receive a show and, specifically, what they do with a musical is as important as the show itself. As a long-running musical, *Wicked* has generated its own set of cultural codes, which go far beyond the Gershwin. Seeing this, Laura MacDonald and Myrtle Halman propose, "*Wicked* has shown greater engagement with the world outside the theaters in which it is performed than many other long-running, globally circulating musicals."[9] In the age of Web 2.0, the possibilities for fan engagement can feel as endless as the interweb itself. Ever-expanding message board forums, YouTube video compilations and bootlegs, and Instagram spam accounts, for example, give the feeling that the mega musical's fandom can't be contained. It's the cultural force that makes the musical a global commodity.

While fans previously flocked to message boards, Tumblr, YouTube, and Instagram, nowadays TikTok is ground zero for new fan engagements with the mega musical. *Wicked* trends on TikTok are expansive. The *Wicked* TikTok archive features *Wicked*-specific challenges, *Wicked* riffs on TikTok trends, and a wide spectrum of fannish video creation. *Wicked* fans have taken to TikTok to stage mini driveway productions of the musical for their friends in quarantine. Digital Ozians have created TikTok makeup tutorials, showcasing how to achieve the perfect lewk as Elphaba, Glinda, or citizens of Oz. Or, take for example a September 21, 2021, TikTok by none other than Kristin Chenoweth (@kristinchenoweth), in which she auditions for the role of Glinda on Broadway. Wielding a scepter, Chenoweth knocks on the stage door of the Gershwin, asking to audition for Glinda, or the Goat, or any role. As a *Wicked* fan, Chenoweth is desperate to be cast. The video, which is underscored by Chenoweth's 2003 rendition of "Popular," is incredibly meta and tongue in cheek. While the video belongs to a series in which Chenoweth auditions for leading roles in *Come from Away* (2017), *Dear Evan Hansen* (2016), *Waitress* (2016), *Chicago*, and *Aladdin*, the *Wicked* iteration reveals just how deep the *Wicked* TikTok community is. Despite her stage and screen fame and storied relationship to *Wicked*, Chenoweth is a theatre nerd at heart and, at the core of this, is her love and fandom for *Wicked*. Her "desire" to be cast as Glinda is not unlike other TikTokers' collective desire to *play Wicked*. Even though Chenoweth is purely playing TikTok for laughs, the Glinda alum shares many sentiments with noncelebrity TikTokers who want to get witchy. The musical has been openly embraced by countless folks who see TikTok as a vehicle to *become* Glinda or Elphaba.

Although teenage girls undoubtedly form the crux of the *Wicked* fandom, the musical also resonates with queer folx, having significant cultural clout in the LGBTQ+ community, mirroring how *The Wizard of Oz* itself is a cultural commodity in queer spaces. Stacy Wolf sees *Wicked*'s divadom as central to this. Queer men are drawn to *Wicked* because of its divas: "These divas are fundamentally nonnormative and nonheterosexual; that is, queer."[10] The relationship between *Wicked* and the queer community mirrors how the musical's themes speak to marginalized peoples. As Wolf recognizes, "Elphaba's difference stands in for all difference."[11] According to Stephen Schwartz, this isn't by chance: "Anyone who is an artist in our society is going to identify with Elphaba. Anyone who is of an ethnic minority, who is black or Jewish or gay, or a woman feeling she grew up in a man's world, or anyone who grew up feeling a dissonance between who they are inside and the world around them, will identify with Elphaba."[12] Even though Schwartz's comments cast a far wider net, there is truth in how people that have been relegated to society's margins connect with Elphaba. As the musical demystifies the Wicked Witch of the West, flipping her original *Wizard of Oz* narrative on its head and fully humanizing the iconic character, audiences who have themselves felt misunderstood, pushed aside, disregarded, and oppressed will inevitably find bits of truths in Elphaba's arc. The musical may not be perfect or high art by any means, but there is something powerful in Elphaba's journey in accepting her outsiderness and finding empowerment in the process. Needless to say, many queer men love them some Elphaba. And rightly so. Elphaba is a queer icon.

Although some scholars have focused on Elphaba's outsiderness as an explanation for why queer men gravitate toward *Wicked*, others see an explicit connection between Elphaba and drag queens. According to literary critic Claude J. Summers, "For many gay men, the centerpiece of the musical was the larger-than-life female star, her persona an exaggeration of femininity that one associates with drag queens."[13] Moreover, one could argue that Elphaba *is* a drag queen. Elphaba troubles normative gender performances. The actor playing Elphaba undergoes an intensive makeup routine before each performance. The process, lasting roughly twenty-five to thirty minutes, mimics the processes that drag queens undergo to achieve their heightened portrayals of femininity.[14] And what does the actor playing Elphaba do once the curtain falls? Well, she must spend another twenty-five to thirty minutes removing the makeup to return to normal, everyday appearance, furthering the point that the actor is essentially doing drag. Achieving a heightened gender performance comes with its costs. But what happens when gender play is remixed through TikTokian aesthetics and cultural norms? What happens to the Wicked Witch of the West when she's TikToked?

TikTok's a Drag . . . Performance Space

In my article "TikTok Is Theatre, Theatre Is TikTok," I propose that TikTok is inherently a performance space, "one that encourages us to re-examine the very ethics and craft of performance."[15] A key facet of this cultural work is reimagining how TikTok serves as a continuum of tried-and-true analog cultures and digital Web 2.0 spaces such as Tumblr and Twitter. In this new, democratized space, performers of all backgrounds make use of the different ways that TikTok privileges a creator's self-determination. In "TikTok Is Theatre," I write, "On TikTok, self-determination allows TikTokers to hone and retain their agency. Self-determination is marked by intrinsic motivation and the ability to control one's own life and public-facing image."[16] Although TikTokian self-determination can take many different forms, as evidenced in the various TikTok Broadway archives seen in this book (*A Chorus Line*, *Beetlejuice*, *Heathers*, and *Six*, for example), in some cases, self-determination is not so much a product of the TikTok platform as it is a hallmark of the specific community of TikTok creators in question. Take, for instance, the drag community. Drag performances are commonplace on TikTok, but TikTok has not necessarily rendered traditional drag performances more popular than they are in other spaces (say, for example, *RuPaul's Drag Race*). Drag has undoubtedly been popularized in recent years, penetrating mainstream US popular culture in ways that may have been unimaginable even decades ago. While RuPaul may have been the face of mainstream drag queens when I was growing up in the nineties, even appearing in the oddball family comedy movies *The Brady Bunch Movie* (1995) and *A Very Brady Sequel* (1996), drag queens in the twenty-first century have had a far greater public presence. Take, for instance, popular drag queens Bianca Del Rio, Trixie Mattel, and

Shangela, to name a few.[17] These queens enjoy widespread public presences, filled with millions of social media followers, headline acts at nationally recognized venues, book deals, television specials, and consistent media coverage.

Just as drag queens have penetrated mainstream US culture, they, too, have become part of the fabric that is TikTok. Since TikTok's early days in the United States, drag has been no stranger to TikTok. Just as drag performers have taken to other social media platforms to lip-sync, do makeup tutorials, walk the runway, and so on, drag TikTokers render the app a critical site for drag performance. Yet, as expansive and inclusive as TikTok is, its mainstream drag community—like with other subcultures of TikTok—largely adheres to Western beauty standards. As media studies scholar Krysten Stein recognizes, TikTok's algorithm privileges drag performers who are White and thin, and it obscures drag queens of color and others who don't fit this model.[18] As a White space, TikTok replicates existing power structures in the United States, and the drag community is no exception to this power imbalance.

Although traditional notions of drag have become pervasive on TikTok, lending a certain queerness to the space, a different form of drag has been baked into TikTok since its early days in the United States. As far back as summer 2018, TikTokers have engaged in drag performances (the practice arose with Musical.ly, even predating TikTok itself). Yet, this isn't the type of drag you will see on *RuPaul's Drag Race*. Oh, no. This is a definitively TikTokian drag.

On TikTok, DIY Drag reigns supreme. DIY Drag is the opposite of traditional drag, which is a heightened gender performance, characterized by over-the-top makeup, wigs, and costumes. Of course, this classic brand of drag fully exists on TikTok, but it is far less common than DIY Drag, which is so pervasive on TikTok that it may not even be seen as a drag performance. It's simply TikTok culture, and nearly everyone engages in it. DIY Drag sees performers fully lean in to TikTok's camp aesthetics. DIY Drag is silly and nonsensical. Rather than elaborate makeup and wigs, DIY Drag makes use of quotidian objects to complete the lewk. Just as I detailed in the opening to this chapter, by my wearing a white bedsheet and wielding a Swiffer WetJet while "Defying Gravity" played, my audience immediately recognized that I was transforming into the Wicked Witch of the West. I didn't need a black cape or a proper broom, much less green makeup. TikTok doesn't require any of this to complete an understandable drag performance. And, of course, Elphaba drag is its own animal; it's a queer performance engaging a queer audience that by and large *gets* the gig once it begins.

DIY Drag is marked by quotidian objects that take on new meanings. That is, a prop can represent more on TikTok. A towel isn't just a towel. Rather, a towel is a radical prop firmly rooted in TikTok's silly aesthetics. For example, boys place towels on their heads to play women, with the towel mimicking long hair. It's an understood TikTokian convention that even casual TikTokers will immediately recognize. A blanket wrapped as a cape achieves the same effect. A pencil becomes a cigarette. A black line over the lip frantically drawn with a permanent marker becomes a mustache that even Burt Reynolds or Ron Swanson would be proud of. Small Post-it notes adhered to fingernails become the world's most elaborate manicured nails. That is, the more DIY, the more campy, the more chaotic the drag performance is, the more effective it is on TikTok, which ultimately can lead to virality.

While traditional notions of drag performance may be relegated to queer communities, DIY Drag is far from a niche TikTok subculture. Rather, DIY Drag can be seen throughout the app, especially by straight TikTokers. Famous TikTok boys such as Noah Beck, Bryce Hall, Chase Hudson, Ondreaz Lopez, and Tony Lopez, to name a few, often engage in TikTokian drag performances. Casual onlookers may miss the queerness of their performances. Yet, these TikTok boys have inevitably used their clout and influence to normalize DIY Drag. Of course, this work can be done in various ways, but these boys principally drag TikTok by means of the towel on the head to encompass girlfriends and moms. Typically, these videos see the TikTok boy having a conversation with a woman. When the video shows Noah Beck (@noahbeck) as a woman, Beck is wearing the exact same clothing from the "Noah Beck as Noah Beck" part of the video. The only difference is that he now has a towel (usually a dishrag) on his head to signify long hair and, as an extension, his playing of a woman. Everyone watching instinctively gets this; Beck doesn't have to do anything else for his audience to grasp it. That Beck is straight—not to mention was in a long-term relationship with Dixie D'Amelio, one of TikTok's biggest stars—only adds to the DIY Drag phenomenon and further blurs the lines around Gen Z's nuanced views toward gender and sexuality. Playing with gender in this way is simply a normal thing that popular TikTok boys do. And, just as the D'Amelio Effect proposes that White girls rule TikTok, TikTok boys like Beck also enjoy a tremendous amount of influence.[19] Even though many of Beck's 34 million followers may be "thirst follows," Beck inevitably influences TikTok culture.[20] Of course, DIY Drag ran rampant on TikTok long before Beck's rise to TikTok fame in 2019–20, but his actions inevitably normalize DIY Drag on the platform. Although some may see this as an extension of the transphobic "man in a dress" trope, DIY Drag isn't played as comedy itself. Rather, DIY Drag helps tell a story. The joke isn't that Noah Beck, for example, is in drag. Rather, the joke is about the story being told. And, of course, this is even if there is a joke at all. DIY Drag isn't just about comedy. It takes place across TikToks of all genres.

Perhaps surprising to TikTok outsiders, drag is built into the TikTok platform itself. That is, the app is a popular site for drag performances that work across various definitions of drag, from traditional to DIY. But, more than that, drag is also integrated into the app through its video effects, which facilitate drag performances. Take, for instance, the Blue & Red Filter, which rose to prominence in June 2021. The Blue & Red Filter allows TikTokers to shift the video color from red to blue each time they blink their eyes. Moreover, when the video is blue, the filter adds a mustache, beard, and full eyebrows to the performer. When using this filter, TikTokers of all genders can easily partake in heightened male gender performances simply by blinking their eyes. There is no need for makeup or crepe hair to fashion into facial hair. The filter does everything.

As soon as it became available, the Blue & Red Filter became synonymous with musical theatre. The filter's popularity rode on the coattails of the *In the Heights* film, directed by John M. Chu.[21] Although the film struggled to attract high box office numbers following its June 2021 release, the film's soundtrack dominated TikTok that summer.[22] The Blue & Red Filter was central to this. A popular TikTok challenge emerged set to a short sound bite from the song "Blackout." Although the film closely follows the stage musical's plot, the film version focuses on Usnavi and Vanessa's relationship (whereas Nina and Benny are arguably the stage version's main pairing). Accordingly, Nina and Benny's fight onstage becomes Usnavi and Vanessa's on film. In some cases, lyrics are adjusted, and in other cases, new lyrics are added. This is precisely where TikTok took notice. Usnavi and Vanessa's heated exchange in the film is as follows:

Vanessa: You abandoned me
Usnavi: Yo, what are you talking about
Vanessa: Usnavi all night, you barely even danced with me

Usnavi: Don't make me laugh, I've been trying all night
You've been shaking your ass for like half of the Heights
Vanessa: Real nice
Usnavi: You barely gave me a chance all evening
Vanessa: What?
Usnavi: Do I get another dance?
Vanessa: I'm leaving
Usnavi: Vanessa

The song's popularity on TikTok was in no doubt due to the platform's collective thirst for Anthony Ramos. While hardcore musical fans and the millions of *Hamilton* fans (thanks to Disney+) were aware of Ramos's talents and raw sex appeal (to say the least), *In the Heights* enabled his career to skyrocket. Screenshots of Ramos in the film coupled with professional modeling pictures in which Ramos serves smoldering lewks populated TikTok videos by way of the green-screen feature. Videos would feature an Anthony Ramos slideshow while TikTokers would seductively dance "on" Ramos, set to the chorus of Destiny's Child's "Bills, Bills, Bills." The performances of Anthony Ramos thirst on TikTok were endless. This is to say that the emergence of the Blue & Red Filter is directly tied to Ramos's popularity, with many TikTokers particularly clinging to Ramos's line deliveries of "Don't make me laugh, I've been trying all night / You've been shaking your ass for like half of the Heights" and "Vanessa" (let's just say, Ramos pleading "Vanessa" is sexy af).[23] As such, this heated exchange from "Blackout" was a fitting sound bite to be paired with the Blue & Red Filter.

In the *In the Heights* Challenge, TikTokers alternate between Usnavi and Vanessa, blinking their eyes at *just* the right moment as the Blue & Red Filter creates a digital drag production. Performers of all genders seamlessly shift between the blue light (a heightened male performance as Usnavi, complete with a mustache) and the red light (a not-so-heightened-but-totally-gets-the-point-across female performance as Vanessa). On TikTok, this is enough. The filter does the work. There is no need for anything else. Because of how drag is embedded into TikTok, drag performances such as these are standard and easily understood.

After weeks of the challenge trending on the app, its virality soon spilled out into other social media platforms, namely Twitter. Soon, *In the Heights*'s original Usnavi and Vanessa (Lin-Manuel Miranda and Karen Olivo) and their film counterparts (Anthony Ramos and Melissa Barrera) joined in on the fun, enabling the challenge to go meta. On July 9, 2021, Ramos (@anthonyramosofficial) uploaded a TikTok duet with Barrera (@melissabarreram), with the screen couple flipping roles. On the right side of the duet, Barrera doesn't do much to *become* Usnavi. Barrera primarily relies on facial expressions and arm movements to encompass Usnavi's machismo in this moment. On the left side of the duet, Ramos goes to town. Shirtless and wearing a baby-blue T-shirt on his head to represent a wig, Ramos leans in to Vanessa, using exaggerated eye rolls and a hair flip to transform into a DIY Drag version of her.[24] All that's missing are the hoop earrings. Ramos and Barrera's video took off, garnering over 11 million views within a few days of being posted. Eleven days later, on July 20, Karen Olivo (@therealkolivo) uploaded a video in which they and Miranda recreate the scene, similarly flipping roles. In the duet, Olivo wears a black baseball hat hiding their long hair, while Miranda wears a long, flowing blonde wig. Adding another layer of DIY to their drag performances, the video is not a true TikTok duet. That is, the video is a screen recording mash-up of Olivo and Miranda, reiterating how celebrities are not always TikTok natives or experts. Regardless of TikTok insiderness, Olivo and Miranda's video fully encompasses both the trend and the ways that TikTok renders drag performances as commonplace on the platform. Although both these videos are messy and reveal a lack of TikTok video-making expertise—not to mention all four stars are either not on TikTok or are TikTok novices—three-fourths of the quartet instinctively "got" that DIY Drag is a core TikTok aesthetic. Ramos, Barrera, and Olivo didn't need a TikTok primer to know about TikTok performance conventions. Rather, their takes on the #InTheHeightsChallenge joined a much larger conversation dictated by noncelebrity TikTokers who create and maintain TikTokian aesthetics and cultures.

These videos of everyday TikTokers and celebrities side by side reiterate DIY Drag as core to TikTokian culture. TikTokers who deeply engage with the platform understand the cultural mores and standards that dictate life on the app. TikTokers understand that the silliness of the Blue & Red Filter does all the work. There is no need for a higher production value, much less for a man to wear an actual wig to play Vanessa. That is, the video of Lin-Manuel Miranda "heightening" his drag performance with an actual wig misses the point. Such drag performances reveal how celebrities are *not* TikTok's trendsetters. As such, TikTok queers traditional media, in which celebrities run the show, dictating trends, culture, and the actions of millions. On TikTok, the power lies in the unknown TikTokers who can go viral at any point due to the platform's powerful and mysterious algorithm. This is precisely how queer men defied gravity in their livings rooms and soon became TikTok trendsetters.

Elphaba DIY Drag

In the Web 2.0 age, queer communities frequently spill into online spaces, extending IRL relationships and identity performances and, effectively, blurring the lines between analog and digital. TikTok is no exception to this. The platform acts as a generative site for queer performance and worldmaking. Media studies scholars Luis Loya and Elaine Almeida understand content creation on TikTok to be "an extension of queer community and identity formation," something that renders "TikTok a fruitful place for queer performance."[25] In the process of facilitating this queer performance, TikTok itself becomes a site of community-building centered on a shared queerness. Loya and Almeida propose that what separates TikTok's queer community from other online queer spaces is the platform's ability to simultaneously serve two purposes. That is, TikTok facilitates "traditional identity expression" while also embracing "absurd and nonsensical humor," the same silly TikTok aesthetics described throughout this book.[26] While silly aesthetics on TikTok can take many forms—from teenagers bouncing on one hip and lip-syncing along with the *Heathers* cast recording to TikTokers choreographing production numbers for the *Ratatouille* musical—in the *Wicked* TikTok archive, one clear trend emerges: DIY Drag.

Wicked DIY Drag is, of course, centered on Broadway diva worship. Musical audiences have long venerated divas, from Ethel Merman and Chita Rivera to Gwen Verdon and Angela Lansbury. Diva worship functions in two ways. On the one hand, we stan the actor herself. On the other hand, we obsess over the larger-than-life characters that they originate: Mama Rose, Velma Kelly, Roxie Hart, and Mrs. Lovett. While these divas and the roles they play have stood the test of time, having long been cemented in the musical theatre canon, our obsession with Broadway's belting ladies continues to inform much of how we embrace and interact with contemporary musicals in the twenty-first century. Enter actors such as Audra McDonald, Kristin Chenoweth, Idina Menzel, Sutton Foster, Kelli O'Hara, Patina Miller, Jessie Mueller, and Cynthia Erivo, who have all created or reimagined iconic leading roles and expanded our notions of what a Broadway diva can encompass.[27]

The relationship between diva worship and queerness has not been lost on musical theatre scholars. For instance, according to Michelle Dvoskin, "diva roles (whether or not they are also diva characters) are productive sites for queer feminist cultural critique, as their excess—their largeness—breaks the bounds of normative femininity and can allow audiences to glimpse it as a construction, rather than a 'natural' state."[28] Like Hamilton's Wicked Witch of the West, the stage version of Elphaba, for instance, is all about excess: extensive green makeup, impossibly high notes, the humanizing of one of pop culture's most notorious villains, and, of course, the camp of the hydraulic lift. The stage character is marked by largeness; she is larger than life, not unlike the over-the-top gender performances of drag queens.

Some scholars understand the relationship between Broadway divas and queer men to be productive. Others, such as D. A. Miller, view queer men's fascination with musical theatre divas as an obsession that, ultimately, can only be partially fulfilled. Miller writes, "We could never be so fully identified with a woman as to get her starring roles."[29] Onstage at the Gershwin, cis men—and trans women, for that matter—are excluded from Elphaba and Glinda casting conversations.[30] Yet, the desires of queer men to *become* Elphaba don't hinge on casting directors; these wishes remain. In *Witch Fulfillment*, Barnette lingers on "the wishes that we fulfill when we put witch characters onstage or on the screen. Whom do we cast in the witch roles, and how do we emphasize their embodiment of this role through design?"[31] While Miller attests that queer men could never get "witch fulfillment" and play divas such as Elphaba or Glinda onstage, TikTok gives queer men the tools to do exactly this: recast *Wicked*'s divas, cast themselves in the process, and recenter Elphaba as a vehicle of empowerment. What wishes do queer men fulfill when they defy gravity? What does their embodiment of Elphaba say about *Wicked*'s mobility in the digital age as well as the possibilities—not to mention the limitations—of TikTok as a drag performance space?

Engaging with the dramaturgy of both *Wicked* and *The Wizard of Oz*, the Elphaba DIY Drag trend sees queer men and nonbinary folks perform the climax of "Defying Gravity." The *Wicked* score includes several notable bangers—"The Wizard and I," "One Short Day," "What Is This Feeling?," "Popular," "For Good." Yet, the musical has become synonymous with its now-iconic act 1 closer, "Defying Gravity." This number is, according to scholar Kelsey Blair, "musical theatre spectacle at its best."[32] Joining landmark belted act 1 finales such as "Everything's Coming Up Roses" (*Gypsy*), "Before the Parade Passes By" (*Hello, Dolly!*), "And I Am Telling You" (*Dreamgirls*), and "Don't Rain on My Parade" (*Funny Girl*), "Defying Gravity" inevitably elicits an emotional response from audiences as we finally see Elphaba "fantastically larger than life, commanding the audience's full attention and controlling the stage through her enlarged presence."[33] Throughout *Wicked*'s first act, audiences bear witness to Elphaba's coming-to-consciousness, from naive baby witch to the powerful "Wicked" Witch of the West that has become immortalized in popular culture.[34] Having finally arrived in the Emerald City, Elphaba soon learns that the Wizard is a fraud and the person behind oppressing the animals of Oz. With Glinda by her side, Elphaba flees the Wizard's chamber, while Madame Morrible warns the citizens of Oz that Elphaba is a "wicked witch," thus making Elphaba Oz's most wanted person. This begins "Defying Gravity," in which Elphaba embraces her wicked side, swearing revenge on the Wizard as she flees the Emerald City, flying on an enchanted broom. According to Gelles, "Elphaba, having been an 'other' her whole life, has just been severely disappointed by her childhood hero. Her whole life she has been pressured to suppress that which made her different in an effort to be accepted. Now, she realises that she must fully embrace her true identity and nature, and what is more, use that which makes her different to change the very world from which she has hidden her gifts."[35] The larger-than-life aspects of the song's plot are matched by Schwartz's score as well as William David Brohn's orchestrations, Joe Mantello's direction, Kenneth Posner's lighting design, and Eugene Lee's scenic design.[36] "Defying Gravity" is a "constellation of intricately arranged and mutually dependent artistic components."[37] Midway through the number, the Oz guards finally discover Elphaba and Glinda in hiding. After the two witches decide on their divergent paths, the guards break in. Elphaba declares that she's the one they want; she's the wicked one. In this moment, the score crescendos and the music builds, pulsating through the theatre. Elphaba then begins to fly high above the stage floor (with the help of some stage magic: a hydraulic lift). A gargantuan black cape expands from the stage floor, giving the illusion that Elphaba is truly larger than life and unstoppable. Stage smoke and lights help complete the scene as the actor playing Elphaba belts the score's most iconic moment.[38] While *Wicked* may have its naysayers, find me someone who doesn't think "Defying Gravity" is a showstopper and I'll show you a liar.

"Defying Gravity," then, is ripe for TikTok adoption, especially by queer men, given how, according to scholar Doris Raab, the song "has become a sort of gay anthem."[39] And, like other "I Am" songs in the musical theatre canon—such as "Don't Rain on My Parade" (*Funny Girl*), "The Impossible Dream"

(*Man of La Mancha*), and "I Am What I Am" (*La Cage aux Folles*)—"Defying Gravity" is rooted in empowerment, "one of the specific manifestations of inspiration in musical theatre."[40] Queer men who perform Elphaba DIY Drag, then, find harmony in the song's empowering qualities, TikTokian aesthetics, and queer culture. As with any trend on TikTok, strategies for recreating the challenge are varied. While some Elphabas defy gravity by performing to the sounds of Idina Menzel on the original Broadway cast recording, this was, in typical TikTok fashion, *not* the most popular audio choice. The trend typically includes bootlegged audio of Broadway replacement Jessica Vosk performing the song. As Elphaba declares, "It's not her. She has nothing to do with it. I'm the one you want. It's me," TikTokers hunch forward, look into the camera, and lip-sync, exaggerating their characterization of Elphaba. As Elphaba belts, "It's me," the drag Elphaba elevates themself, typically by standing fully upright on a chair before finishing the performance. Of course, TikTok encourages creativity, and many TikTokers deviate from the trend's predominant blueprint. Some TikTokers will don black clothing and a black cape. Others will hold an actual broom. Some will even employ analog special effects (e.g., fans to mimic wind) or digital special effects such as TikTok effects and filters. Once the performance is complete, TikTokers use hashtags such as #Wicked, #WickedTok, and #ElphabaDrag to find community and to enable others to find their video. The result is a constantly growing body of queer DIY Drag Elphaba performances that, when viewed in tandem, reveal much about the *Wicked* TikTok archive.

TikTok is not a contained environment. When you see *Wicked* at the Gershwin, at the Apollo Victoria, or on tour, you inevitably know what you're getting into. Or, take for instance the Song, Stage and Screen Conference, where I could do an Elphaba DIY Drag performance and the majority of attendees could immediately place my performance within the dramaturgical world of *Wicked*. Audiences walk into the theatre—or Zoom room—with a built-in syllabus of *The Wizard of Oz* that can't be matched on TikTok. TikTok audiences are more diverse and wide reaching just by the structure of the digital space itself. The audience comprises Ozians, people that hate *Wicked*, casual musical theatre fans, folks who've landed on Gay TikTok, and, of course, people who will quickly scroll past because they accidentally left Straight TikTok and are desperate to return to the land of fit White teens doing dance challenges and posting thirst traps. Despite the algorithm, casual observers will inevitably stumble across videos of Elphaba DIY Drag and *Wicked* TikTok at large. Notably, even if such users arrive entirely by accident, they will likely recognize Elphaba, or the so-called Wicked Witch of the West, when they see her, because she is a known commodity in a way that TikTok musical trends from shows like *Six* and *Heathers* aren't. Moreover, the Wicked Witch of the West is a more iconic cultural figure than Beetlejuice himself; she is easily one of the most recognizable characters in US popular culture history. The Green Girl is everywhere. Because of this, TikTok content engaging with the dramaturgy of Elphaba holds far greater potential to leave its targeted audience base and fan communities and penetrate into TikTok's mainstream.

At its roots, TikTok is a place for playing and for pushing the boundaries of identity performances. TikTok drag work is marked by embodiment. That is, in everyday Web 2.0 interactions such as TikTok, "the body serves as a critical site of identity performance. In conveying who we are to other people, we use our bodies to project information about ourselves."[41] In the case of Elphaba DIY Drag, queer men engage in identity performances that are multipronged. On the one hand, these drag performances enable queer men to project and portray their queerness in a public-facing space. On the other hand, TikTok drag facilitates community-building in which queer musical theatre fans can find other queer musical lovers. That is, these performances are as much about the individual performer as they are about spectatorship. As with other case studies in this book, videos of queer men "defying gravity" often go viral, leading to hundreds of thousands of views (sometimes millions), thousands of shares, and, perhaps most importantly, robust comment sections in which TikTokers discuss *Wicked* as a queer text. In many ways, seemingly irrelevant TikToks are actually critical sites for queer identity and community-building. Speaking of the larger queer TikTok community, Loya and Almeida propose: "Through the process of remixing sounds, queer users affirm their own identity, teach others about their identity, and collectively construct a network of pop culture and symbols toward a 'queer zeitgeist.'"[42] Of course, remixing *The Wizard of Oz* as a queer cultural text is far from a new phenomenon. Yet, queer TikTokers position *Wicked* as part of a new queer TikTok zeitgeist that centers camp drag, Broadway divas, and a lineage of queer iconography to create something wholly new in the TikTok realm.

On TikTok, queer men *become* divas, tapping into the legacy of how Broadway's diva performances have historically appealed to queer men. By "becoming" these divas—whether in a basement, in a drag club, or on TikTok—queer men can embody the fantasy of performing divadom as "the thrills of a femininity become their own."[43] When they are playing Elphaba, this means getting a little wicked—angry and empowered facial expressions, hunched back, forward lean, a broom in one hand held high, and conjuring hands. That is, the mimesis is rooted in physically imitating Elphaba. Embodiment tells the story.

Take for instance a May 2, 2020, TikTok by Tyler Warwick (@tyler_warwick).[44] Covered in a blue light, Warwick's rendition of Elphaba DIY Drag begins with him crouched forward, his knees bent and his face ready to release heaps of tension as he begins to "defy gravity" (Figure 3.3 and Figure 3.4). Warwick is, of all places, in a bathroom, standing in front of a plain white shower curtain, with the edge of the toilet in sight. A blanket is

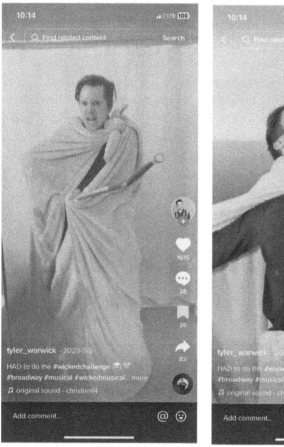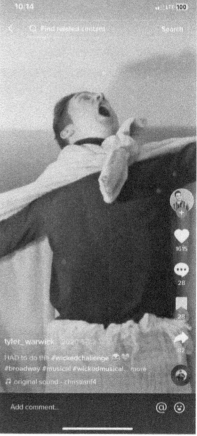

Figures 3.3 and 3.4 Tyler Warwick defies gravity with a blanket and a Swiffer WetJet. Posted on May 2, 2020.

wrapped around him, tied in a larger-than-life knot at his neck. He holds a Swiffer WetJet in his hands. As the music crescendos, Warwick perfectly lip-syncs along with veteran Broadway Elphaba Jessica Vosk's vocals. As soon as Warwick-as-Elphaba declares "It's me" and begins to fly on the broom, Warwick's bathroom light switches to green, basking the entire "stage" in *Wicked*'s signature color and giving Warwick's skin a greenish tone, achieving the effect of Elphaba's intensive makeup routine with the flip of a switch. The DIY, kitschy "makeup design" completes the lewk. Elphaba is ready to soar. And soar she does. As the showstopper kicks into high gear, Warwick slowly rises from his crouched position, extending both arms out as his facial expressions do the heavy lifting, completing the over-the-topness of his performance. In case audiences forget the DIY nature of the performance, once his arms are out, we see the Swiffer WetJet's cleaning-solution cartridge. With arms extended, he continues to rise as the camera zooms in on his face, framing him from below, further giving the impression that Warwick is, in fact, flying. Because, at the end of the day, while Elphaba might need a hydraulic lift to fly at the Gershwin, in the digital space of TikTok it is the camera and the DIY aesthetics that complete the effect.

By using bootleg audio of Vosk, as opposed to Menzel's vocals on the original Broadway cast recording, Warwick's video coincidentally includes the robust audience reaction to the moment. That is, as Warwick rises, the audience—*his* audience—erupts into boisterous applause, cheering and clapping as their diva recognizes her true potential and embraces the power she has always held. Given how "Defying Gravity" is an empowering, uplifting "declaration of self, of intent, of promise, and of a future of fearless existence," Warwick's performance becomes a site in which he taps into these qualities, as well.[45] After all, Warwick isn't just playing Elphaba. Rather, he *is* Elphaba. This performance conveys how musical theatre can be a site of inspiration and idealism, particularly with musical numbers like "Defying Gravity" that, according to Raymond Knapp, "seek to project and embody qualities of courage, heroic resolve, and their capacity to do the right thing and overcome difficulties."[46] For Warwick, an out-of-work actor during the onset of the COVID-19 pandemic, the #WickedChallenge was part of a larger project to take control of his own narrative of using TikTok as a performance space when other, more traditional modes of performance were closed or dramatically altered. It shouldn't be lost that it was (only) in this new, democratized TikTokian space that Warwick was able to find empowerment as a character he wouldn't typically be able to play. In this space,

Warwick demonstrates his agency as a performer, and with every view, like, comment, and follow, Warwick's audiences help him further defy gravity.

The same empowerment narrative can be found throughout the DIY Drag Elphaba archive. Yet, this collection of videos is indicative of TikTok. That is, the variety and expansiveness of queer men's engagements with Elphaba enable each TikToker to put their unique spin on the challenge and dramaturgical world of *Wicked*. While Warwick leans in to an over-the-top rendition of the challenge, from the DIY drag elements to the exaggerated facial expressions, other queer men lean in to realism. Take for instance TikToker Logan Schyvinck's (@lowgy_) April 27, 2020, video (Figure 3.5 and Figure 3.6), in which he presents "a Wicked daydream."[47] Blair proposes

Figures 3.5 and 3.6 Logan Schyvinck has a "*Wicked* daydream." Posted on April 27, 2020.

that "Elphaba's transformation in 'Defying Gravity' begins with the broomstick."[48] Schyvinck's transformation is no different. Set to the original cast recording, Schyvinck's video begins with him sweeping the floor in his foyer. As he casually passes the broom back and forth across the tile floor, the music builds and Schyvinck's daydream begins. He slowly lifts up the broom to eye level, staring at it in amazement and wonder. The music continues to build, and, just when Elphaba is about to reach her greatest height, Schyvinck spreads his arms wide. Once his body is fully open and facing the camera, Schyvinck is immediately transported outside, where he is seemingly standing on a tall ladder. But, of course, we don't see the ladder. We just see this DIY Elphaba soaring high above the ground dressed fully in black, from the shirt and backwards baseball hat to the black cape and long flowing skirt. Just as Schyvinck's daydream transports him to Oz, we are transported to the Gershwin. Schyvinck perfectly lip-syncs to Menzel's vocals as his insanely large cape perfectly billows in the wind. While other renditions of this challenge feature a single take, Schyvinck's video is heavily edited, featuring jump cuts to showcase different angles, close-ups, and pan outs. In short, in just a matter of seconds, audiences bear witness to a multilayered performance of "Defying Gravity" in which our Elphaba fully embodies the empowering qualities of *Wicked*'s titular character while also showcasing his power as a queer man. With Schyvinck clad in a sleeveless shirt, his arm movements accentuate his bulging biceps, his physical power acting as a metaphor for the power he feels while daydreaming about playing the Wicked Witch of the West. Schyvinck soars to new heights, becoming the version of himself he has always longed to be. But, even so, this *is* TikTok, and Schyvinck's video is ultimately a fantasy. After lip-syncing "Everyone deserves a chance to fly," he is immediately transported back to his foyer, where his broom is just a broom and he has a floor to continue sweeping. The daydream is complete.

Whereas Warwick's rendition of Elphaba DIY Drag relied on low production value and everyday household objects to complete the illusion, Schyvinck's take on the challenge conveys how wide reaching TikTokian drag can be. In the case of Schyvinck, audiences can see the relationship between the stage show and the world of TikTok. That is, as Blair posits, "the performance of power is best understood by considering the relationship between the music and other artistic elements–such as props, costume, lighting and staging–which transform Elphaba into the Wicked Witch of the West."[49] In just twenty-seven seconds, Schyvinck's performance gives us all of these production elements, albeit filtered through a TikTokian sensibility, as is never more evident than when he swaps the hydraulic lift for an eight-foot ladder to create his drag showstopper. As a coup de théâtre, or better said a coup de TikTok, this moment inevitably elicits a reaction from unsuspecting audiences, who might be expecting a more traditional—and perhaps more DIY—take on "Defying Gravity." But what we get is something far more complicated and more involved. We quite literally bear witness to Schyvinck's coming-to-consciousness, empowerment, and embrace of his "wicked" identity, all of which is captured in the moment of his taking flight for the first time. While the realities of the mundane world (the domestic labor of sweeping the floor and doing household chores) may be what Schyvinck faces in his daily life, TikTok allows him to soar, reach his full potential. He can engage in some "witch fulfillment" and become his own DIY version of Elphaba.

There is an artistry in the illusion. Both Warwick and Schyvinck are not Elphaba and yet simultaneously are Elphaba. Without the green makeup, there is no hiding the performer, unlike with (most) drag performances. The performer's face is immediately recognizable to anyone that may know him, while the use of DIY props renders the performance legible to anyone familiar with *Wicked* or *The Wizard of Oz*. As such, there is a double consciousness at play, in which the Elphaba in question performs outsiderness and insiderness. They play to both audiences—those in the know and those who have no clue what is happening. Some audiences are in on the joke. Others aren't. Others don't care. They are here for the comedy—or the biceps—that works either way. This is why TikTok works. It's seen by multiple audiences. Yet, for audiences to fully enjoy the performance, they need to know all of the video's contexts. This was immediately apparent to me on April 23, 2022, when I taught a workshop for the nonprofit organization Broadway for Arts Education on the use of TikTok with students. As I showed the video of Warwick in Elphaba DIY Drag, the Zoom chat immediately began to light up with attendees recognizing Jessica Vosk's voice. "Yaaaaaas Jessica Vosk!" and "It's Jessica Vosk for me!" they wrote, revealing how this video—and TikTok trend—had a deeper meaning for them, one with an added layer. It wasn't just a song from *Wicked* or a funny drag performance; it was a moment of knowing the singing actor, as well, something that is surely lost on most TikTok audiences. One attendee even personally knew Vosk, adding yet another and very unexpected layer to the video. And, of course these layers are all part of *Wicked* diva worship. Wolf writes that fans "value the diva who, like them, grows and changes, and they appreciate the actor who can represent that change realistically and convincingly."[50] Vosk is the belting diva who doesn't just play Elphaba, Vosk *is* Elphaba. And as queer men use Vosk's vocals to recreate their own rendition of "Defying Gravity," they are worshiping her as much as they are the fictional character Elphaba. Her realistic and convincing portrayal of Elphaba's character arc gives queer men an outlet to channel their fandom and diva worship. For that, we stan Vosk.[51]

Conclusion

Despite the empowering qualities of DIY Drag, the desire to become Elphaba is potentially a failed promise for queer men. Although TikTok grants them the performance space to play iconic diva roles, queer men are still *not* being cast in these roles onstage, something actors such as Warwick and Schyvinck are surely aware of. Even so, part of the fascination is the insider/outsider positionality that TikTok allows. These dreams can be realized on TikTok, even if they remain fantasies offline, in traditional theatre spaces. Yet, this doesn't alter queer men's fascination with Broadway's belting divas. In a July 3, 2020, TikTok, Warwick (@tyler_warwick) perfectly demonstrates this relationship. As Warwick walks through an industrial park, he reacts to the sounds of Elphaba declaring, "It's not her. She has nothing to do with it. I'm the one you want. It's me." Hearing Elphaba, he moves his head around, looking everywhere until he can spot Elphaba. As she begins to soar, Warwick spins around and reveals pixely footage of Idina Menzel performing "Defying Gravity" onstage at the Gershwin. In typical DIY TikTok fashion, the bootleg video of *Wicked*, the *Wicked* Slime Tutorial if you will, plays on a green screen in the sky above the industrial park.[52] Warwick smiles, looks to Elphaba, and turns to the camera, crying and nodding his head up and down. In this video, viewers can see how Warwick's identity is not simply centered on performing DIY Elphaba himself. Rather, his identity as a musical theatre fan, or better yet a *Wicked* fan, is what gives him power. Even though Warwick had defied gravity himself a few months prior, he now encounters Elphaba in the wild, in the sky high above a CrossFit gym. Now, as an audience member and as a witness to Elphaba's transformation, Warwick sees the power in Elphaba's coming-to-consciousness and empowerment, something that reinforces his own journey of self-determination when *he* defied gravity. On TikTok, her journey is his journey.

While musical theatre fans like Warwick may have kept their fannish identities and diva obsessions private in earlier eras (recall D. A. Miller listening to showtunes clandestinely in his basement as a kid, as I discuss in the introduction), in the TikTok Age, showcasing this part of one's queer identity is an empowering act of declaration and self-determination. DIY Drag enables queer men, and TikTokers at large, to play—with gender, with sexuality, with social norms, with fan identities, with the musical theatre canon. It allows us an accessible venue to engage with our favorite musicals in a low-frills, campy, and kitschy way. As musical theatre further infiltrates TikTok's mainstream, we must continue to unpack how theatre fans use platforms such as TikTok as spaces to perform fan identities and find empowerment in their favorite musical stories and characters. While the Grimmerie might be Elphaba's tool of empowerment, TikTok plays that role for this cohort of queer men, these DIY Elphabas if you will. With a phone in their hand, a blanket, and a broom, TikTok enables them to defy gravity.

Interlude

Mamma Mia! Here We Cosplay Again

In the TikTok age, there is one thing I *always* do when I see my niece Charlie—make a video. My journey with TikTok and other digital dance apps began in 2018, just as Charlie was about to turn six. As I grew in my dance abilities (thanks to my very patient students), Charlie did, too (thanks to growing up and the added coordination that comes along with it). Over the years, Charlie and I have done many dance challenges, from Jalaiah Harmon's Renegade and Doja Cat's "Say So" to Hip Hop Harry's Who's Next Challenge and all iterations of the staple Gen Z dance move—the Woah.[1] But when I saw Charlie on April 23, 2020, we decided to do something a bit different: TikTok cosplay, or the practice of making costumes inspired by fictional characters. Cosplay is a portmanteau of "costume" and "play," and that is exactly what we did. We got into costume and played. In this case, we traded in our dance skills for all things ABBA.

Now, dear reader, you should know something important about me; I'm an ABBA fan. A big one. Some would say it's a problem, but I think it's something to celebrate. What lived as a guilty pleasure for me has finally emerged as a very honest, very public part of my identity. Love me some ABBA! So, as I began researching for this book (i.e., spending far too much time on TikTok "researching"), I quickly noticed that there was a growing body of *Mamma Mia!* TikToks, forming a sizable archive that perhaps is only topped by *Hamilton*.[2] I didn't complain about having to spend time in this archive. Not. At. All. Considering that *Mamma Mia!* is one of the "icons of global culture," as scholars Terence Tsai and Shubo Liu suggest, it should come as no shock that the ABBA property would find a home on TikTok.[3] After all, TikTok is a site where seemingly unrelated chunks of popular culture coalesce and find new afterlives.

Like with their ABBA counterparts, *Mamma Mia!* fans' love for the film franchise only seems to grow with time. As more arenas to express their fandom emerge, their fandom grows stronger. Like ABBA TikTok, *Mamma*

Mia! TikTok is expansive.[4] Although *Mamma Mia!* TikTok runs the gamut, with fans of the film, stage musical, and, of course, ABBA, engaging in various popular trends as well as using the 2008 film's vast array of sound clips and memeable content to create wholly original digital content, several trends have emerged.[5] Trending *Mamma Mia!* content has included fans recreating Anthony Van Laast's choreography from the films, TikTokers storming into their bedrooms and slamming their doors as the opening notes to "Mamma Mia" play (and text reads "when you slept with three guys this summer and don't know who got you pregnant"), and teens channeling Amanda Seyfried by crawling on the beach as they lip-sync "Lay All Your Love on Me." And, by summer 2020, there was a sizable body of work engaging with TikTok cosplay, which, like its drag counterpart, is incredibly DIY (most fans are not donning ornate costumes reminiscent of those seen in filmic or stage versions of the *Mamma Mia!* franchise). This is precisely where Charlie and I would begin this particular TikTok journey.

While scrolling through the hashtag #MammaMia, we noticed a trend in which couples wear robes and sunglasses, with their heads wrapped in towels, while holding a very full glass of red wine in one hand (sometimes the wine is juice, sparkling water, or a soft drink, depending on the age of the TikToker). During the trend, *Mamma Mia!* fans lip-sync to "Angel Eyes" from the enormously popular 2018 *Mamma Mia!* sequel *Mamma Mia! Here We Go Again*. In the film scene, Tanya (Christine Baranski) and Rosie (Julie Walters), as always, offer counsel to Sophie (Amanda Seyfried), who is struggling to reconcile her dream of opening up her mother's bed-and-breakfast with her husband's job prospects in New York City. This scene, of course, is set in the bed-and-breakfast's spa, because, well, why the hell not? Since the stage musical *Mamma Mia!* debuted in 1999 on the West End, Tanya and Rosie have been two of the property's breakout characters, something cemented in both films. Theatre scholar Malcolm Womack sees their popularity as intrinsically tied to the brands of feminism they espouse: "Tanya can be seen as the liberal feminist who works inside the matrimonial, and legal, system, using her gender and sexuality to attain financial security and personal freedom; Rosie as the cultural feminist who has raised her consciousness (and clearly it has stayed raised, as she is operating what must surely be a feminist bookstore)."[6] From Tanya's "Does Your Mother Know?" to Rosie's "Take a Chance on Me" in *Mamma Mia!* to their respective scenes in the film sequel, Tanya and Rosie have frequently captured the attention of the ABBA TikTok fandom. "Angel Eyes" is no different.

MAMMA MIA! 119

Cosplay includes four components: "a narrative, a set of clothing, a play or performance before spectators, and a subject or player."[7] Each of these elements was at work as Charlie and I began to create. To make our entry into the *Mamma Mia!* TikTok Broadway archive (Figure 3.7 and Figure 3.8) with "Angel Eyes," Charlie and I recruited two more members to round out our rendition of the Dynamos—my partner, Kayla, and Charlie's little brother, Michael. "Mom, how many robes do you have? . . . Do you have extra pairs of sunglasses? . . . What about a hair wrap?" My mom, as always, was confused, amused, and supportive. She quickly rounded up our supplies, and we

Figures 3.7 and 3.8 Author and family members don bathrobes, towels, and sunglasses to cosplay "Angel Eyes" from *Mamma Mia!: Here We Go Again*. Posted on April 25, 2021.

headed to the bathroom to get the spa lewk in addition to the unparalleled lighting that bathrooms provide for TikTok videography.[8] As we got into costume, rehearsed, and recorded the video countless times to get the perfect take, we did something else that is characteristic of making TikToks—we laughed. Shauna Pomerantz and Miriam Field observe as much in writing about her TikToking experiences with her daughter, and my work with my niece and nephew supports Pomerantz and Field's findings.[9] Indeed, creating something as silly as a *Mamma Mia!* TikTok in full, DIY cosplay can be a powerful tool to build relationships through musical theatre fandom.

While we were cosplaying as the Dynamos on the fictional Greek island Kalokairi, TikTok was quickly becoming a de facto breeding ground for musical theatre cosplay. Almost immediately after TikTok entered the US market in fall 2018, cosplayers recognized the app as a fundamental site to perform their fandom. The app is filled with cosplay, from Harry Potter and Star Wars to Spiderman and Sailor Moon. The opportunities for TikTok cosplay are limitless, providing a home for fannish performances as well as the opportunity to find community with other cosplayers, who discover this fan-specific content due to how the platform's algorithm sorts its users into tight-knit communities. And, what is more, the nature of the platform itself is well suited for cosplay. Fans make use of tools like duets, stitches, effects, hashtags, audio, and other trends that encourage casual TikTok viewers to take on a more active role and become TikTok creators themselves.

Theatre-critic-turned-sci-fi-books editor Jen Gunnels proposes that "few venues exist for adults to play dress-up" and cosplay.[10] Although Gunnels wrote these words in 2009, well before social media became the powerhouse that it is today, they still ring true: beyond fan conventions, there *aren't* many venues to cosplay in analog spaces. But as digital cultures began spilling into these analog spaces, such fan conventions increased in number, variety, and scale, expanding in-person opportunities for fans to become their favorite characters. Look no further than Comic-Con, and the increasing exposure the mega event gets as the United States' most famous opportunity to celebrate comic books and, by extension, dress as comic-book characters. Although Comic-Con launched in 1970, the event boomed in the social media age, and, as comic-book fans across the world began to see footage from Comic-Con on Facebook, Instagram, Twitter, and the like, other fandom conventions began to appear. There are no bounds to the type of fandom conventions that exist. Musical theatre fans even have a fandom convention of their own now—BroadwayCon.[11]

But if analog cosplay venues are few and far between, any number of digital venues can be transformed into a space to dress up: whether AOL and Myspace, as in the early years of social media, or Facebook and especially Tumblr, in more recent years. But perhaps chief among these venues, especially as social distancing and quarantining practices became commonplace in 2020 and 2021 and people sought to escape from the realities of the COVID-19 pandemic, has been TikTok. Like baking, sewing, reading, or playing *The Sims*, TikToking provides a way to mentally check out and take a break from the anxieties that have become standard. TikTok was and remains an escape. But the platform also has the benefit of bringing cosplayers (like any other subculture on the site) together, helping specific cosplay fandoms find *their people* via the platform's algorithm. No longer must fans seek out fan communities. Rather, on TikTok, the community comes to them.

Now, of course, TikTok didn't invent musical theatre cosplay. Nor was it the first platform to serve as a home for musical cosplayers. For instance, musical lovers have long donned show-specific costumes when attending performances, whether it's *Hedwig and the Angry Inch* fans (HedHeads) dressing as Hedwig to see the original Off-Broadway or Broadway revival productions of the show, or *Wicked* lovers wearing enough green to be a naturalized citizen of Oz.[12] And if you stop at legendary New York Broadway showtunes "sing-along" piano bar Marie's Crisis Café on Halloween, I guarantee you will find Broadway fans in musical theatre costumes singing their favorite showtunes at the top of their lungs. But as TikTok expanded into a global social media powerhouse, musical fans—and cosplayers, in general—began viewing the platform as a space to engage in cosplay, from incredibly detailed costumes to ridiculously DIY riffs on iconic musical theatre characters. The phenomenon has only grown in the four years since 2019, when *Beetlejuice* cosplayers helped ensure that musical theatre was a TikTok staple. Today, TikTok is home to cosplayers engaging with a wide array of musicals. Like DIY Drag Elphabas, this cohort of cosplayers explicitly plays within the world of the musical in question. This is a far cry from the stealth musicals that become TikTok standards.

Nicolle Lamerichs proposes that "expression through a costume of a fictional character is actually self-expression."[13] Gunnels suggests that cosplay isn't escapism as much as it is a critical exploration and performance of identity that isn't so far removed from someone's non-cosplay, colloquial identity.[14] That is, while musical cosplayers may have used TikTok as a way to escape from the pandemic, they were at the same time engaging in a practice of embracing identity. TikTok cosplay became a more accurate representation of identity, not to mention a form of community belongingness. In my case, my love of ABBA and *Mamma Mia!* didn't begin in 2020. Rather, TikTok gave me the confidence to publicly display something that had always lived inside me, albeit as a guilty pleasure that I only rarely talked about on social media. But, seeing other *Mamma Mia!* fans use TikTok as a critical site to perform their fannish identities inspired me to begin performing my own ABBA-influenced identity. After I posted my collaborative "Angel Eyes" TikTok (@official_dr_boffone), the video immediately caught traction, amassing tens of thousands of views within a day and accumulating significant engagements from other *Mamma Mia!* fans who found joy in the video.[15] Seeing how TikTok spectators engaged with our video made me self-actualize my interests in ABBA even more. This was *not* something to hide. After all, fandoms have lived in the mainstream for decades (if not longer). Sports fans wear face paints and jerseys, learn dances and cheers, and engage in a wide variety of performance practices to conspicuously inhabit their identity as fans. This behavior is expected, encouraged, and part of the canon of the particular team. Take, for instance, Liverpool Football Club's use of "You'll Never Walk Alone" from *Carousel* as its anthem or the New Orleans Saints "Who Dat?" battle cry. If these cosplay performances are so firmly ingrained throughout popular culture then why shouldn't musical theatre fans have a similar experience of inhabiting their fannish identities in the public domain? Shouldn't we be allowed and encouraged to be musical theatre lovers out in the open just as Liverpool and Saints fans are expected to do?

When my niece Charlie and I put on bathrobes and lip-sync to songs from *Mamma Mia! Here We Go Again*, we are not trying to hide our showtune obsession. Nor are we trying to obfuscate the ABBA of it all. Our actions are quite the opposite. We are showing our commitment to a specific culture.[16] And we are displaying just how far we are willing to go to do that and to make our fandom legible. We are expressing our love for musicals, *Mamma Mia!*, and the dramaturgy of Kalokairi. Not to mention, we are worshipping the Holy Book (aka *ABBA Gold*).[17] ABBA is joy. ABBA is having fun. ABBA is dancing like nobody's watching. ABBA is loving yourself for who you are. And aren't these qualities precisely what cosplay is? Are they not the same qualities I've used to describe TikTok throughout this book?

4

Anyone Can Cook, Anyone Can Create

Ratatouille: The TikTok Musical

The year 2021 began with the unlikeliest of new musicals. While live musical performances typically take place on New Year's Day across the world (from Broadway to the West End and Madrid's Gran Via to Seoul's Daehangno), this year, with the majority of the world's theatres dark, the musical theatre world's attention was squarely on one new show—*Ratatouille: The TikTok Musical*. What began as a TikTok joke about Pixar's 2007 animated film *Ratatouille* soon became a trend on the ultra-popular short-form video app. In August 2020, longing to visit Disney World and ride the soon-to-open Ratatouille ride at Epcot, TikToker Emily Jacobsen posted a video singing "Ode to Remy" in a high-pitched voice: "Remy, the ratatouille, the rat of all my dreams / I praise you, oh ratatouille, may the world remember your name." The nonsensical lyrics soon drew the attention of composer Daniel Mertzlufft, who scored them and created a video of his own, which promptly went viral, spawning a collection of TikTok videos that built on the "rataturgical" world of *Ratatouille* the musical. Gen Z and Millennial TikTok composers wrote songs riffing off characters and plot points from the film. Other TikTokers added to the show: costumes, scenic design, choreography, marketing, and the like (the possibilities were endless). Soon, there was a swelling collection of "rataturgy" that encompassed nearly every aspect of the film in a musical format ready for the stage.[1]

At first glance, the *Ratatouille* TikTok archive seemed like an absurd joke. At the end of the day, no app does ridiculous jokes that go too far quite as well as TikTok does. But, once viewers began to scroll, it became all too apparent that something magical was cooking in this TikTokian kitchen. Soon, Disney and Pixar were engaging in the *Ratatouille* musical universe, posting to social media and uploading TikToks that informally endorsed the project, lending an air of credibility to the musical and sparking the belief that this could actually become something more than a TikTok phenomenon. With Disney and Pixar's blessing, the musical "premiered" on January 1, 2021, as

Ratatouille: The TikTok Musical, a benefit concert performance under the direction of Lucy Moss for the Actors Fund.[2]

In just five months, *Ratatouille* went from TikTok phenomenon to a fully fledged workshop concert starring the likes of Wayne Brady, Tituss Burgess, Adam Lambert, Priscilla Lopez, Ashley Park, André De Shields, and Mary Testa. In four days of streaming, the musical sold over 350,000 tickets and raised over $2 million. The event was widely covered in national media, with outlets such as *Good Morning America*, the *Today Show*, the *New York Times*, the *Washington Post*, and the *Los Angeles Times* profiling and reviewing the show. Although most media and casual social media users poked fun at the experiment and eagerly waited to hate-watch it, once the opening chords to the *Ratatouille* overture began to play, spectators soon recognized that this phenomenon was indeed worthy of our attention and even held artistic value.[3] As a definitively twenty-first-century way of creating a musical that privileged open access and collaboration, *Ratatouille: The TikTok Musical* offered a shining example of how TikTok can be a platform to crowdsource a musical. As reviewer Christian Lewis noted, "TikTok inverted and democratized" the traditional process of creating a new musical.[4] While *Ratatouille* was not the first crowdsourced musical on the platform, it was the first example to enter mainstream popular culture in the digital age, presenting a possibility for how musical theatre development and production might thrive in a pandemic and postpandemic world. As Jesse Green wrote in the *New York Times*, "As bad as the pandemic has been for plays, it has been even worse for musicals, which are not only intensely collaborative but also inherently unhygienic. The next 'A Chorus Line' won't emerge while everyone is standing six feet apart. No new 'Hamilton' can spit its rhymes from behind a wall of masks."[5] Yet, *Ratatouille* defied the odds.

Throughout this book, I have detailed the myriad ways that musical theatre fans use TikTok to perform fandom. Each of these trends focuses on individual fan performances that, in tandem, create an archive of repetitions. *Ratatouille* broke open this mold, revealing how the app can facilitate a branch of fandom that promotes and relies on collaboration and crowdsourcing. That is, *Ratatouille* was made possible by dedicated musical theatre fans and artists who wanted to participate and collaborate. The immediate goal was to have fun, but as the project continued to grow at an exponential rate, creators became more and more serious, always with the goal of developing a fully realized Broadway musical, even if the idea might have been lunacy for anyone with knowledge about how musicals are built, produced, and brought to Broadway.

Ratatouille's central theme is that "anyone can cook."[6] Despite being a rat, the film's protagonist, Remy, can become a world-renowned chef. Outsiders, regardless of how far from the mainstream they are, can achieve greatness. It should be no surprise that the film has been widely embraced by queer communities, for example.[7] The film rejects barriers and gatekeeping. Although the world of Broadway musicals may have barriers that exclude certain types of artists (women and people of color, for instance) from offstage creative roles, Ratatouille the musical reveals how crowdsourced platforms such as TikTok enable anyone to create—or "cook," as Chef Gusteau would say. All an aspiring musical theatre creator needs is a cell phone, some tech savvy, and an idea, and they, too, can cook. Indeed, Ratatouille the musical is a phenomenon and an exception to the rules of Broadway. And, the musical's rise to pop culture glory parallels the very theme of the show, demonstrating that a composer doesn't need to be Stephen Schwartz, Stephen Sondheim, or Jeanine Tesori to write a "Broadway" musical. This was not lost on most spectators. As the final credits rolled across our screens on January 1, musical theatre scholar Barrie Gelles texted me, "'The #RatatouilleMusical Community'—that as a credit is literally a musical theatre changing moment." But then again, very little about Ratatouille: The TikTok Musical is conventional. The musical pushes against the very idea of what a musical is and how it can come into existence.

This chapter charts the journey of Ratatouille the musical from TikTok trend to benefit concert. I question the possibilities and limits of crowdsourcing on TikTok. By means of the algorithm, TikTok allows anyone to create. Aspiring musical theatre artists from composers and designers to actors and dancers were able to join the #RatatouilleMusical community by simply creating TikTok videos, using the appropriate hashtags, dueting one another, commenting on one another's videos, and the like. The typical process of building a musical was flipped on its head. This was of the people by the people for the people. As such, I argue that TikTok democratizes the musical theatre development process. That this happened with a Disney property is even more noteworthy. This was something new and different, and throughout the lead-up to the benefit concert, the musical theatre community took notice. What was this recipe that was changing musical theatre creation at a time when musical theatre development had all but ceased? Ultimately, as Ratatouille: The TikTok Musical illustrates, the question is not *can* a TikTok meme-musical become a fully fledged Broadway musical, but, *how* does TikTok make this form of fandom a reality? How does TikTok work as a space to develop new musicals?

Crowdsourcing on TikTok: *Grocery Store: A New Musical*

TikTok is known as a hub for collaboration and crowdsourced trends, mirroring the ways that the internet at large encourages community-building and participatory cultural interaction. One way that TikTokers engage with this culture is through crowdsourcing, or "the deliberate blend of bottom-up, open, creative process with top-down organizational goals." A portmanteau of "crowd" and "outsource," crowdsourcing privileges "cooperation, aggregation, teamwork, consensus, and creativity."[8] This new way of performing work lends itself especially well to TikTok, given that it provides users with equal access to the platform and facilitates geographically diverse connections. While crowdsourcing and devising (or, collective creation) share many similarities, devising traditionally relies on co-presence and a facilitator of some kind. Crowdsourcing rejects these requirements, instead relying on a more organic form of building something new from the ground up, one that puts all participants on equal footing. That is, the internet enables a form of collaborating that can only exist in a digital space. TikTok, therefore, does what musical theatre development labs can't. TikTok musicals don't have to wait for grants or rehearsal spaces. They don't require funders and producers. And they don't necessarily need time. All they require is creative thinking and a network—and a new musical, big or small, can be developed at a rapid clip. In a review of *Ratatouille: The TikTok Musical*, theatre scholar Lusie Cuskey recognized how TikTok's "ecosystem removes the challenge of sending large audio or video files back and forth, risking corruption and requiring download, upload, and encoding time or attempting to work around a Zoom lag; creators can share and respond to content nearly instantly in the app, generating an immediate record of their work."[9] Thus, TikTok removes several roadblocks that complicate both traditional, face-to-face theatre-making and theatre-making in digital spaces. On TikTok, things are just easier. And, of course, with TikTok comes the opportunity to go viral and launch into the pop culture zeitgeist.

Ratatouille: The TikTok Musical perhaps best exemplifies the unique capabilities of TikTok to facilitate a pop-culture phenomenon. Because of TikTok's interface, collaboration is easier to achieve than on other social media platforms, such as Facebook, Twitter, and Instagram. TikTok's duet feature makes this possible: it allows TikTokers to work together to create original content featuring two distinct parts, with each TikToker doing part of the video. Media studies scholars Luis Loya and Elaine Almeida assert, "The duet function allows creators to capitalize on a sound's success to gain views while also providing opportunity for alternative interpretation."[10] The TikTok duet effect allows users to not only duet with another user's video, but also create an endless loop in which an unlimited number of people can "duet" with the original and subsequent videos. As the original duet grows, so, too, does the virality of the trend. Casual TikTokers are likely to see several versions of the same duet trend while scrolling on the app. The duet effect speaks to the possibilities of the internet, specifically the speed, reach, and instant nature of digital collaboration. According to Daren C. Brabham, the internet enables "idea exchanges" that "can travel so fast along its channels that the medium virtually erases the issue of time and therefore accelerate[s] creative development."[11] As such, dueting on TikTok enables creators to speed up the collaboration process and see results in far less time than musical theatre creators are accustomed to.

Frances Johnson (@johnson_fran) unintentionally kicked off one of the best examples of this sort of process in fall 2020. On November 8, she uploaded a video (Figure 4.1) commenting on one of the most uninspired trends on TikTok: dueting a video without adding anything to it. In this trend, users duet a popular video to try to land on the coveted For You Page (FYP). While Charli D'Amelio dances or Jojo Siwa shows off her special Jojo Siwa birthday-party merchandise, creators stare into the camera from the other half of the screen. The gimmick is that viewers will stay around to engage with the original video, with the hope that something interesting will happen. Of course, some individuals have found success with reaction videos, but they can also be a large source of frustration for the TikTok audience.[12] In Johnson's video, she looks into the camera and states, "Can we stop dueting videos when we have absolutely nothing to add to them? I don't need to know what you looked like watching that TikTok." The video soon caught like wildfire on the app, leading to an unprecedented string of duets that poked fun at Johnson's video while also dueting it and actually adding context to the original video (Figure 4.2). Initial duets to Johnson's video add her missing (that is, off-screen) hand, gesturing next to her as she asks TikTokers

128   TIKTOK BROADWAY

Figures 4.1 and 4.2 Frances Johnson calls for TikTokers to stop creating meaningless duets. Posted on November 8, 2020.

to stop making meaningless duets. The next duet adds her torso. Then her other arm. Then her legs. Then a dog walking across the room. Then a full film crew from the boom mic operator and cue card holder to the director and cameraman. Soon the duet chain became so large that it was impossible to see the original video. And, of course, there were several different duet chains that were unique, yet entirely in the same scope. In the course of a few months, Johnson's original video was viewed over 3.3 million times and the sound bite was used for over 58,000 duets. The duet chains were then cross-posted on Twitter and Facebook, reinforcing TikTok's stature as the go-to place for generating and spreading meme culture.

Throughout 2020, TikTokers expanded on how duets could work on the app. Johnson's unexpected trend revealed that even the most mundane video could lead to an incredible level of creativity and crowdsourced collaboration. As the larger TikTok community was leaning in to the collaborative nature of the app that emerged during the COVID-19 pandemic, musical theatre creators and fans took notice, beginning their own experimental journey on TikTok.

Enter Daniel Mertzlufft (@danieljmertzlufft). On September 23, 2020, the composer and musical theatre fanboy uploaded the first song in *Grocery Store: A New Musical*. In the video (Figure 4.3 and Figure 4.4), Mertzlufft

Figures 4.3 and 4.4 Daniel Mertzlufft performs *Grocery Store*. Posted on October 7, 2020.

stands in front of a green-screen grocery-store aisle, singing the rousing act 1 finale about the experience of being in one of the most everyday places, a grocery store, but as if it lived within the world of a contemporary musical. As he sings the lyrics—"And we're fighting in a grocery store. And I love you, but I don't know if I like you anymore"—text appears on the video, informing viewers about what a full production of this scene might look like. The text reads, "Just the MOST dramatic. Gotta have the back-up singers belting too." Much like the opening number of *[title of show]*, which quite literally explains the music and directing choices while the actors perform the same techniques they are explaining, Mertzlufft's text reads, "DRAMATIC PULLBACK!!!" as he opts down after his "diva tenor" high notes. "We're fighting in a grocery store," he sings, displaying his full vulnerability and "#ACTINGGGG" chops." The writer includes a "really extra riff to display how emotional they are." As the song comes to a dramatic close, Mertzlufft turns around and walks down the green-screen grocery-store aisle, his body glitching as he moves farther away from the screen. Although this may seem like a funny TikTok gag, Mertzlufft's forty-second video spawned several noteworthy collaborations that built out the world of this brief scene. Through the crowdsourcing that TikTok enables, *Grocery Store: A New Musical* went from a one-off joke into something that seemed like it could be part of an existing musical or, perhaps, even become a new, stand-alone musical.

On September 23, 2020—or the very same day that Mertzlufft posted his video—Megan (@another.blonde) added to the original video, creating a dramatic duet. While Megan largely sings alongside Mertzlufft, adding her own unique riffs to the score, she also adds text to demonstrate what her character, his girlfriend (or soon-to-be ex-girlfriend?), is thinking. He sings about them fighting; she states, "we are." Orange text hovers over the video: "Speaking over singing to show that they are NOT on the same page in the relationship." "Daniel, please. We are better than this. We can make this work," she pleads. At the video's climactic finish, Mertzlufft walks down the aisle; she pleads, "Please. No. I—" as text tells us, "That moment when he leaves her in the bread aisle without saying if he wants white or wheat." With the musical's central protagonists set, other users added supporting characters to the scene. On September 34, 2020, Kelsey Jade (@kaputkali) dueted the video as their child, singing about how she loved her mom and dad and was sad to see them fighting and potentially separating/divorcing. Another duet played the role of the grocery store employee who bears witness to the fight—commenting about the action but then announcing at the end of the video, in dramatic fashion,

"We close at nine!"[13] Other duets added the perspectives of "a can of soup," which sang the lyrics "I'm a can of soup" (just in case it wasn't already evident) (@alexengelberg); the squeaky wheel of the shopping cart, which was just a TikToker singing in a high-pitched belt (@themichaelspencer); the automatic door with the too-loud bell going "ding dooo0oonngg" (@stevenglukas); the random voice that comes over the speaker, "attention shoppers, 201" (@rikygalvin); and the water sprayers that always mist when you're reaching for kale, which was TikToker @igorandwheezy spraying water out of his mouth in front of a produce section green screen at the song's climax. In addition to such duets, which built out the world of *Grocery Store: A New Musical* detail by detail, there were other examples that achieved their own level of virality and demonstrated just how far the musical could reach on TikTok. For example, Broadway and film veteran Skyler Astin (@skylarastin) added his perspective as Daniel's lover on October 6, 2020. As TikTokers added duets to *Grocery Store* "One Day More" style, perhaps the most remarkable thing of all was that the micro musical was fully built in just ten days, with the core parts being cemented within twenty-four hours of Mertzlufft's original video. *Grocery Store* was musical theatre development at hyper speed, something that TikTok crowdsourcing not only facilitates, but encourages.

Yet, while musical theatre artists and fans were using TikTok to create and engage with musical theatre during the pandemic, this phenomenon was still largely out of the purview of the larger musical theatre world. As such, when *Ratatouille: The TikTok Musical* debuted, arts writers and journalists tended to refer to it (and not *Grocery Store*) as the first crowdsourced musical. These writers showed a lack of knowledge about the platform and a lack of research, but this situation wasn't helped by the fact that TikTok is notoriously difficult to search for old content. Trends pass so quickly that it's hard to know what was popular during the time before someone joined the app. Despite how much *Grocery Store* grew, and despite the virality it achieved on TikTok (and Twitter, through cross-sharing), it was still a quiet phenomenon. And yet, it offered a new model for how musical theatre artists might create and fans might fan-out during the pandemic, when traditional models of musical theatre development and in-person spectatorship had ceased to exist. Mertzlufft revealed that TikTok can be a place where creativity thrives and, perhaps most significantly, where serious musical theatre writing and artistic collaboration can take place, even under the silliest of circumstances. This was not lost on TikTok insiders. For instance, Twitter user Emma Lynn wrote, "TikTok's duet feature can result in the most hilarious and creative collaborations. Pretty much a guy wrote a musical number about a grocery store and everyone is adding onto it and I am deceased."[14]

Mertzlufft, it seems, had found the secret to musical theatre–making and fandom during the pandemic. Others soon took notice of this trend, and of Mertzlufft himself, who was invited in November 2020 to create the mini-musical *Thanksgiving: The Musical* for *The Late Late Show with James Corden*.[15] Meanwhile, another dish was cooking in the kitchen, one that would flip the musical theatre world on its head.

"Ode to Remy": How *Ratatouille* Went from a Silly Joke to the Toast of TikTok

In 2007, Pixar captured audiences' and even the most-skeptical critics' attention with its latest animated film, *Ratatouille*, directed by Brad Bird and Jan Pinkava. The film tells the story of an aspiring and supremely talented chef, Remy, whose major roadblock is that he just so happens to be a rat. Being a culinary wiz in the rat world helped him save his dad from eating rat poison, but in the cutthroat world of Parisian haute cuisine, being a rat won't fly. Remy teams up with another aspiring (if not-so-talented) chef, Linguini, who works as a lowly garbage boy. Working together, the duo defies the odds, wowing notorious food critic Anton Ego with a ratatouille that brings humanity back to the hardened critic. According to Pixar scholar Eric Herhuth, the film "explores how sensorial events, such as fine dining and physical comedy, contribute to radical changes to communities and individuals."[16] This parallels how the world of *Ratatouille* the musical fostered collaboration that disrupted and reimagined musical theatre–making. Indeed, the rise of *Ratatouille: The TikTok Musical* embodied the very themes that the source material espouses. Rats are largely "considered to be an ugly, filthy, dangerous and disease-carrying specimen of vermin" and are often seen as unwanted intruders.[17] Yet, by the end of the film Remy has bested these stereotypes and won adoration, therefore representing the ultimate underdog. Much like outsiders who have long been unwelcome in certain spaces, Remy epitomizes what it feels like to be a dreamer and to infiltrate and succeed in a world that was not designed for your inclusion or prosperity.[18]

Naturally, an animated film that invokes a visceral experience holds much power to both wow audiences and stay with them long after the credits finish rolling. The film was a critical and commercial success, making $620 million at the box office and winning the Academy Award for Best Animated Feature, in addition to garnering four other Oscar nominations (no small feat for an animated film). Although *Ratatouille* underperformed at the box office compared to other Pixar features such as *Toy Story* and *Finding Nemo*, the film has become part of the Disney canon and, thus, has demonstrated some veritable staying power even in the crowded world of Disney. A theme park ride, Remy's Ratatouille Adventure, opened at Walt Disney Studios Park, Disneyland Paris, in 2014, allowing *Ratatouille* fans to shrink down to the size of a rat and navigate the kitchen. The ride was set to open at the France Pavilion in Epcot's World Showcase at Walt Disney World in Florida in 2020, before the pandemic delayed opening plans.

For Disney fans, the pandemic meant canceled or severely altered Disney vacations. And, visitors to the theme parks were met with new safety restrictions that affected the experience: guests had to wear masks at all times and were only permitted to eat and drink in certain places, for example, while live performances were put on hiatus and character meet-in-greets were canceled.[19] It also meant that several new marquee attractions were delayed. Such was the case with Remy's Ratatouille Adventure. The ride seemed like a perfect addition to the France Pavilion, given the film's iconic Parisian setting and focus on French cuisine, which is a major selling point of the pavilion. Remy, then, would be at home.

And so, we arrive back at the starting point of our story: with Emily Jacobsen, a Disney fan who spent the summer of 2020 wanting to be in the "most magical place on earth" after her much-anticipated Disney vacation was canceled due to the pandemic. The twenty-six-year-old elementary school teacher was cleaning her apartment one day when she started making a nonsensical jingle celebrating Remy, much like previous odes she had created (and posted to TikTok) praising iconic Disney characters. While she wished she could be at Epcot riding Remy's Ratatouille Adventure, singing about it would have to be the next best thing. Jacobsen was inspired by lyrics and words indicative of traditional Catholic hymns. She later commented, "We [my brother and I] think it's hysterical to blend the idea of a fictional Disney character with words like 'praise,' 'salvation,' and 'remember his name,' things like that."[20] On August 10, 2020, like so many TikTokers, Jacobsen (@e_jaccs) uploaded the sound bite to the app. "I made the song, put it on TikTok, added some crazy effects, changed my voice to be more cartoon-like and sent it off to family and friends as a joke," claimed Jacobsen, adding, "I never thought anything of it."[21] The "Ode to Remy" video draws from TikTok aesthetics, from the silly, high-pitched singing and the lyrics that don't exactly make sense (Remy is *not* a ratatouille) to the use of text and the green screen, which features extreme close-ups of Remy from the film.

TikTok virality can occur in various ways. There is no formula. Jacobsen observes, "TikTok is so unique with the algorithm, anyone can kind of go viral for anything, as I found out."[22] Sometimes it's luck; the famed algorithm can pluck videos from anonymity and make people "TikTok famous" overnight. Other times, virality depends on a larger creator taking notice of a trend and sharing it with their audience, who will inevitably recreate and engage with the sound bite, dance, or trend. This is precisely the journey that "Ode to Remy" took. On October 10, 2022, shortly after Jacobsen uploaded the song, popular TikToker Brittany Broski (@brittany_broski) used the sound bite in a TikTok video that accumulated over 2.4 million views as of March 2024. Broski, also known as the "kombucha girl," had over 5 million followers at the time, and many of them, too, began interacting with "Ode to Remy."[23] Her followers engaged with her video while also clicking on the sound bite and then immersing themselves in Jacobsen's song. Jacobsen's video would hit 1 million views within a few weeks, no small feat for a small creator. Soon, there was an archive of repetitions that helped cement the clip as part of the TikTok repertoire. From there, the possibilities were endless, even the possibility of a Broadway musical riffing off "Ode to Remy." TikTok is a place of creativity, playfulness, and ambition, so why not a crowdsourced musical that would eclipse *Grocery Store* in nearly every way?

On October 19, 2020, two months after Jacobsen posted her video, Daniel Mertzlufft (@danieljmertzlufft) would post his own response to "Ode to Remy" (Figure 4.5 and Figure 4.6). He had come across the sound clip and decided that Remy needed the Disney treatment. Inspired by the music of legendary Disney composer Alan Menken, Mertzlufft reimagined Jacobsen's ditty in the style of the grand finale of *The Hunchback of Notre Dame*. After a friend tagged him in Jacobsen's video, asking him whether this was perhaps the next *Grocery Store*, Mertzlufft went to work. He later recalled, "I thought what she put up was charming and silly, and perfect to be a fun little parody for an act 2 finale. What better way to end Act 2 in a show than the line, 'May the world remember your name?'"[24] Mertzlufft leaned in to the Disney aesthetic—specifically Menken's classic scores from *The Little Mermaid*, *Beauty and the Beast*, and *The Hunchback of Notre Dame*—to embody the Disney feeling and sound.[25] His composition was filled with piano, strings, and plenty of bells, effectively matching the grandiosity of Jacobsen's lyrics

ANYONE CAN COOK, ANYONE CAN CREATE 135

Figures 4.5 and 4.6 Daniel Mertzlufft performs the title song from what would become *Ratatouille: The TikTok Musical*. Posted on October 19, 2020.

("praise," "may the world remember your name"). The new rendition included a forty-person choir to make the song feel big.[26] Throughout the short video, Mertzlufft again used text to explain what this would look like in a full production: "Big Act II finale. Lots of glitter, Remy centerstage, listening to his adoring fans praise him"; "CONFETTI EVERYWHERE! LIGHTS GOING CRAZY! REMY ON A LIFT FLYING OVER THE AUDIENCE!!!" If Mertzlufft's take on "Ode to Remy" feels like something larger than life, that is a testament to his success. The song is meant to invoke an emotional response, and, for Gen Z and younger Millennials, the film *Ratatouille* holds the potential to conjure nostalgia. As such, "Ode to Remy" worked as a double agent. On the one hand, TikTokers were reminded of their childhoods, much like Anton Ego when he finally tastes Remy's ratatouille, which immediately transports him to the simpler times of his childhood. On the other hand, Mertzlufft's video functioned as a call to action for creators to add to the musical, imagining what a Disney musical could look like. TikTokers were given the green light to build a musical version of one of their favorite childhood films.

With a properly scored and incredibly catchy tune, *Ratatouille* the musical was primed to be the next crowdsourced TikTok musical experiment. Mertzlufft's "Ode to Remy" was an immediate viral sensation, yielding 2.4 million views within two months. The comment section for the October 19, 2020, video ballooned, evidencing the interest from the TikTok musical theatre fandom at large in both collaborating on this project and witnessing it come to fruition. For example, @andiebahm commented, "ok but why do i have goosebumps" (30,000 likes); @megan.audreyyy commented, "i'm so excited for when gen z is in charge of everything" (24,000 likes); @ginavol.6 commented, "now all i want is a broadway musical version of ratatouille" (13,000 likes); and @tyler_warwick commented, "Not me singing this under my breath while teaching theatre today" (3,000 likes). And, of course, many TikTokers took up the topic of Jacobsen's lyrics, noting that since Remy isn't a ratatouille, the lyrics don't entirely make sense. Others noted how the lyrics would make sense depending on who was singing them and how the number was staged. At all moments on Mertzlufft's post, musical fans engaged in rataturgy that sought to build out the show, tease out the staging specifics, and troubleshoot any snags in the process of making a new musical. Ratatousical TikTokers were motivated to respond and join the fandom because of the chance for virality, TikTok fame, clout, and a hand in the making of the musical.

TikTokers caught the *Ratatouille* bug. The archive of #ratatouillethemusical quickly grew, accumulating hundreds of videos in just a few weeks. The submissions to the musical ran the gamut. American Idol contestant Sophia James (@sophiajamesmusic) submitted a song. *Dear Evan Hansen* alum Andrew Barth Feldman (@andrewbfeldman_) covered part of the score. Actors interpreted the songs. High school musicians played different instruments as part of the show's orchestra. Dancers choreographed the songs. Designers showcased their costume renderings. Directors pitched their concepts for what the show would look like. Scenic design and marketing approaches were all part of the *Ratatouille* archive. Even Broadway producer

Ken Davenport (@kendavenportbway) made a tongue-in-cheek pitch to produce the show on Broadway.[27] As videos began to add to the dramaturgical world of *Ratatouille* the musical, several hallmarks of crowdsourcing began to take place. Most notably, there was an overwhelming number of submissions to the musical, only ten songs of which would later be canonized as part of the benefit concert. This "peer-vetted creative production approach" enabled any TikToker (not just the Broadway veterans, who had no real advantage here) to submit an idea, with the superior ideas—the cream, as it were—rising to the top. Brabham suggests, "The peer-vetting process simultaneously identifies the best ideas and collapses the market-research process into an instance of firm-consumer cocreation. It is a system where a 'good' solution is also the popular solution that the market will support."[28] Not surprisingly, the most viral videos became accepted as the *Ratatouille* musical canon. These songs, performers, and concepts would ultimately make up the "finished" show as it was performed at the Actors Fund benefit concert.

Notably, this process of crowdsourcing, peer-vetting, and canonization mirrored a traditional way of making musicals—the out-of-town tryout. Musical theatre scholar Laura MacDonald explains, "original musicals in particular need to be developed and tested in other venues and in front of other audiences before being deemed worthy of Broadway."[29] By staging the development of the *Ratatouille* musical in real time, always in front of an audience that knew it was watching the equivalent of an out-of-town tryout, the musical's crowdsourced creative team and energized leaders were able to home in on what *Ratatouille* would eventually become. As this book has chronicled, the way musicals are made and the way that audiences interact with musical theatre have shifted in the TikTok Age. *Ratatouille* is proof that, as MacDonald affirms, "the places musicals are tried out prior to Broadway openings, and the reasons producers and creative teams conduct their work out of town, have changed over the course of the twentieth century," something that continues into the third decade of the twenty-first century.[30]

Although "Ode to Remy" energized this process, it was soon joined by several other undisputed canonical songs in the musical's burgeoning score. These other songs emerged during the "out-of-town" TikTok tryout. Among those was "Trash Is Our Treasure" (Figure 4.7 and Figure 4.8), with music and lyrics by Gabbi Bolt (@fettuccinifettuqueen). The song is written for Remy's father, Django, as he details how rats don't need haute cuisine, much less interaction with humans (the worst!). All they need is trash. Like Mertzlufft's contribution, Bolt's song has a high production value by TikTok standards.

138   TIKTOK BROADWAY

Figures 4.7 and 4.8 Composer Gabbi Bolt performs "Trash is Our Treasure" from *Ratatouille: The TikTok Musical*. Posted on October 27, 2020.

Bolt, who is a composer beyond her work with *Ratatouille*, sings in her recording studio, using a microphone and recording setup that is rarely seen on TikTok. She wears homemade rat ears, and her video features pictures of Django and Remy throughout, demonstrating that she "gets" TikTok aesthetics. The song has, according to Bolt, a definitive "Disney parental big-bad-world-whimsy." Like "Ode to Remy," "Trash Is Our Treasure" riffs off the Disney sound. Bolt points out that it is "very Chim-Chimney, waltz, ooky-spooky vibes."[31] Bolt uploaded the song on October 27, 2020, and woke up to 80,000 likes the next morning. The video amassed over a million views in two months. Much like other canonical *Ratatouille* TikToks, Bolt's had become an overnight sensation and unquestionably part of the canon. Composer R. J.

Christian (@rjthecomposer), who wrote Anton Ego's solo song "Ratatouille" (featured in the benefit concert), confirms this, commenting on the video, "The melody slaps. The arrangement slaps. The performance slaps. You killed this."

Broadway veteran and Tony Award nominee Kevin Chamberlin (@chamberlin_kevin) is far from a Zoomer, much less a Millennial. But that didn't stop him from joining in on the phenomenon. His inclusion in the *Ratatouille* musical canon is noteworthy, representing how inclusive TikTok Broadway can be. Although many arts journalists, musical theatre fans, and casual onlookers attributed *Ratatouille* the musical to Gen Z (and, in fact, they did account for the bulk of contributions), this was a movement that spanned several generations. Chamberlin didn't need to look far for his inspiration to join the crowdsourcing experiment. While watching the film, he noticed Chef Gusteau and his cookbook, aptly titled *Anyone Can Cook*. Other TikTokers had also noticed the need for a song embodying the movie's mantra, but Chamberlin's submission (posted November 18, 2020) became the canonical Gusteau song. When it was time to cast the benefit concert, director Lucy Moss (co-creator of *Six*) looked no further than Chamberlin himself, who was born to play the part. To craft "Anyone Can Cook," Chamberlin began rhyming cooking terms from the film, jotting down everything on a yellow legal pad: "Boil and broil. Deglaze and braise. Casserole can be drole."[32] His husband was out shopping, and Chamberlin asked him to make a pit stop—kitchenware store Sur La Table for an authentic chef's hat. That night, Chamberlin recorded the song at the piano. In the video, Chamberlin sings along as he plays the piano, dressed all in white. Within twenty-four hours the video had 1.4 million views, and it hit 5 million within two months. There was little doubt that Chamberlin was immediately part of the rataturgy universe. One user (@toodarling) commented, "oh the role is YOURS," amassing 90,000 likes in agreement. Another TikToker (@zoinketh) went all in on their Chamberlin advocacy: "YALL IF HE ISNT CASTED AS GUSTEAU IM SUING AND IM SUING HARDDDDD" (17,000 likes). Chamberlin's submission accumulated nearly 50,000 comments, most of which praised the song, his performance, and the way that "Anyone Can Cook" fit into the rataturgical universe. Throughout the comment section, users repeatedly acknowledged Chamberlin and "Anyone Can Cook" as the definitive Gusteau and Gusteau song, respectively. As with other submissions to the musical, virality dictated how the canon was formed. TikTok fame was the name of the game. Views, likes, comments, and shares all contributed to canon formation and helped the eventual *Ratatouille* creative team, spearheaded by Jacobsen and Mertzlufft, easily identify the musical's core composers and corresponding score.

Like many *Ratatouille* fans, Josh Abram Lloyd was actively keeping track of the musical's development and eagerly awaiting the new submissions that were seemingly coming in every few hours at a certain point in November 2020. Lloyd noticed that there was no one formally organizing the musical or hosting a community conversation as to what had been created, what needed to be created, and what had already become ratatousical canon. Lloyd created an official TikTok account for the musical: Ratatouille The TikTok Musical (@ratatouillemusical). Lloyd claims, "The first video that I posted was a call to action, asking for help from any and everybody: lighting designers, technicians, actors—literally whatever you can do. We just wanted people to make this a reality."[33] The account served as a hub for the ratatousical fandom, highlighting other users' content and showcasing new videos while also documenting the building of the show. The @ratatatouillemusical account amassed over 500,000 followers in just two months, placing it only behind *Hamilton* as the most followed account associated with a musical production. TikTok creators such as Alex Powell, Nathan Fosbinder, and Blake Rouse created profile videos for the account. Moreover, the account was able to grow organically by authentically engaging with popular TikTok trends. For example, a December 30, 2020, video engages with the "What's your favorite celebrity interview moment?" trend by stitching Gusteau's TV interview from the film after the prompt. A January 14, 2021, post does the "What's a video that lives in your head rent free?" challenge, splicing Priscilla Lopez's performance from the benefit concert after the prompt. A January 17, 2021, video featured Gritty (the bright orange dumpster fire of a mascot that calls the Philadelphia Flyers home) auditioning for his role in the musical by dancing Tristan Michael McIntyre's choreography to "Ode to Remy" while the song blasts through the loudspeakers at the Wells Fargo Center. Videos such as these helped solidify the musical's pop culture status even after the benefit concert went dark, proving that *Ratatouille* the musical was, in fact, more than just a TikTok trend and an eventual fundraiser for the Actors Fund. Rather, it had become a regular fixture in the US cultural zeitgeist.

Any official musical needs branding. Seeing this need and recognizing her lack of musical ability (her words, not mine), thirty-three-year-old graphic designer Jess Siswick (@siswij) made the official *Ratatouille* playbill. In a TikTok posted on November 13, 2021, Siswick designs the *Ratatouille* logo to the sounds of "Ode to Remy." The Playbill features a fork with ratatouille on its end. But this is no ordinary ratatouille; it's shaped like Remy. The smoke billowing off the steamy food takes the shape of his chef's hat. The colorful design manages to encompass both the franchise's main character and its signature dish in one powerful image. Siswick's design quickly became canon and was adopted as the Actors Fund benefit concert's official branding. It was even put on a real Broadway marquee (St. James Theatre), made feasible by the marquee's digital LED screen. Siswick admits, "A few days after I posted my playbill on TikTok, I saw it being shared everywhere. I saw it on Twitter. People saying, 'This playbill looks legit.' "[34] Playbill even took notice, asking Siswick for permission to use her design to make an official playbill for the show. During the benefit concert, attendees and ratatousical fans could download the digital playbill and read more about the production details in addition to profiles on the creatives, and dramaturgical essays about how *Ratatouille* the musical came to fruition.

The aforementioned videos are only a handful of the thousands that dedicated musical theatre aficionados created. Throughout the community, from creators to audiences, there was a drive to participate in this crowdsourcing experiment, something that mirrored the participatory culture of other community-based digital platforms such as YouTube, Wikipedia, and Flickr. This wasn't *just* about creators. *Ratatouille* thrived because of the way that general TikTok spectators embraced the musical. Jacobsen's, Mertzlufft's, and Chamberlin's content became canon by accumulating shares, comments, likes, and favorites. This community support reflected the creators' enthusiasm for the project and vision to see the musical become a fully integrated book musical that maybe could make it to the Broadway stage one day. Director Lucy Moss recognizes how organic the development of the musical was, confirming, "I think the best theater comes from people who have an idea of something and are like, 'I want to make this, I want to see this.' Rather than trying to artificially create what you think people are going to want to see it or what you think will be successful."[35] The development of *Ratatouille* was not motivated by producers. No one had to be pitched to participate. No one had to make a certain amount of money or have a certain group of collaborators for the project to be green-lit. Making money and building audiences were never the goal of the creative process. The equation was about the joy, pleasure, and labor that goes into creating a musical outside of the commercial realm, which, as Stacy Wolf sustains in *Beyond Broadway*, is a testament to how amateur theatre is made and thrives in the United States.[36]

Although it may have seemed like a long shot in October 2020, if Remy could climb the ranks of Parisian haute cuisine, then *Ratatouille* the musical could achieve comparable greatness. After all, anyone can cook. *Ratatouille* the musical's success was that the leading creatives leaned in to TikTok. Throughout the process, *Ratatouille* was meant to live and thrive on TikTok. It was only taken offline when it had become something larger than TikTok, something semi-stageable that needed more space to live and grow, beyond the confines of a brief TikTok video. Something that could be presented for the public at large and consumed by general audiences.

Ratatouille: From TikTok to the Actors Fund

"You must be imaginative, strong-hearted. You must try things that may not work, and you must not let anyone define your limits because of where you come from. Your only limit is your soul. What I say is true—anyone can cook—but only the fearless can be great," proclaims world-renowned Chef Gusteau at the beginning of the *Ratatouille* film. Although Gusteau speaks to the world of the culinary arts, his mantra can readily be applied to the vision of TikTokers, who didn't let traditional models of musical theatre creation and fandom dictate what potential *Ratatouille* the musical held. By November 2020, *Ratatouille* the musical had entered the mainstream. It had penetrated the US cultural zeitgeist, becoming not just niche musical theatre culture but *culture* culture. On November 14, 2020, Patton Oswalt, who voiced Remy in the film, tweeted about the musical, declaring, "My . . . God . . ." and tagging director Brad Bird.[37] On November 20, 2020, the official Disney Parks TikTok account (@disneyparks) even shared a behind-the-scenes video of the making of Remy's Ratatouille Adventure, with Disney Channel actors Milo Manheim (*Zombies*) and Pearce Joza (*Zombies 2*) rapping and beatboxing, respectively, adding their own submission to the musical's archive. The next day, on Instagram, Pixar shared a screenshot of Remy from the film, with the caption, "The rat of all our dreams," letting everyone know that they approved and were in on the joke.[38] When *CBS This Morning* reported about the trend, Gayle King sang "Ode to Remy." Suddenly, *Ratatouille* the musical was everywhere. Ellenore Scott, who choreographed the benefit concert, recognizes this growing popularity: "Even people in my life who were not on TikTok knew that this musical was being developed on TikTok."[39]

As the *Ratatouille* TikTok archive was exponentially growing, many TikTokers—both creators and spectators—discussed their collective dream for the musical to become a fully fledged, fully staged Broadway musical. This dream seemed incredibly unrealistic to anyone with knowledge about how musicals are made, especially Disney musicals. Disney is notoriously guarded about intellectual property. In *Disney Theatrical Productions: Producing Broadway Musicals the Disney Way*, musical theatre scholar Amy S. Osatinski stresses that Disney is synonymous "with consumer capitalism and commodification."[40] As such, the idea that a group of TikTokers could twist Disney's arm into turning *Ratatouille* into a bona fide Broadway musical felt like a long shot (to put it nicely). Even so, Disney seemed entertained by what was transpiring on TikTok. Emily Jacobsen admits that there was a level of concern and nervousness that Disney "was going to come in with some kind of legal notice to stop, even though all I had done was create an original song about the character, and I wasn't profiting in any way off it. But then suddenly things started popping up that made me think, all right, they're not angry. It started when they quoted my lyrics on various social media platforms."[41]

Seaview Productions soon entered the picture, with an offer to produce the musical as a one-off benefit concert to support the Actors Fund. Surprising to many, Disney granted permission.[42] In an official statement, Disney responded: "Although we do not have development plans for the title, we love when our fans engage with Disney stories. We applaud and thank all of the online theatre makers for helping to benefit The Actors Fund in this unprecedented time of need."[43] That this permission was so readily granted is likely partially due to the fact that there were no plans in the pipeline for Disney to develop *Ratatouille* as a Broadway musical. Too, perhaps, *Ratatouille* the musical presented what was a convenient opportunity for Disney to appear more inclusive, which Osatinski states has been a goal of Disney in recent decades.[44] Moreover, Seaview had no goals for *Ratatouille* beyond the benefit concert; this was an isolated phenomenon. For Seaview producer Greg Nobile, the spontaneous nature of *Ratatouille* the musical is what made it so exciting: "This isn't something that's taking five years to develop. The benefit is the end of the road, and this production is as realized as it's going to get, and we feel a great honor and responsibility in that."[45] Once Seaview announced the benefit concert, social media—in particular Twitter—blew up, with many questioning how and why *Ratatouille* was coming to fruition. Moreover, many were skeptical of how the project would treat its creators. Writing for *Vox*, TikTok journalist Rebecca Jennings asserted that "TikTok is not exactly a notable platform when it comes to crediting creators," pointing to how much of the app is filled with users mimicking popular trends, "doing the same dance or making the same joke without naming the originator, whether that's out of a desire to falsely claim credit or because it's nearly impossible to determine who the originator even is." Jennings added that because of how "litigious Disney" is, "it seemed highly unlikely to me that anything resembling an actual musical would fairly recognize the dozens of people who invented it."[46] Yet, *Ratatouille: The TikTok Musical* not only credited all creators, but also *paid* everyone involved. Seaview paid all creators the equivalent of Off-Broadway rates, which, admittedly, is vague, but means that everyone involved made between $1,000 and $5,000, depending on the role they played in the production (as actor, designer, composer, etc.).[47] Moreover, all creators were prominently featured throughout the process as well as in the final concert. The entire process from conception of producing the musical to opening night lasted thirty-one days, with a budget of $200,000.[48]

The musical follows the film's plot. Michael Breslin and Patrick Foley, who created one of 2020's most riotous digital theatre offerings in the Pulitzer Prize for Drama finalist *Circle Jerk*, adapted the film into a sixty-minute musical.[49] Given three weeks to write the book, Breslin and Foley correctly chose to highlight the songs that made *Ratatouille* a TikTok phenomenon.[50] Foley reveals, "We approached it as a classical memory play. Remy, our protagonist, played by Tituss Burgess, takes us through this incredible story, and—in almost a Fleabaggy but also Shakespearian way—is able to step in and out of the dramatic action." Breslin adds that some of the film's plot points "had to be heavily truncated, but the central plot has been the same."[51] Throughout the musical, Remy recalls his adventure from aspiring chef to the toast of the Parisian culinary scene. Along the way, Remy is separated from his family and ends up in Paris, at the doorstep of famed chef Gusteau, who also happens to be his imaginary friend. As Gusteau's mantra and song posit, "anyone can cook," even a rat. But a rat still needs some help to take over Gusteau's kitchen. Enter Linguini, an aspiring chef and incredibly clumsy garbage boy who doesn't exactly have culinary talent. After a chance encounter in which Remy makes a delicious bisque that is credited to Linguini, the two decide to pair up. Remy will stand in Linguine's chef hat, pulling Linguini's hair to control his movements and create award-winning cuisine. In the end, Remy defies all odds, wowing renowned and feared food critic Anton Ego by serving him a ratatouille that immediately transports him to his childhood.

With this adventure complete, Remy's next venture will be as head chef at Ego's new restaurant—La Ratatouille.

Despite being composed by ten different writers—much like *SpongeBob SquarePants: The Broadway Musical*, *Working*, or most jukebox musicals—the score to *Ratatouille* is surprisingly cohesive. While there is a certain je ne sais quoi that makes the score click, much credit must be given to the Broadway Sinfonietta, which provided orchestrations and a lush twenty-person orchestra composed entirely of women. Notably, many of the songs—and, in particular, the songs that achieved more widespread virality—pay homage to musical theatre songwriting. That is, songs such as "Anyone Can Cook," "A Rat's Life," and "I Knew I Smelled a Rat" all sound familiar, even to the first-time listener. Seasoned musical theatre fans will inevitably recognize how "Anyone Can Cook" plays off *Beauty and the Beast*'s "Be Our Guest" (not to mention the "Ratical songs for ratical rats" section, which, of course, pays homage to *Cats*). Colette and Linguini's "Kitchen Tango" riffs off *Rent*'s "The Tango Maureen." Skinner's "I Knew I Smelled a Rat" reminds viewers of *Catch Me If You Can*'s "Don't Break the Rules." The culminating song ("Finale") harks to another Disney property: *The Hunchback of Notre Dame*. Homages to musical theatre such as these permeate the score. These songwriting techniques play directly into TikTok spectatorship, which privileges sound bites and trends that are both familiar and unfamiliar at the same time. That is, *Ratatouille*'s score is instantly hummable, and Remy's theme, "Ode to Remy," is an earworm that will stay with audiences long after they have viewed the TikTok or the musical itself. When *La Cage aux Folles* composer Jerry Herman declared that the "simple, hummable show tune" was "alive and well at the Palace" (upon his receiving the 1984 Tony Award for Best Original Score over the much-celebrated score to Stephen Sondheim's *Sunday in the Park with George*), Herman never could have imagined that the simple, hummable Broadway score could be alive and well on TikTok, of all places.

Being a project generated from TikTok, the production leaned in to the TikTok form, in production quality, dance aesthetics, and video editing. A TikTok ethos was thoroughly ingrained in nearly every aspect of the production, including all of Lucy Moss's directing choices. That is, it looked and felt like a sixty-minute TikTok video, an authentic Gen Z and Millennial creation that leaned in to camp, messiness, and queer chaos to create something that felt entirely original despite being a (mostly) faithful adaption of a Disney animated film. Whereas many Disney stage adaptations maintain the film's aesthetics and ethos as much as they can (*The Lion King* aside), *Ratatouille* was something different.[52]

Playing Remy, Tituss Burgess performed in front of a green screen with images of Paris and the inside of a chef's hat behind him. Per the TikTok norm, part of the joke is how unrealistic the backgrounds are. It's supposed to look bad, cheesy, and even cringey. Priscilla Lopez performed from her guest bedroom, complete with singing a reimagined—not to mention dark and menacing—version of "What I Did for Love," her signature song from *A Chorus Line*. Rather than having a cohesive costume design, the musical looked, well, it looked like TikTok. Tituss Burgess's gray sweater told us that although he didn't look like a rat, he was. His father, Django, played by Wayne Brady, wore rat ears and full DIY rat makeup. Mary Testa's Skinner wore a chef's hat and a pencil mustache drawn with a magic marker. Some of the rat ensemble wore rat ears (read: Mickey ears) and others did not, with some even creating rat ears by putting their hair in buns. This could potentially be jarring to the typical musical theatre spectator, but on TikTok, this is a fundamental aspect of the camp aesthetic that the app encourages.

For instance, during the dance break in Emile's song "Rat's Way of Life," choreographer Ellenore Scott borrowed from the TikTok dance tool kit, lending a sense of authenticity to the production that reminded viewers that although they were viewing the musical on TodayTix, it was indeed a TikTok product. The ensemble (the queens from the original Broadway company of *Six*) performed signature Gen Z TikTok moves such as the Woah, the Mop, the Wave, the Dolphin Dance, and the Roll.[53] Admittedly, the dance moves didn't match the song in tone or thematic content (TikTok dance trends are typically literal to the song lyrics and heavily reliant on the beat). Even so, including these dance moves was a special wink that reminded viewers that what they were witnessing was a campy ratatousical romp. As Remy said to the audience after the song: "Say what you want about rats, but we know how to sell a musical number: just the right amount of cheese." The production knew exactly what it was and who its audience was.

Moreover, production numbers made use of TikTok editing. During "Anyone Can Cook" and "I Knew I Smelled a Rat," dancers JJ Niemann and Joy Woods were joined by two of their clones using the Clone Trio Effect, allowing Moss and Scott to build a full Broadway chorus line. Niemann and Woods began "Anyone Can Cook" dressed as rats, and a jump edit allowed for a seamless costume change into chef costumes. The type of costume change that typically relies on stage magic was facilitated by a simple TikTok edit to produce the same effect. Kevin Chamberlin's Gusteau captured the dreamlike quality of his imaginary friend via the Beauty Aura Effect, complete with Chamberlin's TikTok handle in the corner of the screen, in case anyone forgot how they achieved this effect. These video effects transformed what potentially could have been a flat production into something that was visually interesting and entirely authentic to TikTok and digital video-making.

During the musical's finale, the professional artists were joined by the TikTok creators. Moss included a montage featuring the musical theatre fans and creators whose passion had ignited this project and made it the most talked-about new musical of winter 2020–21. During the curtain call, "Ratamix," Broadway vets took their bows alongside the TikTokers who had created the music, reminding us of the "ratical" nature of how this musical was developed. *Ratatouille*, while not perfect, perfectly captured the beauty of TikTok, the silliness and joy that it enables, and the power that the app holds to catalyze new musical creation and collaboration. As *Ratatouille* the musical conveyed, with the power of TikTok, anyone can cook.

The benefit concert was, by any measure, a massive success. The event raised over $2 million in just four days, making it the most successful fundraiser in the history of the Actors Fund. Grossing over $2 million in one week would put *Ratatouille* in elite company, with hugely popular musicals such as *The Lion King* and *Hamilton*. Over 350,000 people watched the musical, which doesn't account for multiple viewers on one device, as was the case when I watched it with my partner. It would take a Broadway musical playing in a 1,500-seat theatre at full capacity twenty-nine weeks to amass 350,000 audience members. It would take an Off-Broadway musical playing in a 499-seat theatre fifty-seven weeks with eight shows per week to draw these numbers.[54] While it is impossible to know the grosses and audiences numbers of an actual twenty-nine-week or open-ended streaming run, the raw data is undeniable, revealing the immense capacity of digital theatre to attract viewers and turn a profit. With this data in mind, *Ratatouille: The TikTok Musical* forces us to question how—and whether—digital streaming musical theatre can become the norm. As the ratatousical fandom of *Ratatouille* conveys, it is certainly a conversation worth having.

Ratatouille's Aftermath and Subsequent Projects

Ratatouille: The TikTok Musical could have been a flash in the pan, much like previous musical theatre digital offerings during the pandemic: the *Rosie O'Donnell Show* reboot, the *Saturday Night Passover Seder*, numerous cast reunion specials, and, of course, live-streamed engagements of Broadway shows such as *Allegiance* (2015), *Bandstand* (2017), and *The King and I* (2015 revival).[55] But the *Ratatouille* musical collaboration had broken open many previously understood Truths—what musical theatre could be, how it could be made, how it could be experienced. Moreover, the musical unveiled the unparalleled power that TikTok harbors to be a place not only of individual creation, but of community creation through crowdsourcing. That the musical benefit concert had so many cooks in the kitchen and still managed to have such a cohesive score, aesthetic, and ethos is no small feat. With Mertzlufft's initial vision that the TikTok community could create a musical, in tandem with the support and leadership of Jacobsen and numerous TikTok creators, a new model for theatre-making was discovered during a period in musical theatre history when nearly all the norms of creation were disrupted and, in many cases, disbanded altogether. That the *Ratatouille* musical was able to do this within a time span of roughly three months is even more noteworthy, considering that musicals take many years to develop from idea to a public-facing presentation. Even fast-tracked musicals such as *Show Boat* (1927) and *Hair* (1968) took years to make it from the page to the stage.[56]

Following *Ratatouille: The TikTok Musical*'s success, the industry at large began to take TikTok more seriously, a rise in interest that paralleled TikTok's own growth in import for the arts and entertainment industry. Just as the *Ratatouille* film "expresses how sensation, creativity, and vulnerability are central to transitions to new media and new democratic formations," so, too, did the *Ratatouille* musical help usher in a new way of making, viewing, and imagining musical theatre, one that took place on TikTok.[57] When 2020 began, very few Broadway musicals or musical theatre performers had TikTok accounts, for example, but by the end of the year, most Broadway productions had TikTok accounts (to varying success). Moreover, Broadway talent from Tony Award–winning divas Kristin Chenoweth and Laura Benanti to dancers Ian Joseph Paget and JJ Niemann all had successful accounts that enabled musical theatre to thrive in 2020 even if the industry was dark. This momentum hit a second gear following *Ratatouille*'s benefit concert. TikTok was no longer seen as mostly a joke. Although many still discussed TikTok in a joking way, the larger musical theatre community had seen that it was a game changer in the industry. On the eve of the benefit concert, for example, producer Greg Nobile noted that he had taken to using TikTok to seek out undiscovered talent. One of his goals—and also that of Seaview—is to make theatre more accessible and diversify the pipeline of theatre-makers.

Nobile reported that the process of "staging" *Ratatouille* had "been a learning lesson for me in, 'Oh my god, TikTok is an extraordinary platform to meet artists.' "[58] Emily Jacobsen echoes these thoughts, advocating for TikTok to be taken more seriously: "There's a lot of talent out there that isn't coming from these already famous or established professionals. I've seen so many things from normal people that are just extraordinary."[59]

Lucy Moss sees the creation of *Ratatouille* the musical to be a landmark moment in musical theatre history and hopes that it is a beacon of things to come. Moss acknowledges, "I hope it opens the doors and/or eyes of producers and the gatekeepers to democratize theater even further, and to show them that something of real merit can be created not in the 'traditional' ways. It's really a big deal."[60] Theatre critic Jonathan Mandell, reviewing *Ratatouille*, wrote that the musical validates TikTok as a bona fide incubator of new musicals in addition to speaking to "the hope and the promise of theater."[61] Writing for the *New York Times*, Jesse Green added, "Whether the novel development process will change the way musicals are made in the future remains to be seen, but 'Ratatouille' serves the moment admirably." That said, Green was skeptical of TikTok's ability to change the way musicals are made. He saw *Ratatouille* as a fluke, a one-time phenomenon more than a model to be emulated: "I am not convinced that the TikTok mind-set can be applied to musical theater content (as opposed to its process) going forward."[62] Green's thoughts mirror the disregard for TikTok that non-TikTokers harbor en masse. There is a tendency to minimize it, not unlike how social media platforms such as Facebook, Instagram, and Twitter were minimized in their infancy. Even so, Green recognized the benefits of reimagining musical theatre development: "Certainly it would be healthier for the theater if Broadway musicals can be built, like 'Ratatouille,' in just a few months, by individuals, not conglomerates. Our current process, which takes years and more money than anyone but a corporate behemoth can muster, too often squashes idiosyncrasy and cuts off artists from their communities of inspiration."[63]

The musical also had a profound effect on members of the creative team. Just weeks after the benefit concert, Daniel Mertzlufft signed with CAA and Kraft-Engel management. Speaking on behalf of Kraft-Engel, Richard Kraft commented, "Who would have thought that the next generation of songwriters would have come from TikTok? We are really looking forward to working with Dan in association with CAA."[64] Mertzlufft, whose original works include *Breathe: Portraits of a Pandemic*, *Dot and the Kangaroo*, and *House Rules: A New Musical*, continues to develop musicals, original films, and adaptations across various mediums. What audiences witness on his TikTok account is just the tip of the iceberg. His work on *Ratatouille: The TikTok Musical* is a testament to this, from his coming up with the arrangement of "Ode to Remy" and energizing the phenomenon to his arranging the musical score and writing a new song under pressure for the benefit concert. Although some may reduce Mertzlufft's achievements due to him being a Zoomer and the platform on which he got his start, *Ratatouille: The TikTok Musical* reveals that he has the goods and the drive to make his mark on the US musical theatre industry.[65] While Mertzlufft has enjoyed the most post-ratatousical success, other composers involved with the project benefited from the phenomenon's expanded audience base. Composers Gabbi Bolt, Blake Rouse, and R. J. Christian all gained TikTok clout in the form of followers, which directly leads to more exposure, more networking, and, of course, more opportunities to expand their personal brand. These composers regularly produce new micro performances that showcase their ideas, whether these are concepts for new material or fully composed songs for imaginary-but-not-out-of-the-realm-of-possibility new musicals. If *Ratatouille* can make the leap from TikTok to an internationally recognized musical theatre phenomenon, then why can't something else? As musical theatre–makers continued to struggle with new musical development following *Ratatouille*, largely due to the COVID-19 pandemic, TikTok composers did not skip a beat. They already had everything they needed to write the next hit musical, and the success of *Ratatouille* inspired them to get to work.

Shortly after *Ratatouille* "closed," TikTokers began circulating the hashtag #2020themusical in an effort to crowdsource another musical phenomenon, this one depicting the major moments from 2020.[66] Although the hashtag accumulated many submissions, the bulk were not up to the quality seen in the *Ratatouille* archive. Only one submission stuck: "We Did It, Joe" (posted January 3, 2021), a song by TikToker Tori Romo (@toriromo) dramatizing the iconic moment in which Kamala Harris realized she was going to be "the first Vice-President that isn't white" and called Joe Biden, telling him the much-memed "We did it. We did it, Joe." Any hopes of *2020: The Musical* soon fizzled out. It seems, not surprisingly, that TikTokers were collectively eager to forget about 2020 and imagine greener pastures.

From here, another TikTok Broadway phenomenon emerged—*Bridgerton: The Musical*. As opposed to relying on crowdsourcing, *Bridgerton* functioned as a sort of TikTok Age concept album in which a single composer wrote songs for each of the characters in the ultra-popular Netflix series, which had premiered in December 2020. In this case, Abigail Barlow (@

abigailbarlowww) wrote the score and posted it on her TikTok account in a serial fashion. Her writing partner, Emily Bear, orchestrated and produced the official tracks. As a riff on the concept album, *Bridgerton* featured high production quality and seemed to take TikTok musical-making to a new, more serious level. And, like with crowdsourced shows, other TikTokers built out the dramaturgical world of *Bridgerton: The Musical*, dueting Barlow's content and adding choreography, scenic design, and the like.[67] Later, Barlow and Bear produced an album version of the score, *The Unofficial Bridgerton Musical*, winning the 2022 Grammy Award for Best Musical Theater Album.[68] Barlow and Bear's *Bridgerton* experiment further marked a shift in TikTok's relationship to the world of musical theatre, given that the *Bridgerton* musical has experienced success and acclaim yet sorta kinda doesn't actually exist... at least not yet. As Sarah Bay-Cheng recognizes, "*The Unofficial Bridgerton Musical* was an unusual musical theatre adaptation without theatre. They didn't even need a live performance."[69] Yet, in the digital world, does a musical need a production to be considered theatre?

The Unofficial Bridgerton Musical's fans will argue that a musical doesn't need a full production. And they don't have much of a choice. After a wave of critical milestones in the musical's development, the *Bridgerton* musical team announced a for-profit concert staging of the musical at the Kennedy Center in Washington, DC. Netflix promptly sued Barlow and Bear for copyright infringement, claiming that the duo's conduct "stretches 'fan fiction' well past its breaking point."[70] *Bridgerton* show creator Shonda Rhimes released a statement explaining how Barlow and Bear took a TikTok experiment turned musical theatre development too far. Rhimes claimed, "What started as a fun celebration by Barlow & Bear on social media has turned into the blatant taking of intellectual property solely for Barlow & Bear's financial benefit.... Just as Barlow & Bear would not allow others to appropriate their IP for profit, Netflix cannot stand by and allow Barlow & Bear to do the same with *Bridgerton*."[71] Ultimately, Barlow and Bear settled with Netflix, effectively putting the possibility of staging the musical to rest. *Bridgerton: The Musical*, it seems, will live as a musical theatre TikTok experiment and concept album. A fully realized stage production is not on the horizon.

Conclusion

Perhaps the secret to TikTok musical theatre development is to not use copyrighted intellectual property? Composer Jorge Rivera-Herrans is attempting to answer this question. Since January 2021, Rivera-Herrans has been developing *EPIC*, an adaptation of *The Odyssey* by Homer. In early January 2021, Rivera-Herrans began documenting his writing process via TikTok, much like Barlow and Bear did. His song clips and development process videos went viral across social media, garnering the creator 742,000 followers on TikTok (@jorgeherrans) and over 70 million views across TikTok, YouTube, and Instagram (as of March 2023). Demonstrating the social in social media, *EPIC* enjoys a robust Discord fan community of over 17,000 fans who closely follow Rivera-Herrans while sharing fan art, memes, fan theories, and other fannish creations. That is, *EPIC* is already enjoying a level of digital support that few well-established musicals ever see. Riding this wave, on December 25, 2022, Rivera-Herrans released *EPIC: The Troy Saga*, an EP consisting of the first five songs from *EPIC*. The streaming album quickly reached the top spot on the iTunes soundtracks chart. A sound bite from the song "Warrior of the Mind" amassed over 116,000 TikTok videos in three months. Although it remains too early in Rivera-Herrans's journey to know what will become of his experiment, *EPIC* further conveys how TikTok can be a serious platform to develop musical theatre in a very public way, one that involves fans at every step of the process.

In the wake of *Ratatouille*, *Bridgerton*, and *EPIC*, if musical theatre fans, practitioners, and producers learned anything from the ratatousical experiment, it's that TikTok should be taken seriously as both a place to develop new material and a platform for fan engagement. That these two things, which almost never transpire in conversation, can take place together in an entirely organic way is a testament to the potential that TikTok and similar social media platforms hold to imagine new ways of musical theatre creation and fandom. In the final moments of *Ratatouille: The TikTok Musical*, Anton Ego tells us, "I now know that not anyone can cook, but a great cook can come from anywhere." So, too, can musical theatre.

Interlude

We ~~Don't~~ Talk about TikTok: The Cultural Power of *Encanto*

Coming off the successes of *Ratatouille: The TikTok Musical* and *Bridgerton: The Musical*, there was suddenly more mainstream attention on TikTok's role in the musical theatre world. Much like the cases of *Beetlejuice*, *Heathers*, and *Six*, crossover successes of musicals began to feel commonplace on TikTok. In 2021 the film musicals *In the Heights*, *tick, tick... BOOM!*, and *West Side Story* all enjoyed their own level of TikTok virality, further cementing these films' role in US popular culture. In fact, as I learned one day in my seventh-period high school class when I mentioned *In the Heights* and my students instinctively began to sing Usnavi and Vanessa's back-and-forth exchange during "Fireworks," none of my students had actually seen *In the Heights*.[1] They all only knew the song from TikTok. And, recognizing the song, knowing the lyrics, and being able to talk about its corresponding TikTok challenge was a form of cultural competency and inner-group knowledge for them. Knowing TikTok Broadway trends is about fitting in, even if you're not a musical fan. TikTok enables musicals to go far beyond their intended audiences. Just like in the early days of TikTok, musical theatre continues to show its import to TikTok culture while also conveying the general role of musical theatre in pop culture at large.

And then in walks *Encanto* and the game completely changes.

Encanto opened in cinemas on November 19, 2021, to limited fanfare. As the United States was still embroiled in the COVID-19 pandemic (the Omicron wave would decimate public life throughout the winter months), *Encanto*—the film and the soundtrack—had apparently missed its mark, becoming a rare flop among animated Disney films, with a low box office and lukewarm reviews. Like other films that were initially released in cinemas during the COVID-19 pandemic, *Encanto* didn't truly find an audience until it was released for streaming, on December 24 of that year. Viewers could log on to Disney+ from the safety of their homes and finally watch Walt Disney

Animation Studios' latest animated feature. *Encanto* quickly went from forgotten Disney quasi-flop to one of the biggest hit films in the studio's history. As the film gained steam in US popular culture, Lin-Manuel Miranda's score became the centerpiece of our collective obsession with *Encanto*. Songs such as "Surface Pressure," "La Familia Madrigal," and the Oscar-nominated "Dos Oruguitas" became hit songs in their own right, landing on the Billboard Hot 100 and streaming charts. And then there is the film's standout song, the earworm that lives rent free in our brains—"We Don't Talk about Bruno."

"We Don't Talk about Bruno" is one of Disney's biggest crossover hits in its sixty-five-year history. In February 2022, the song peaked at number 1 on the coveted Billboard Hot 100, staying in the top spot for four weeks and firmly surpassing *Frozen*'s "Let It Go" as the highest-charting Disney single since 1995 (when "Colors of the Wind" from *Pocahontas* held the honor). It should come as no surprise that TikTok factors highly into the rise of "We Don't Talk about Bruno." TikTok has rewritten the book on how hit songs get made. Look no further than the commercial successes of artists like Lil Nas X, Lizzo, Doja Cat, Dua Lipa, Megan Thee Stallion, Cardi B, and The Weeknd, who have been able to ride TikTok virality to the top of the charts.[2] Even though "We Don't Talk about Bruno" may not be the catchy club anthem that "Old Town Road," "Levitating," or "Savage" are, the Lin-Manuel Miranda tune somehow did the impossible and topped the charts.[3]

"We Don't Talk about Bruno" is far from the first Disney crossover hit song. Even so, the song flips the traditional script. Previous crossover hits have included the titular song from *Beauty and the Beast*, *The Lion King*'s "Can You Feel the Love Tonight," *Aladdin*'s "A Whole New World," and, as mentioned "Colors of the Wind" and "Let It Go." These tend to be generic songs that fit into multiple contexts. That is, they are marketable. They can easily be performed in a number of venues, like, for instance, on stage at the Academy Awards. "We Don't Talk about Bruno" is far from that type of catchy tune.

"We Don't Talk about Bruno" is an exposition-heavy ensemble number in which the Madrigal family and the townspeople share gossip and anecdotes about Mirabel's ostracized uncle, Bruno Madrigal. The song, which is puro *chisme*—or *bochinche* (aka tea or hot goss)—reveals how Bruno's gift, his *encanto*, for prophecy is commonly believed to be the source of everyone's misfortune. As a result, Bruno is estranged from his family and, by extension, the town. Hiding is Bruno's way of surviving.[4] Voiced by Carolina Gaitán, Mauro Castillo, Adassa, Rhenzy Feliz, Diane Guerrero, and Stephanie Beatriz, the song repeatedly reminds us "we don't talk about Bruno" for all the misfortune he has caused. Supposedly, Bruno is the villain of this story, but, as viewers soon learn, Bruno is far from the villain. Miranda's song is filled with Latin music styles like salsa and guajara, with pop, hip-hop, dance, and Broadway sounds infused throughout. Much like Miranda's other hit songs "96,000" from *In the Heights* and "Non-Stop" from *Hamilton*, "We Don't Talk about Bruno" climaxes on a polyphonic outro.[5]

The story of how we went from *never* talking about Bruno to *always* talking about Bruno is intricately connected to TikTok. Like other popular songs, "We Don't Talk about Bruno" is a hit generated by TikTok rather than by a traditional media outlet such as radio or television. As of February 2023, there were over 1 million unique videos using just one sound bite from "We Don't Talk about Bruno." This doesn't factor in other sound bites from the song or consider the ecosystem of the *Encanto* soundtrack at large, which permeated mainstream TikTok during the film's monumental climb to the upper tier of US popular culture.

But why did "We Don't Talk about Bruno" become the runaway TikTok hit, as opposed to the more standard pop song "Surface Pressure" or the Oscar-nominated "Dos Oruguitas"? I propose that the plurality of the song gives TikTokers a lot of material to play with. That is, the song is a mélange of voices, stories, character quirks, musical stylings, and sound effects. "We Don't Talk about Bruno" is a sonic playground. And, let's be honest, the song is weird, and, on TikTok, weird works. As such, the song's weirdness is part of its allure. The song has different levels of engagement. There are different characters to latch on to. Creators can lip-sync to sections of the song. They can dance to sections, either mimicking the film's choreography or coming up with their own original TikTok dances. Fans can cosplay as the characters. So, whereas other Disney standards like "Colors of the Wind" and "Let It Go" may have just one or two levels of engagement, "We Don't Talk about Bruno" lends itself to myriad dramaturgical interpretations and remixes on TikTok. Of course, I would be remiss to not acknowledge that TikTokers can take any song or sound clip and do *literally anything* with it, but "We Don't Talk about Bruno" *encourages* this sort of playful creativity and ridiculousness.

Look no further than Guamanian dancer and choreographer Brian Esperon (@besperon), whose TikTok account was dedicated to all things "We Don't Talk about Bruno" in January and February 2022.[6] Esperon is no stranger to virality. As the creator of the dance to "WAP," by Cardi B featuring Megan Thee Stallion, Esperon knows firsthand the power that dance challenges and trending sound bites have on TikTok and their potential to become thoroughly ingrained in popular culture. "WAP" became one of the biggest hit songs of 2020, and its corresponding dance challenge became one of TikTok's biggest viral dance challenges in the platform's short history. With over 97 million views on his original video as of March 2023, Esperon was at the root of the "WAP" craze. Although "WAP" (wet-ass pussy) and "We Don't Talk about Bruno" (Uncle Bruno) share little in common thematically speaking (to say the least!), the two songs do share a similar blueprint for TikTok virality. Just like with "WAP," as Esperon began playing with the *Encanto* soundtrack, his millions of followers began interacting with him, revealing their fandom of both Esperon and *Encanto*. As they egged him on to continue creating "We Don't Talk about Bruno" content, the song's popularity on TikTok grew.

After Esperon had posted a series of videos mimicking Luisa's choreography from "Surface Pressure," his fans began requesting that he do other songs from the film. Bolstered by his fans' requests and support, Esperon uploaded his first BrunoTok on January 22, 2022 (Figure 4.9 and Figure 4.10). The rest was history. In the initial video, Esperon stands in front of his TV in his living room, wearing red pants, a white T-shirt, and a red bandana around his forehead. On the television screen, we see Dolores leaning over, telling Mirabel about Bruno. Shit's about to get real. In the video, Esperon perfectly mimics Dolores's movements as he lip-syncs her verse from the song. In this DIY Drag performance, Esperon *becomes* Dolores, even nailing her infamous shoulder-shimmy choreography. The video had over 25.8 million views as of March 2022, but what is more telling are the 10,800 comments it received, many of which requested future videos. Such requests are a well-established genre of TikTokian comments on the videos of favorite creators, and they drive additional engagement. Choosing one of these requests, the creator then makes a new video that features the comment while also doing what the comment requests the creator to do. In this case, Esperon's followers began demanding more videos of him playing with "We Don't Talk about Bruno." And that's exactly what Esperon gave them.

Esperon soon posted videos responding to the comments on his videos. "Now with the dress," demanded one TikToker (@_vamp_alex_). And that is exactly what Esperon did. His January 23, 2022, video features him in a long red skirt and red leather high heel boots recreating Dolores's lines and choreography. Then came a perfectly executed video of Camilo's part ("seven foot frame, rats along his back"; January 24, 2022). But, of course, Esperon's fans were not fully satisfied. They didn't just want Camilo's part; they wanted transitions. TikToker @pendelau7 suggested, "You should do a transition every time it switches between Camilo and bruno." Esperon's January 25,

WE ~~DON'T~~ TALK ABOUT TIKTOK   157

Figures 4.9 and 4.10 Brian Esperon transforms from Bruno to Camilo while recreating a segment from "We Don't Talk About Bruno" from *Encanto*. Posted on January 25, 2022.

2022, TikTok features Camilo's part but with flawless transitions in which Esperon switches back and forth between Camilo and Bruno. In the background, their animated counterparts seem to be mimicking Esperon at this point: he is the spotlight, demonstrating his dance technique and his deft editing skills. The video, which had over 45 million views as of March 2023, is truly a TikTokian masterpiece, highlighting what makes the app a virtual playground of endless entertainment. Esperon's video is technically advanced and perfectly executed. In this video and others, Esperon plays with trending content and mainstream popular culture in a playful and new way.

He engages with followers, drawing them back to the space and transforming them from followers to *fans*. And, of course, as with any viral TikTok, the comments section is a robust message board in which fans engage with both Esperon and one another. The more than 25,000 comments posted to the January 25, 2022, video included hand-clapping emojis from the official TikTok for Walt Disney Records (@disneymusic), praise for the transitions (@misslucycarrington: "This was that smooth I didn't even realise you were changing outfits"), and, of course, requests for more videos recreating "We Don't Talk about Bruno" (@hello__hi65: "Hahaha... now do Isabellas part"). Esperon would create dozens of BrunoTok videos, mimicking nearly every part of the song.

Esperon's performance hit its crescendo on February 11, 2022. After weeks of mixing and matching characters and scenes from "We Don't Talk about Bruno," Esperon posted a TikTok video declaring that he would be playing *every* part in the song. The video uses the audio meme of Cher's 1978 television performance in which she announces that she will be performing every role in *West Side Story*. Esperon's Cher-esque TikTokian coup couldn't be contained to just TikTok. Nope. Esperon needed more space, and so he sent his audiences to Instagram, which, at the time, allowed videos longer than TikTok's three minutes. The full-length video is truly a masterpiece, with frequent jump cuts in which Esperon transforms into each new character through wardrobe choices and physical movement. The performance climaxes with the song's well-known polyphonic outro at the Madrigal family dinner table. In this final feat of digital video editing, Esperon appears on screen simultaneously as different members of the family, with fades and cuts to transform into other pairs and trios from la familia Madrigal. The entire 3:32 minute video gives dancing, editing, costumes, characterizations, and, of course, Lin-Manuel Miranda's infectious song.

Although Brian Esperon's serial TikTok foray into the world of "We Don't Talk about Bruno" became the song's most well-known and widely circulated collection of videos on the platform, Esperon was far from the only TikTok creator turned *Encanto* fan. The million-plus TikTok videos using the hashtag #WeDontTalkAboutBruno hashtag have over six *billion* views. What is more, videos using #Encanto have over thirty billion views. These videos are far reaching, thoroughly tapping into the app's subcommunities, particularly through the way that TikTokers remix *Encanto* with existing TikTok trends, effectively harmonizing the dramaturgical world of *Encanto* with TikTokian aesthetics and cultures. And, of course, TikTok's upper echelon of influencers and celebrities hold much power to make things go viral. In addition to Esperon, take for instance dancing duo Austin and Marideth Telenko, better known for their stage names Cost n' Mayor (@cost_n_mayor), who created a dance challenge for Dolores's verse; their initial video has over 22 million views as of March 2023. Much like with Esperon, Cost n' Mayor's fans encouraged them to continue choreographing other parts of the song. Although they didn't go quite as far as Esperon, Cost n' Mayor's continued entries into the BrunoTok archive convey how responding to fan comments via video is just one route to TikTok virality and extended account growth. Pre-TikTok celebrities also engaged with "We Don't Talk about Bruno," further adding to the song's influence. On January 11, 2022, Stephanie Beatriz (@stephaniebeatriz), who plays Mirabel in the film, posted a duet lip-syncing Pepa and Felix's intro to the song, accumulating over 12 million views as of March 2023. And in a Janaury 26, 2022, TikTok with over 10 million views as of March 2023, Colleen Ballinger (aka Miranda Sings, @mirandasings) uses the DIY Drag Blue & Red Filter to transition between Pepa and Felix. These are but a few examples of both the expanse of the *Encanto* TikTok archive and the ways that TikTokers with large followings continue to influence the app's mainstream culture.

Although the case studies throughout this book reveal much about musical theatre's role in dictating and influencing TikTok culture, "We Don't Talk about Bruno" and the larger *Encanto* universe convey how musicals are the mainstream on TikTok. When TikTokers scroll their For You Page (FYP) and stumble across BrunoTok, there is no doubt that they are engaging with *Encanto*, a musical. This isn't the land of stealth musicals that penetrate TikTok's mainstream in a largely covert way. Not at all. "We Don't Talk about Bruno" is clearly musical theatre fodder created by a world-renowned theatre nerd (Lin-Manuel Miranda) living in the upper echelon of US popular culture. As TikTok moves forward, further cementing its role in nearly every aspect of life in the United States, musical theatre will continue to play a part in this cultural work. Whether it's Mirabel and Bruno or the priest who lost his hair and the woman whose fish dies, there's a role for everyone on TikTok Broadway.

Conclusion

The musical *KPOP* was supposed to take Broadway by storm.[1] After a commercially and artistically successful Off-Broadway run at Ars Nova in 2017, there was energy to extend the life of *KPOP* and possibly bring it to Broadway one day. When producers announced that the musical would debut at Broadway's Circle in the Square in October 2022, it seemed that New York theatre audiences were finally ready to join the worldwide K-pop revolution.

But *KPOP* never found success. Throughout its long and rocky preview period, the production dealt with incredibly low grosses, cancellations due to COVID-19 and other sicknesses, and a host of other roadblocks. The production had poor ticket sales and struggled to fill one of Broadway's smallest theatres (776 seats), even with heavily papered tickets. The show opened on November 27, 2022, to mixed reviews. Nearly all of them cited the infectious score and choreography while recognizing how the show's libretto weighed down the entire evening, making it difficult for the musical to appear as anything more than a series of dynamite musical performances with book scenes that stopped the show cold. Given the show's low grosses, it was no surprise that *KPOP* announced it would close on December 11, after only seventeen performances (not including forty-four previews), making *KPOP* one of Broadway's biggest flops in recent decades.

Despite its commercial failures, *KPOP* sparked much online debate about how ineffective traditional Broadway marketing playbooks can be to curate audiences for shows that don't cater to upper-class, White theatregoers. While tried-and-true marketing strategies might put butts in seats for Hugh Jackman and Sutton Foster in the 2022 revival of *The Music Man*, and Michael Jackson's name alone can generate interest in *MJ: The Musical* (2022), those same strategies don't necessarily work with shows about marginalized populations in the United States, especially populations that haven't historically been represented on Broadway. Such shows—*KPOP* and *A Strange Loop* (2022), for example—struggle to find footing because they quite literally aren't being supported in an authentic way for those productions or their prime audience demographics.[2] The *KPOP* team recognized this and saw the potential in connecting to the rabid online fandoms that real-world K-pop idols have. By any measure, the digital presence of K-pop artists and fans alike is incredibly expansive. *KPOP* attempted to connect to these K-pop lovers. Yet, as Monica Chin noted, "At the end of the day, technology alone is not enough. The artist still needs to connect."[3] It should come as no surprise that the primary point of connection for *KPOP* ended up being TikTok, even if the experiment did get cut short.

Although *KPOP* began using TikTok on August 30, 2022, to promote the show's fictional K-pop groups F8 and RTMS, the account (@kpopbroadway) didn't find much traction until November 10, 2022. In the first few months of *KPOP*'s TikTok account, it posted a mix of content that showed how marketing a musical by creating a viral fan-first social media campaign requires TikTok—and social media—acumen. Posts that felt authentic to TikTok performed well, drumming up interest in the musical, but many of the posts felt like Broadway marketing forcing a tired playbook into the TikTok apparatus (for example, uploading a YouTube video onto TikTok, complete with large black bars above and below the video). This was until *KPOP* did something that made too much sense for no other Broadway production to have done it before: it hired a prominent theatre TikToker to run the account. In this case, TheatreTok personality Brandon Powers (@brandon_powers), an accomplished director and choreographer in his own right, was hired by marketing agency SpotCo to be the *KPOP* TikTok account's lead content creator. Powers led the TikTok strategy, created content alongside the *KPOP* cast, and posted all the videos. The shift from tepid TikTok engagement to increased video views and higher engagement rates was almost immediate. Under Powers's artistic direction, the account began posting native TikTok content, much like *Beetlejuice* had done in 2019. Suddenly, *KPOP* was giving (potential) fans an inside look into the world of the musical. Fans were able to meet the stars who would become their new K-pop idols. Zachary Noah Piser, who played Brad, answered seven questions while walking down the street and into the Circle in the Square Theatre. A November 29, 2022, video used the new TikTok picture format to introduce several members of the cast: the video begins with a shirtless Jinwoo Jung (Juny) in his dressing room, fully playing into how thirst traps perform well with the TikTok algorithm. A December 1, 2022, video features RTMS teaching a dance tutorial of their song "Gin & Tonic," leaning in to TikTok's robust trending dance challenge culture. These authentic TikTok videos were mixed with footage from the show itself, offering a glimpse into how electric the musical was while also encouraging musical lovers to get to know the world backstage at *KPOP*. Indeed, *KPOP* TikTok worked to transform followers into fans into ticket buyers into long-term supporters of the musical.

The feather in the *KPOP* TikTok bucket hat was the live stream of the last fifteen minutes of the final performance, on December 11. The musical follows K-pop artists as they prepare for a concert presentation to wow US American audiences. In the final fifteen minutes, spectators view the concert, which features arguably the strongest section of the musical itself (in my opinion and as evidenced by reviews). During this powerhouse section, audiences see MwE, F8, and RTMS in all of their power. Helen Park's score, Jennifer Weber's choreography, Teddy Bergman's direction, and *all* design elements coalesce to offer audiences one of best finales on Broadway. To be sure, the musical itself had its challenges, but nearly every reviewer and much word of mouth signaled the music numbers as intoxicating. But potential fans just didn't get to see this, and, perhaps most importantly, few full-price ticket buyers had been willing to take the gamble on a new show. Brandon Powers recognized how captivating this final moment could be on social media and how it could help ensure the musical's longevity beyond Broadway. Seeing the TikTok account experience rapid growth, Powers petitioned for the musical to go live on TikTok and Instagram for just fifteen minutes, thus ensuring that the production didn't violate Actors' Equity contracts.[4] At the time of the live stream, the Instagram account had about 14,500 followers (compared to nearly 6,000 TikTok followers). The live stream reached 4,895 total accounts on Instagram and 2,600 accounts on TikTok. At one point 2,560 people were viewing it on Instagram, and 743 more were watching it on TikTok. Although Instagram drew more viewers, then, TikTok offered better margins (with a higher percentage of followers watching the event). While these numbers are undoubtedly low by social media standards, over 3,000 concurrent digital spectators is a number that nearly matched the total number of seated audience members in attendance across all shows during one of its eight-show weeks.

The fact that 7,500 people viewed the musical online conveys how musical theatre fans are hungry for this type of radical digitality. Audiences want to engage with musical theatre from the convenience of their cell phones. They want to be a part of something new, something exciting, something that hasn't been done before. They want to see shows that they otherwise wouldn't be able to see because of how prohibitive travel to New York City (or London, or Seoul, or Madrid, etc.) can be. By any measure, digital media is the future, and, accordingly, the more musical theatre as a genre and an industry leans in to this digitality, the more change-makers can move the art form further into the digital age, into the future.

While, for *KPOP*, TikTok may have generated the moment, per usual much of the conversation took place on Twitter. Following the live stream, Brandon Powers tweeted, "SO glad we got to make this happen and to have people all over the world tune in to celebrate this epic amazing show. Let this be only an early chapter for this show and the possibilities for digitally sharing theatre!"[5] Digital theatre-maker and advocate Jared Mezzocchi also celebrated the experiment on Twitter, in multiple tweets:

Two phones from different angles, I watched both feeds and thought "by simply doing this for 15mins, we are able to learn a tremendous amount about how to strengthen the experience at such a low cost." Yes, contracts, compensation, and so many other topics to debate..but..[6]

The act of just DOING THIS so that we can discuss ACTUAL things is so important to this moment, just like when Clyde's did streaming at a pro-film level. Now we have two very different case studies and can grow.[7]

Mezzocchi further acknowledged how important this moment was for not just commercial Broadway theatre, but theatre at large. While commercial Broadway theatre may often be poorly positioned to be a change-maker for industry standards, the capabilities of social media live-streaming expand conversations around access, engagement, and marketing. In *KPOP*'s case, the experiment—while successful—ultimately didn't help the longevity of the show. But, perhaps as Mezzocchi alludes, productions can capitalize on these strategies by incorporating them into productions from the beginning (that is, well before the show sets a closing date).

While productions may lament low capacity since the dawn of COVID-19, digital methods have clearly shifted the needle, bringing theatre directly into people's homes. But, while COVID-19 changed the reality for streaming theatre at large,[8] it admittedly didn't shift the culture around live streaming of Broadway productions.[9] And yet, as theatre collective Fake Friends has demonstrated through commercially and critically successful digital productions of *Circle Jerk* (2020, 2022) and *This American Wife* (2021), live-streamed theatre can be an event that sparks a robust digital conversation.[10] In a similar vein, aren't live television musicals like *The Sound of Music* (2013), *The Wiz* (2015), and *Jesus Christ Superstar* (2018) high-budget live-streamed theatre? Despite these successes, the idea of live streaming a Broadway musical pushes against the commercial confines of being a Broadway musical. On the one hand, the *KPOP* live streams didn't generate income for the production; the live stream may have helped more fans see the musical, but those fans didn't buy tickets that day (of course, had the musical stayed open, it's very likely the live stream would have led to ticket sales, but we can only speculate). On the other hand, Actors' Equity rules meant to protect its union make things tricky when trying to expand a show beyond the confines of the theatre building itself. Indeed, Broadway has its limits.

KPOP's failures and successes both on TikTok and beyond convey how there is indeed a potentially robust fan community for just about any musical on TikTok, one that can help fill theatres, stream cast albums, and create viral video content expanding the reach of the musical in question. The result of these fannish behaviors can potentially canonize a show, ensuring its longevity far beyond its Broadway run. The marked shift in *KPOP*'s marketing strategy under the leadership of Brandon Powers speaks to how musical productions must consider TikTok as a serious marketing weapon. TikTok is not merely a frivolous virtual playground for chronically online Zoomers (and cringey Millennials). Rather, when TikTok is authentically used from even before a musical opens, it can generate real interest in a musical production.

In the case of *KPOP*, the final weeks of the musical's Broadway run saw an explosion on TikTok, in which the account grew by thousands of followers in just a few days (no small feat on any platform, much less for a musical set to close at the end of the week). Of course, this growth partially owes credit to the digital #SaveKPOPBroadway campaign across various social media platforms, which ensured that the final week of performances was sold out (even if the average ticket price only rose to $51.12, equating a total gross of $281,757.10).[11] Yet, social media success, especially on TikTok and especially for a musical, requires growth strategies within the app itself. Aside from perhaps *Hamilton*, the bulk of musical theatre fans do not necessarily seek out different productions on TikTok. Rather, the TikTok algorithm feeds musical lovers recommended musicals they might enjoy. Given these facts, it is conceivable that *KPOP*'s growth fortuitously shadowed the musical's reach on other social media platforms like Twitter and Facebook, where the theatre community maintained a robust conversation about the musical, the challenges it faced throughout its development and subsequent Broadway run, and its abrupt closing. In any case, TikTok proved to be a fundamental site for celebrating *KPOP* in its final weeks and in the immediate aftermath of its closing. While becoming a commercial Broadway flop typically is the nail in the coffin for new musicals, *KPOP*'s TikTok popularity conveys how this musical can have life after Broadway. Perhaps there is far more to musical theatre than *just* a production on the Great White Way.

As TikTok continues to grow, musical theatre on the platform expands, as well. Much of this expansion has its roots in the early days of TikTok Broadway. New TikTok musicals like *For You, Paige* and *Mexican Pizza: The Musical* likely don't exist in a universe sans *Ratatouille: The TikTok Musical*. Trending challenges such as the "Revolting Children" dance set to the "little bit naughty" segment from the *Matilda* film and the "Holy Mary" dance from the hit television show *Wednesday* connect to a lineage of TikTok dance that includes the MUNY *Legally Blonde* dance call and the "Rich Man's Frug" from *Sweet Charity*. All the while, *Six* upholds its stature as a TikTok commodity in which TikTok creators—and musical lovers—continue to mine the musical's cast recording for viral audio memes. Prominent TheatreTok vloggers like Brandon Powers, Broadway Bob, Bryan the Business Analyst, Ashley Hufford, Katherine Quinn, and Kate Reinking use the platform to give fans constant breakdowns of all the latest theatre news, show reviews, and hot takes. And, as *KPOP* reveals, Broadway productions might find that they can use TikTok live streaming as a low-cost way to reach more fans. By any measure, the myriad ways that TikTok intersects with musical theatre fandom are just the beginning.

As always, at the heart of TikTok Broadway lies the fans. Musical theatre lovers, show queens, and the like are the driving force behind musical theatre's popularity on TikTok and on social media at large. As I've detailed throughout this book—and in my writing in general—TikTok brings people together. Sometimes it's Broadway actors like Amber Ardolino and their castmates making silly TikToks within the world of their show. Sometimes it's Disney fans coming together to collectively generate a bizarre and heartfelt musical adaptation of *Ratatouille*. And other times it's a fifteen-year-old musical fan sitting in my third-period Spanish 2 class scrolling through my TikTok page, landing the video of my niece and me doing *Mamma Mia!* cosplay to "Angel Eyes." That student says, "Dr. Boffone, can we make this TikTok?" And so you do. You assemble the *Mamma Mia!* lovers in the class together. You bring bathrobes, towels, and sunglasses from home. You perfectly lip-sync to ABBA because musicals are your happy place and because performing your fandom on TikTok is an immediate serotonin boost.

My fannish experiences are but a few in the robust community that is TikTok Broadway. TikTok has revolutionized musical fan practices. Musical theatre fans engage in an incisively critical practice that has great potential to shape the future of musical theatre—as form, as commodity, as cultural practice. In the social media age, we have the power. And, on platforms like TikTok, we can do this cutting-edge cultural work in an incredibly public way. No longer are we secretly singing and dancing to vinyl records of *Follies* and *Chicago*. No longer are we anonymously chatting on the BroadwayWorld message board. No longer are we hiding deep in the Tumblr rabbit hole. Those days are long gone. In the TikTok Age, musical theatre fandom can be front and center. It can be incredibly public. And, it can all be fed directly to you on your For You Page. The algorithm knows. You can't hide it. Nor should you. You love musical theatre. And you're ready for TikTok to give you your fix. Curtains up. It's showtime.

Notes

Preface

1. Dubsmash is primarily known as a dance challenge app. Although Dubsmash began its life as a lip-syncing app, in 2018 the company moved from Berlin to Brooklyn and began focusing on the one demographic that was still using the app—Black teenage girls in the United States. The app remains central to the digital dance community and continues to expand its reach across the globe. In terms of the interface, Dubsmash shares many similarities with TikTok. For more on Dubsmash, see Trevor Boffone, *Renegades: Digital Dance Cultures from Dubsmash to TikTok* (New York: Oxford University Press, 2021). Triller is also an important app in the digital dance world, but the app features a wider range of content than Dubsmash. Triller is known for edits. Users will upload several videos, and the app will create a cutting that mixes the uploaded video. Triller is also popular with video bloggers.
2. The Microwave Challenge was a popular TikTok trend throughout 2019. To mimic the trend, TikTokers sit on the ground. As the beat drops, TikTokers spin in place, using their back arm, hidden behind them, to make it appear as if they are magically rotating.
3. There is a rich body of autoethnographic fan studies. See, for example, Ika Willis, "Keeping Promises to Queer Children: Making Space (for Mary Sue) at Hogwarts," in *Fan Fiction and Fan Communities in the Age of the Internet*, ed. Karen Hellekson and Kristina Busse (Jefferson, NC: McFarland, 2006), 153–70; Shannon K. Farley, "Translation, Interpretations, Fan Fiction: A Continuum of Meaning Production," *Transformative Works and Cultures* 14 (2013), https://doi.org/10.3983/twc.2013.0517; Kristina Busse, "The Ethics of Studying Online Fandom," in *The Routledge Companion to Media Fandom*, ed. Melissa A. Click and Suzanne Scott (London: Routledge, 2018), 9–17; and Will Brooker, Mark Duffett, and Karen Hellekson, "Fannish Identities and Scholarly Responsibilities: A Conversation," in Click and Scott, *The Routledge Companion to Media Fandom*, 63–74.
4. Matt Hills, *Fan Cultures* (London: Routledge, 2002), 65–89.
5. Brooker, Duffett, and Hellekson, "Fannish Identities and Scholarly Responsibilities," 63.
6. For more on the ethics of fan studies, see Lucy Bennett, "Surveying Fandom: The Ethics, Design, and Use of Surveys in Fan Studies," in Click and Scott, *The Routledge Companion to Media Fandom*, 36–44; Busse, "The Ethics of Studying Online Fandom"; and Brooker, Duffett, and Hellekson, "Fannish Identities and Scholarly Responsibilities."

168   NOTES

Introduction

1. Rice (@chrisriceny) is one of the more successful musical theatre performers on TikTok, with over 210,000 followers as of February 2024. Although Rice may be a relatively little-known actor, his success on TikTok reflects the democratized nature of the app. TikTok's most famous actors do not necessarily reflect those who are famous outside of the app.
2. Bob Avian is billed as *A Chorus Line*'s co-choreographer. The historical record shows that Avian's role was more in line with that of Bennett's assistant.
3. Stacy Wolf, *Changed for Good: A Feminist History of the Broadway Musical* (New York: Oxford University Press, 2011), 117.
4. For example, for the 2006 Broadway revival, Charlotte d'Amboise played this "leading" role but was nominated for the Tony Award for Best Supporting Actress in a Musical.
5. For a critical overview of *A Chorus Line*'s body politics and casting, see Ryan Donovan, *Broadway Bodies: A Critical History of Conformity* (New York: Oxford University Press, 2023), 27–54.
6. Bryan M. Vandevender, "They're Playing My Song: The American Musical in the Me-Decade," in *The Routledge Companion to the Contemporary Musical*, ed. Jessica Sternfeld and Elizabeth L. Wollman (London: Routledge, 2020), 34.
7. While going through the archive, I stumbled across my own *A Chorus Line* TikTok fan practice. Months earlier I had commented on this video from Liotine, "Donna [McKechnie, the original Cassie] has been real quiet since you posted this." In another *A Chorus Line* TikTok, I commented, "commenting so I can stay on A Chorus Line TikTok." In the course of writing this book, I had many similar experiences in the TikTok Broadway archive, where my own fan practices undergirded the research I was doing.
8. Warren Hoffman, *The Great White Way: Race and the Broadway Musical* (New Brunswick, NJ: Rutgers University Press, 2014), 143.
9. Hoffman, *The Great White Way*, 145.
10. For a critical analysis of *A Chorus Line*, see Brian Eugenio Herrera, "Little Steps: The Absurdity of *A Chorus Line*," *Studies in Musical Theatre* 10, no. 1 (2016): 105–15; Hoffman, *The Great White Way*; David Roman, *Performance in America: Contemporary US Culture and the Performing Arts* (Durham, NC: Duke University Press, 2005); and Wolf, *Changed for Good*.
11. Hoffman, *The Great White Way*, 145.
12. Herrera, "Little Steps," 109.
13. As of February 2024, TikTok has not influenced Broadway casting practices. Although a number of Broadway performers have sizable followings on TikTok (as well as other social media platforms), the gold standard remains talent and the ability to perform eight shows per week.
14. Notably the musical *Ride the Cyclone* has been able to ride TikTok virality to a second life. *Ride the Cyclone* tells the story of six teenagers who were killed in a roller-coaster accident. The musical began its life in 2008 in Victoria, British Columbia, before

productions at the Chicago Shakespeare Theater and Off-Broadway in 2016. Written by playwright Jacob Richmond and musician Brooke Maxwell, *Ride the Cyclone* found a second wave after clips and songs from the show began circulating on TikTok in 2022 and 2023. Much like other examples throughout this book, fans created a rabid fandom on TikTok, making a wide variety of videos playing with the musical. The musical's 2023 production at Arena Stage in Washington, DC, was an immediate success, extending multiple weeks and signaling that *Ride the Cyclone* was perhaps ahead of its time when it first premiered. With a robust TikTok fan community, *Ride the Cyclone* appears primed for new productions and a transition from a cult favorite to part of the musical theatre popular culture canon.

15. For more on TikTok's relationship to trending music, see Trevor Boffone, *Renegades: Digital Dance Cultures from Dubsmash to TikTok* (New York: Oxford University Press, 2021); D. Bondy Valdovinos Kaye, "Make This Go Viral: Building Musical Careers through Accidental Virality on TikTok," *Flow Journal* 27, no. 1 (2020), https://www.flowjournal.org/2020/09/make-this-go-viral/; Arantxa Vizcaíno-Verdú and Crystal Abidin, "Music Challenge Memes on TikTok: Understanding In-Group Storytelling Videos," *International Journal of Communication* 16 (2022): 883–908; Arantxa Vizcaíno-Verdú and Ignacio Aguaded, "#ThisIsMeChallenge and Music for Empowerment of Marginalized Groups on TikTok," *Media and Communication* 10, no. 1 (2022): 157–72.

16. For more on the role of digital theatre in 2020 and 2021, during the onset of the COVID-19 pandemic, see Dani Snyder-Young, "We're All in This Together: Digital Performances and Socially Distanced Spectatorship," *Theatre Journal* 74, no. 1 (2022): 1–15.

17. Zoomers frequently refer to the summer of 2019 as the Golden Age of TikTok because this was a time when the app was almost exclusively a Gen Z space in the United States. Given the relatively small size of the TikTok community at the time, trending content was more widespread and cohesive. Moreover, the likelihood of going viral and getting "TikTok famous" was higher. That is, the app was less saturated, giving off the idea that it was a more tight-knit and like-minded community.

18. Jessica Hillman-McCord, "Musical Theatre in the Digital Age," in *iBroadway: Musical Theatre in the Digital Age*, ed. Jessica Hillman-McCord (London: Palgrave Macmillan, 2017), 2.

19. Hillman-McCord, 2.

20. For more on digital musical theatre fan practices, see Ryan Bunch, "'You Can't Stop the Tweet': Social Media and Networks of Participation in the Live Television Musical," in Hillman-McCord, *iBroadway*, 173–205; Kathryn Edney, "Let's Misbehave: Cell Phone Technology and Audience Behaviors," in Hillman-McCord, *iBroadway*, 95–117; Jessica Hillman-McCord, "Digital Fandom: *Hamilton* and the Participatory Spectator," in Hillman-McCord, *iBroadway*, 119–44; and Kirsty Sedgman, "No-Object Fandom: *Smash*-ing Kickstarter and Bringing *Bombshell* to the Stage," in Hillman-McCord, *iBroadway*, 145–72.

21. D. A. Miller, *Place for Us: Essay on the Broadway Musical* (Cambridge, MA: Harvard University Press, 1998), 2–3, 16.

22. Fan studies is a robust discipline that understands fandom as a critical identity performance. Major interventions in fan studies include Henry Jenkins, *Textual Poachers: Television Fans and Participatory Culture* (London: Routledge, 1992); Henry Jenkins, *Convergence Culture: Where Old and New Media Collide* (New York: New York University Press, 2006); Matt Hills, *Fan Cultures* (London: Routledge, 2002); Paul Booth, *Digital Fandom: New Media Studies* (London: Peter Lang, 2010); Louisa Ellen Stein, *Millennial Fandom: Television Audiences in the Transmedia Age* (Des Moines: University of Iowa Press, 2015); and Melissa A. Click and Suzanne Scott, eds., *The Routledge Companion to Media Fandom* (London: Routledge, 2020).
23. Hills, *Fan Cultures*, viii.
24. Stacy Wolf, *Beyond Broadway: The Pleasure and Promise of Musical Theatre across America* (New York: Oxford University Press, 2019), 15.
25. Hills, *Fan Cultures*, x.
26. See, e.g., Laura MacDonald, "Connection in an Isolating Age: Looking Back on Twenty Years of Engaging Audiences and Marketing Musical Theatre Online," in Hillman-McCord, *iBroadway*, 17–42; Laura MacDonald, "Have I Done Enough? Lin-Manuel Miranda and *Hamilton*'s Culture of Generosity," *Performance Research* 23, no. 6 (2018): 40–49; Laura MacDonald, "Rising in the East: Disney Rehearses Chinese Consumers at a Glocalised Shanghai Disneyland," in *Performance and the Disney Theme Park Experience: The Tourist as Actor*, ed. Jenny Kokai and Tom Robson, 127–48 (London: Palgrave Macmillan, 2019); and Laura MacDonald, "Seasons of Love: Chinese Millennials' Affective Amateur Musical Theatre Performance," *Performance Research* 25, no. 1 (2020): 112–20.
27. See Wolf, *Changed for Good*; and Wolf, *Beyond Broadway*.
28. Kelly Kessler, "'Rash Talk and Virtual Protests': The Musical Genre's Personal and Political Interactivity in the Age of Social Media," in Sternfeld and Wollman, *The Routledge Companion to the Contemporary Musical*, 335–44.
29. Holley Replogle-Wong, "The Great Generational Divide: Stage-to-Screen Hollywood Musical Adaptations and the Enactment of Fandom," in Sternfeld and Wollman, *The Routledge Companion to the Contemporary Musical*, 345–54.
30. Sam O'Connell, "Mediated Musical Theatre," in *The Routledge Companion to Musical Theatre*, ed. Laura MacDonald and Ryan Donovan (London: Routledge, 2022), 464–77.
31. Gabriella Giannachi, *Virtual Theatre: An Introduction* (London: Routledge, 2004); Matthew Causey, *Theatre and Performance in Digital Culture* (London: Routledge, 2006); Michael Kustow, *Theatre@Risk* (London: Methuen Drama, 2007); Rosemary Klich and Edward Scheer, *Multimedia Performance* (London: Red Globe Press, 2011); Bill Blake, *Theatre and the Digital* (London: Red Globe Press, 2014); Amy Petersen Jensen, *Theatre in a Media Culture: Production, Performance and Perception since 1970* (Jefferson, NC: McFarland, 2007); and Valerie M. Fazel and Louise Geddes, eds., *The Shakespeare Multiverse Fandom as Literary Praxis* (London: Routledge, 2021).
32. Patrick Lonergan, *Theatre and Social Media* (London: Red Globe Press, 2016), 5.
33. Lonergan, *Theatre and Social Media*, 4–5.
34. Wolf, *Changed for Good*, 223.

35. Other social media apps used to create short-form video content include Dubsmash, Triller, Zoomerang, and Funimate.
36. For more on TikTok's short history and global import, see Boffone, *Renegades*, 26–34; Melanie Kennedy, "'If the Rise of the TikTok Dance and E-Girl Aesthetic Has Taught Us Anything It's That Teenage Girls Rule the Internet Right Now': TikTok Celebrity, Girls and the Coronavirus Crisis," *European Journal of Cultural Studies* 23, no. 6 (2020): 1069–76; Andreas Schellewald, "Communicative Forms on TikTok: Perspectives from Digital Ethnography," *International Journal of Communication* 15 (2021): 1437–57; Crystal Abidin, "Mapping Internet Celebrity on TikTok: Exploring Attention Economies and Visibility Labours," *Cultural Science* 12, no. 1 (2021): 77–103; Crystal Abidin, *TikTok and Youth Cultures* (Bingley, UK: Emerald, 2024); D. Bondy Valdovinos Kaye, Jing Zeng, and Patrik Wikstrom, *TikTok: Creativity and Culture in Short Video* (Cambridge: Polity Press, 2022); and Jing Zeng, Crystal Abidin, and Mike S. Schäfer, "Research Perspectives on TikTok and Its Legacy Apps," *International Journal of Communications* 15 (2021): 3161–72.
37. TikTok, however, has been around in China since 2016. The Chinese version of the app is named Douyin. TikTok became available internationally in 2017.
38. Although Zoomers are digital natives, having been born with this technology doesn't mean that young people understand it or know how to effectively use it.
39. For more on BeReal, see Trevor Boffone, "Do You Want to Make a TikTok? Is It Time to BeReal? Gen Z, Social Media, and Digital Literacies," *Journal of Language and Literacy Education* 18, no. 2 (2022), http://jolle.coe.uga.edu/volume-18-2/.
40. Wallaroo, "TikTok Statistics," last updated February 6, 2021, https://wallaroomedia.com/blog/social-media/tiktok-statistics/.
41. Wallaroo, "TikTok Statistics—Updated October 2020."
42. Yunan Zhang and Tom Dotan, "TikTok's U.S. Revenues Expected to Hit $500 Million This Year," *Information*, June 17, 2020, https://www.theinformation.com/articles/tiktoks-u-s-revenues-expected-to-hit-500-million-this-year.
43. Kyesha Jennings, "City Girls, Hot Girls and the Re-Imagining of Black Women in Hip Hop and Digital Spaces," *Global Hip Hop Studies* 1, no. 1 (2020): 49.
44. Raymond Williams, *Culture* (London: Fontana Press, 1981), 200.
45. Paige Leskin, "The Ultimate Guide to TikTok, the Hot App Gen Z Is Obsessed with and Facebook Is Terrified Of," *Business Insider*, October 24, 2019, https://markets.businessinsider.com/news/stocks/tiktok-how-to-use-short-form-video-app-gen-z-2019-6-1028319047.
46. Sejla Rizvic, "Everybody Hates Millennials: Gen Z and the TikTok Generation Wars," *Walrus*, February 9, 2021, https://thewalrus.ca/everybody-hates-millennials-gen-z-and-the-tiktok-generation-wars/.
47. Rizvic, "Everybody Hates Millennials."
48. Kennedy, "If the Rise of the TikTok Dance and E-Girl Aesthetic Has Taught Us Anything," 1072.
49. Tom Lamont, "'It's Hard to Put the Brakes on It. We Doubled Down': Charli D'Amelio and the First Family of TikTok," *Guardian*, June 6, 2020, https://www.theguardian.

com/lifeandstyle/2020/jun/06/its-hard-to-put-the-brakes-on-it-we-doubled-down-charli-damelio-and-the-first-family-of-tiktok.
50. Deanna Ting, "'Every Kid Wants to Be an Influencer': Why TikTok Is Taking Off with Gen Z," *Digiday*, February 7, 2020, https://digiday.com/marketing/every-kid-wants-influencer-tiktok-taking-off-gen-z/.
51. Louisa Ellen Stein, "Tumblr Fan Aesthetics," in Click and Scott, *The Routledge Companion to Media Fandom*, 86.
52. Rizvic, in "Everybody Hates Millennials," lists "ethos, aesthetics, and attitudes" as core tenets of Gen Z TikTok.
53. Rizvic, "Everybody Hates Millennials."
54. The lyrics are quoted from Richard Rodgers and Oscar Hammerstein II, "In My Own Little Corner" from *Cinderella*, Genius, accessed February 20, 2023, https://genius.com/The-original-broadway-cast-of-cinderella-in-my-own-little-corner-lyrics.
55. TikTok's critics have recognized how the platform replicates many of the same systems of oppression that exist in analog spaces. Even so, marginalized communities still use TikTok as a site of activist work, self-fashioning, and community-building. See, e.g., Cienna Davis, "Digital Blackface and the Troubling Intimacies of TikTok Dance Challenges," in *TikTok Cultures in the United States*, ed. Trevor Boffone (London: Routledge, 2022), 28–38; Wendyliz Martinez, "TikTok for Us by Us: Black Girlhood, Joy, and Self-Care," in Boffone, *TikTok Cultures in the United States*, 39–46; Tom Divon and Tobias Ebbrecht-Hartmann, "#JewishTikTok: The JewToks' Fight against Antisemitism," in Boffone, *TikTok Cultures in the United States*, 47–58; and Elle Rochford and Zachary D. Palmer, "Trans TikTok: Sharing Information and Forming Community," in Boffone, *TikTok Cultures in the United States*, 84–94.
56. For more on TikTok's Whiteness, see Boffone, *Renegades*, 26–34; and Trevor Boffone, "The D'Amelio Effect: TikTok, Charli D'Amelio, and the Construction of Whiteness," in Boffone, *TikTok Cultures in the United States*, 17–27.
57. Sam Biddle, Paulo Victor Ribeiro, and Tatian Dias, "Invisible Censorship," *Intercept*, March 16, 2020, https://theintercept.com/2020/03/16/tiktok-app-moderators-users-discrimination/.
58. Jessica Sage Rauchberg, "TikTok's Digital Eugenics: Challenging Ableism and Algorithmic Erasure through Disability Activism," *Flow Journal* 27, no. 1 (2020), http://www.flowjournal.org/2020/09/tiktok-digital-eugenics/; and Jessica Sage Rauchberg, "#SHADOWBANNED: Queer, Trans, and Disabled Creator Responses to Algorithmic Oppression on TikTok," in *LGBTQ Digital Cultures: A Global Perspective*, ed. Paromita Pain (London: Routledge, 2022), 196–209.
59. Safiya Umoja Noble, *Algorithms of Oppression: How Search Engines Reinforce Racism* (New York: New York University Press, 2018), 36.
60. Ruha Benjamin, *Race after Technology: Abolitionist Tools for the New Jim Code* (Boston: Polity Press, 2019), 3.
61. Elizabeth Ellcessor, "Accessing Fan Culture: Disability, Digital Media, and Dreamwidth," in Click and Scott, *The Routledge Companion to Media Fandom*, 204.

NOTES   173

62. Similarly, Rauchberg proposes that TikTok is an ableist place while also recognizing that disability activism is happening on the platform. See Rauchberg, "TikTok's Digital Eugenics."
63. Trevor Boffone, "The Rise of TikTok in US Culture," in Boffone, *TikTok Cultures in the United States*, 1–2.
64. Wolf, *Changed for Good*, 223.
65. Schellewald, "Communicative Forms on TikTok," 1439.
66. Jensen, *Theatre in a Media Culture*, 4.
67. Wolf, *Changed for Good*, 223.
68. Hillman-McCord, "Musical Theatre in the Digital Age," 3.
69. Zachary Pincus-Roth, "The Most Exciting Theater Now Is a Figment of Our Imagination," *Washington Post*, December 22, 2020, https://www.washingtonpost.com/arts-entertainment/2020/12/22/tiktok-broadway-musical-theater-ratatouille/.
70. Jared Mezzocchi (@JaredMezzocchi), "It is. On TikTok. [. . .]," Twitter, September 5, 2021, 8:07 a.m., https://twitter.com/JaredMezzocchi/status/1434503502303215616.
71. Elizabeth L. Wollman, *A Critical Companion to the American Stage Musical* (London: Methuen Drama, 2017), xi.
72. Wolf, *Beyond Broadway*, 5.
73. Barrie Gelles, "*Glee* and the 'Ghosting' of the Musical Theatre Canon," *Popular Entertainment Studies* 2, no. 2 (2011): 90.
74. Broadway Bob (@broadwaybob) had 72,000 followers as of February 2024. Pablo David Laucerica (@pablodlaucerica) had over 452,000 followers as of February 2024.
75. JJ Nieman's TikTok account (@jjniemann) had over 1M followers as of February 2024. Nieman has been integral to the TikTok Broadway community, from his videos disclosing what actors do onstage when we can't hear or see them to his involvement with *Ratatouille: The TikTok Musical*.
76. Shoebox Musicals (@shoeboxmusicals) had 103,000 followers as of February 2024.
77. Alexa Chalnick's TikTok account (@alexachalnick) had over 1.1 million followers as of February 2024.
78. Katie Johantgen's TikTok account (@katiejoyofsho) had 73,000 followers as of February 2024.
79. Bryan the Business Analyst's TikTok account (@bryantheba) had 37,000 followers as of February 2024.
80. As of February 2024, Kate Reinking (@theatreislife) had 37,000 followers, Ashley Hufford (@ashleyhufford) had 57,000 followers, and Katherine Quinn (@itskatharinequinn) had 76,000 followers.
81. Brandon Powers (@brandon_powers) had 71,000 followers as of February 2024.
82. Grace Walker (@notkristenbell) had 32,000 followers as of February 2024. In a similar vein, Gabriel Rodriguez (@genuinelygabriel) uses TikTok to highlight Latinx plays, albeit to a far smaller audience than Walker. For more on Rodriguez, see Elena Machado Sáez, "Hype It Up: US Latinx Theater on TikTok," in Boffone, *TikTok Cultures in the United States*, 117–25.

83. Other notable TikTok accounts in this category include: @themeparksentertainment (39,000 followers), @genwithahardg (10,000 followers), @musicaltheatreprof (Mathew Miller, 11,000 followers), @dankuhlman (15,000 followers), @eli.bway (13,000 followers), and @the_theater_lovers (19,000 followers) (all numbers as of March 2024).
84. "TikTok Apologizes after Inadvertently Giving Platform to Thousands of Theater Kids," *Onion*, June 8, 2020, https://www.theonion.com/tiktok-apologizes-after-inadvertently-giving-platform-t-1843955237.
85. For more on WitchTok, see Jane Barnette, "Hocus-Pocus: WitchTok Education for Baby Witches," in Boffone, *TikTok Cultures in the United States*, 97–107; and Chris Miller, "How Modern Witches Enchant TikTok: Intersections of Digital, Consumer, and Material Culture(s) on #WitchTok," *Religions* 13, no. 2 (2022): article 118, https://doi.org/10.3390/rel13020118. For more on BookTok, see Sarah Jerasa and Trevor Boffone, "BookTok 101: TikTok, Digital Literacies, and Out-of-School Reading Practices," *Journal of Adolescent & Adult Literacy* 65, no. 3 (2021): 219–26; and Trevor Boffone and Sarah Jerasa, "Toward a (Queer) Reading Community: BookTok, Teen Readers, and the Rise of TikTok Literacies," *Talking Points* 33, no. 1 (2021): 10–16.
86. Hills, *Fan Cultures*, xii.
87. Popular blogger Eugene Wei likens the TikTok algorithm to the Sorting Hat from *Harry Potter*, which sorts first-year students into Gryffindor, Hufflepuff, Ravenclaw, and Slytherin houses. TikTok's algorithm sorts users into subcultures. Eugene Wei, "TikTok and the Sorting Hat," *Remains of the Day*, August 4, 2020, https://www.eugenewei.com/blog/2020/8/3/tiktok-and-the-sorting-hat.
88. Abidin, "Mapping Internet Celebrity on TikTok," 88.
89. Tanya Kant, *Making It Personal: Algorithmic Personalization, Identity, and Everyday Life* (Oxford: Oxford University Press, 2020), 2–3.
90. Zeng, Abidin, and Schäfer, "Research Perspectives on TikTok and Its Legacy Apps," 3163.
91. Schellewald, "Communicative Forms on TikTok," 1439.
92. Andrea Ruehlicke, "All the Content, Just for You: TikTok and Personalization," *Flow Journal* 27, no. 1 (2020), http://www.flowjournal.org/2020/10/content-just-for-you/.
93. Jenkins, *Textual Poachers*, 86.
94. Ting, "Every Kid Wants to Be an Influencer."
95. Hills, *Fan Cultures*, 20.
96. José van Dijck, *The Culture of Connectivity: Critical History of Social Media* (Oxford: Oxford University Press, 2013), 77.
97. Limor Shifman, "Memes in a Digital World: Reconciling with a Conceptual Troublemaker," *Journal of Computer-Mediated Communication* 18, no. 3 (2013): 365.
98. Jonathan Miller, *Subsequent Productions* (New York: Viking Adult, 1986), 1.
99. Alicia Corts, "(Un)limited: Virtual Performance Spaces and Digital Identity," *Theatre Symposium* 24 (2016): 113.
100. Jessica Sternfeld and Elizabeth L. Wollman, introduction to Sternfeld and Wollman, *The Routledge Companion to the Contemporary Musical*, 1.

101. Boffone, "The Rise of TikTok in US Culture," 5–6.
102. Howard Gardner and Katie Davis, *The App Generation: How Today's Youth Navigate Identity, Intimacy, and Imagination in a Digital World* (New Haven, CT: Yale University Press, 2013), 32.

Chapter 1

1. Alan Siegal, "How 'Beetlejuice' Was Born," *Ringer*, March 30, 2018, https://www.theringer.com/movies/2018/3/30/17178786/.
2. In the film, the title character's name is spelled "Betelgeuse," whereas the musical simplifies things by using "Beetlejuice" in all instances. To be consistent with the musical, I refer to the character as Beetlejuice in this chapter.
3. Jacob Stolworthy, "Day-O: How Beetlejuice Conquered Its Strangeness to Become a Cult Classic," *Independent*, October 28, 2018, https://www.independent.co.uk/arts-entertainment/films/features/beetlejuice-30-years-michael-keaton-tim-burton-winona-ryder-cinema-release-film-a8602251.html.
4. Mark Salisbury and Tim Burton, *Burton on Burton* (London: Faber and Faber, 2006), 54.
5. Salisbury and Burton, *Burton on Burton*, 54.
6. *Beetlejuice's Graveyard Mash-Up* factored heavily into my childhood trips to Universal Studios Florida. The live musical revue combined all of my favorite things as a young child—musicals, camp aesthetics, theme parks, you name it! The show ran from 1992 to 2016 in Orlando and from 1991 to 1999 at Universal Studios Hollywood as *Beetlejuice's Rock and Roll Graveyard Revue*.
7. Laura MacDonald, "Connection in an Isolating Age: Looking Back on Twenty Years of Engaging Audiences and Marketing Musical Theatre Online," in *iBroadway: Musical Theatre in the Digital Age*, ed. Jessica Hillman-McCord (London: Palgrave Macmillan, 2017), 18.
8. Elizabeth Titrington Craft, "'Is This What It Takes Just to Make It to Broadway?!': Marketing *In the Heights* in the Twenty-First Century," *Studies in Musical Theatre* 5, no. 1 (2011): 51.
9. Matt Hills, *Fan Cultures* (London: Routledge, 2002), 123.
10. Jessica Hillman-McCord, "Musical Theatre in the Digital Age," in Hillman-McCord, *iBroadway*, 2.
11. Trevor Boffone, "Taking *Hamilton* to the Streets: Lin-Manuel Miranda, Latinidad, and the Aesthetics of Accessibility," in *Dueling Grounds: Revolution and Revelation in the Musical "Hamilton,"* ed. Paul Laird and Mary Jo Lodge (New York: Oxford University Press, 2021), 95.
12. Boffone, "Taking *Hamilton* to the Streets," 95.
13. MacDonald, "Connection in an Isolating Age," 29.
14. Jessica Hillman-McCord, "Lin-Manuel Miranda: Digital Diva," *Studies in Musical Theatre* 12, no. 1 (2018): 109–22.

15. Craft, "Is This What It Takes Just to Make It to Broadway?!," 50. Notably, however, as Craft (53) explains, *In the Heights* augmented these digital methods with traditional, tried-and-true methods of marketing a musical on Broadway: "They continued to rely on traditional methods like direct mailings, newspaper ads, radio and television commercials, and a Times Square billboard."
16. Boffone, "Taking *Hamilton* to the Streets."
17. *The Search for the Next Elle Woods* (2008) was a reality show in which actors competed to become the next lead in *Legally Blonde* on Broadway.
18. CubbyBernstein, "Cubby Bernstein—Xanadu—Episode One," YouTube video, uploaded May 12, 2008, 3:34, https://www.youtube.com/watch?v=qa8sPwfdn9g.
19. YouTube is also home to a legion of musical theatre fans who create their own content, specifically designed for the platform. For example, MacDonald documents how Japanese musical fan Kaho Kidoguchi sings showtunes on YouTube, often in costumes invoking the dramaturgy of the musical. For more on YouTube fan performances, see Laura MacDonald, "The Border and Boundary Crossings of Musical Theatre Fans in Europe and East Asia," in *Theatre Fandom*, ed. Kirsty Sedgman (forthcoming). Also, see Aya Esther Hayashi, "'YouTube! Musicals! YouTubesicals!': Cultivating Theater Fandom through New Media," in *The Routledge Companion to the Contemporary Musical*, ed. Jessica Sternfeld and Elizabeth L. Wollman (London: Routledge, 2020), 374–83.
20. *Next to Normal*'s Twitter handle is @n2nbroadway. The Twitter account grew to over 145,000 followers by the end of the experiment, no small feat in the early days of Twitter.
21. MacDonald, "Connection in an Isolating Age," 29.
22. Kathryn Edney, "Let's Misbehave: Cell Phone Technology and Audience Behaviors," in Hillman-McCord, *iBroadway*, 96.
23. Elena Machado Sáez, "Debt of Gratitude: Lin-Manuel Miranda and the Politics of US Latinx Twitter," *archipelagos: a journal of Caribbean digital praxis* 4 (2020), https://archipelagosjournal.org/issue04/machado-gratitude.html.
24. Laura MacDonald, "Have I Done Enough? Lin-Manuel Miranda and *Hamilton*'s Culture of Generosity," *Performance Research* 23, no. 6 (2018): 40–49.
25. See Boffone, "Taking *Hamilton* to the Streets."
26. For more on Ham4Ham, see Boffone, "Taking *Hamilton* to the Streets"; and MacDonald, "Have I Done Enough?"
27. Quoted in Alexander Vuocolo, "Gen Z Looks for Authenticity in TikTok Viral Marketing, Says Creative Agency CEO," *Cheddar*, December 28, 2020, https://cheddar.com/media/gen-z-looks-for-authenticity-in-tiktok-viral-marketing-says-creative-agency-ceo.
28. In April 2021, Broadway enthusiasts on TikTok began performing the choreography to "Rich Man's Frug" and "The Heavyweight" from the 1969 *Sweet Charity* film. The trend was a micro trend, accumulating only a little more than two thousand videos at its height. While this barely qualifies as a trend in the world of TikTok, it nevertheless linked a small community of Fosse fans on the platform.

29. Zoe Paskett, "From *Six* to *Heathers*, the Best Musical Theatre TikToks," *Evening Standard*, February 26, 2020, https://www.standard.co.uk/culture/theatre/best-musical-theatre-tiktoks-six-heathers-hamilton-a4372251.html.
30. Vuocolo, "Gen Z Looks for Authenticity."
31. Maria Sibirtseva, "Insightful Tips on TikTok Marketing to Reach Generation Z and Millennials," *Deposit Photos* (blog), August 4, 2020, https://blog.depositphotos.com/tips-on-tiktok-marketing.html.
32. Ben Brantley, "In 'Beetlejuice,' the Afterlife Is Exhausting," rev. of *Beetlejuice*, dir. Alex Timbers, *New York Times*, April 25, 2019, https://www.nytimes.com/2019/04/25/theater/beetlejuice-review-broadway.html.
33. Peter Marks, "'Beetlejuice' Cleans Up Its Act for Broadway. It's Not a Raging Success, but It'll Do," rev. of *Beetlejuice*, dir. Alex Timbers, *Washington Post*, April 25, 2019.
34. Frank Rizzo, Rev. of *Beetlejuice*, dir. Alex Timbers, *Variety*, April 26, 2019, https://variety.com/2019/legit/reviews/beetlejuice-review-broadway-musical-1203194763/.
35. Sara Holdren, "*Beetlejuice* Is Best When It's at Its Most Antic," rev. of *Beetlejuice*, dir. Alex Timbers, *Vulture*, April 25, 2019, https://www.vulture.com/2019/04/review-beetlejuice-is-best-when-its-at-its-most-antic.html.
36. E. J. Dickson, "Can TikTok Save 'Beetlejuice,' the Broadway Musical?," *Rolling Stone*, December 16, 2019, https://www.rollingstone.com/culture/culture-features/beetlejuice-broadway-musical-tiktok-trend-920184/.
37. David Edelstein, "'Beetlejuice': Tim Burton, Michael Keaton on the Ghoulish Masterpiece," *Rolling Stone*, June 2, 1988, https://www.rollingstone.com/movies/movie-features/mixing-beetlejuice-78733/.
38. Presley Ryan's TikTok account (@prezryan) had over 230,000 followers as of February 2023.
39. Shauna Pomerantz and Miriam Field, "A TikTok Assemblage: Girlhood, Radical Media Engagement, and Parent-Child Generativity," in *Visual and Cultural Identity Constructs of Global Youth and Young Adults: Situated, Embodied and Performed Ways of Being, Engaging and Belonging*, ed. Fiona Blaikie (New York: Routledge, 2021), 139–57; Shauna Pomerantz and Miriam Field, "Watching TikTok, Feeling Feminism: Intergenerational Flows of Feminist Knowledge," in *TikTok Cultures in the United States*, ed. Trevor Boffone (London: Routledge, 2022), 61–71.
40. Craft, "Is This What It Takes Just to Make It to Broadway?!," 50.
41. For more on the Woah, see Trevor Boffone, *Renegades: Digital Dance Cultures from Dubsmash to TikTok* (New York: Oxford University Press, 2021).
42. Brendan Wetmore, "'Beetlejuice' on Broadway Is Breaking TikTok," *Paper Mag*, October 3, 2019, https://www.papermag.com/beetlejuice-broadway-tiktok-trend-1-2640689936.html.
43. Quoted in Dickson, "Can TikTok Save 'Beetlejuice,' the Broadway Musical?"
44. Chris Stokel-Walker, "Presley Ryan's TikToks Have Made *Beetlejuice* Broadway's Hottest Ticket," *FFWD* (blog), *Medium*, December 20, 2019, https://ffwd.medium.com/presley-ryans-tiktoks-have-made-beetlejuice-broadway-s-hottest-ticket-fa9c76b1f123.

45. Foxberri's TikTok handle (@foxberri.cosplay) had over 1.4 million followers as of May 2022.
46. Quoted in Dickson, "Can TikTok Save 'Beetlejuice,' the Broadway Musical?"
47. Quoted in Dickson, "Can TikTok Save 'Beetlejuice,' the Broadway Musical?"
48. For more on *Dear Evan Hansen*'s digital presence, see Adam Rush, "#YouWillBeFound: Participatory Fandom, Social Media Marketing and *Dear Evan Hansen*," *Studies in Musical Theatre* 15, no. 2 (2021): 119–32. For more on the confluence of musical theatre fans and marketing, see Adam Rush and Stephanie Lim, "From Stage Door to Cyber Space: The Digital Evolution of Musical Theatre Fandom," in *The Routledge Companion to Musical Theatre*, ed. Laura MacDonald and Ryan Donovan (London: Routledge, 2022), 231–46.
49. Quoted in Stokel-Walker, "Presley Ryan's TikToks."
50. James Deaville, "Play It Again (and Again, and Again): The Superfan and Musical Theater," in Sternfeld and Wollman, *The Routledge Companion to the Contemporary Musical*, 360.
51. Hayashi, "YouTube! Musicals! YouTubesicals!," 374.
52. Caitlin Mullen, "Brands Look to Employees to Engage Gen Z on TikTok," *Biz Women*, November 13, 2020, https://www.bizjournals.com/bizwomen/news/latest-news/2020/11/brands-look-to-employees-to-engage-gen-z-on-tiktok.html.
53. The virality of @oompa_loompa_dobadido's video prompted a resurgence in the "Say My Name" challenge. As of April 2021, there were over 11,700 TikTok videos using the original video's audio, many of these videos going viral themselves and further leading to *Beetlejuice*'s TikTok afterlife.
54. Quoted in Stokel-Walker, "Presley Ryan's TikToks."
55. Brent Lang, "How 'Beetlejuice: The Musical' Became a Broadway Turnaround Story," *Variety*, November 18, 2019, https://variety.com/2019/legit/news/beetlejuice-the-musical-broadway-1203407953/.
56. Quoted in Stokel-Walker, "Presley Ryan's TikToks."
57. Quoted in Stokel-Walker, "Presley Ryan's TikToks."
58. Stokel-Walker, "Presley Ryan's TikToks."
59. Dickson, "Can TikTok Save 'Beetlejuice,' the Broadway Musical?"
60. Lang, "How 'Beetlejuice: The Musical.'"
61. Some theatres have standing-room tickets which allows productions to play at above 100 percent capacity. Productions can also earn above their gross potential by means of premium tickets and flex ticket pricing.
62. Craft, "Is This What It Takes Just to Make It to Broadway?!," 57.
63. Quoted in Dickson, "Can TikTok Save 'Beetlejuice,' the Broadway Musical?"
64. Quoted in Marc Hershberg, "Broadway Marketers Fear TikTok Ban," *Forbes*, July 19, 2020, https://www.forbes.com/sites/marchershberg/2020/07/19/broadway-marketers-fear-tiktok-ban/.
65. Quoted in Hershberg, "Broadway Marketers Fear TikTok Ban."
66. *Hamilton* has the most successful TikTok account for a musical production, with over 2.2 million followers as of March 2024. While TikTok has certainly factored into *Hamilton*'s success, the musical was a global phenomenon years before TikTok

was founded. As such, although I consider the relationship between *Hamilton* and TikTok, the expansiveness of the dramaturgical world of *Hamilton* clouds the role of TikTok, thus problematizing an understanding of how TikTok can lead to ticket sales and ultimately to turning a profit, such as was the case with *Beetlejuice*.

Interlude

1. Lin-Manuel Miranda and Jeremy McCarter, *Hamilton: The Tevolution* (Hachette, UK, 2016), 234
2. Amber Ardolino's TikTok handle is @ambernicoleardolino. As of March 2024, she had 578,000 followers and was performing in the ensemble of *Funny Girl* on Broadway.
3. For a comprehensive overview of twerking, see Kyra D. Gaunt, "YouTube, Twerking & You: Context Collapse and the Handheld Co-Presence of Black Girls and Miley Cyrus," *Journal of Popular Music Studies* 27, no. 3 (2015): 244–73; Aria S. Halliday, "Twerk Sumn! Theorizing Black Girl Epistemology in the Body," *Cultural Studies* 34, no. 6 (2020): 874–91; and Aria S. Halliday, *Buy Black: How Black Women Transformed US Pop Culture* (Urbana: University of Illinois Press, 2022).
4. As of February 2024, there were over twenty-six billion views on the #WAP hashtag, and over 5 million videos had been created using the official "WAP" sound bite.
5. Saturday Night on Broadway is a tradition in which occupants of the August Wilson Theatre and the Neil Simon Theatre wave at each other from their respective dressing room windows every Saturday night at 7:30 p.m.
6. Elena Machado Sáez, "Debt of Gratitude: Lin-Manuel Miranda and the Politics of US Latinx Twitter," *archipelagos: a journal of Caribbean digital praxis* 4 (2020), https://archipelagosjournal.org/issue04/machado-gratitude.html.
7. Shoutout to Stephen Sondheim's *Follies*.
8. Indeed, this was my experience with these videos. When I first noticed the series, I favorited the videos, saving them in a special *TikTok Broadway* folder. When I returned to the folder months later to write this interlude, the videos had disappeared. This led me down a rabbit hole to find the videos and learn about what had happened (although I had a strong hunch).
9. Devereaux's TikTok account had 163,000 followers as of February 2024.
10. Bootleg videos of Broadway productions frequently appear on YouTube. Since a video titled "Fun Home Bootleg" would be easy to find and eventually be taken down, bootleggers are clever with their titles. It has become common practice to title bootlegs with any riff on "slime tutorial," aka "Head Over Heels Slime Tutorial." In the case of the original Broadway production of *Fun Home*, one bootleg is titled, "How to Make a Cheesecake with Only a Handful of Cheese (Fun Home Edition)."
11. For more on musical theatre's bootleg culture, see Peter C. Kunze, "Bootlegs over Broadway: Musical Theatre (Re)Productions, Digital Circulation, and the Informal Media Economy," *Creative Industries Journal*, 2021, https://doi.org/10.1080/17510694.2021.1996984.

Chapter 2

1. DiTanna's TikTok account (@dominicditanna) had 4.1 million followers as of March 2024. Born in 1988, DiTanna is a Millennial, but his series engages in mainstream Gen Z culture. In 2019, non-Zoomers were still in the minority on TikTok.
2. *Billy on the Street* (2011–22) is a comedy game show hosted by Billy Eichner in which he stops people walking down the sidewalk in New York City and asks them questions with the chance to win money.
3. "Another Day of Sun" was composed by Justin Hurwitz, with lyrics by Benj Pasek and Justin Paul.
4. Notably, "Another Day of Sun" was commonly used on Musical.ly before its acquisition by TikTok, demonstrating the integration of Musical.ly culture into TikTok's mainstream.
5. Herrera identifies as "stealth Latinos" such actors as Ricardo Montalbán, Juano Hernandez, Mel Ferrer, and Rita Moreno, who were able to maneuver in and around Hollywood (playing characters of a variety of races and ethnicities) due to the legibility of Latinx nonwhiteness. See Brian Eugenio Herrera, *Latin Numbers: Playing Latino in Twentieth-Century U.S. Popular Performance* (Ann Arbor: University of Michigan Press, 2015), 60.
6. Tin Pin Alley refers to a group of songwriters and music publishers—such as Irving Berlin and George Gershwin—who dominated the music scene in late nineteenth- and early twentieth-century New York City.
7. Machinima is a portmanteau of machine and cinema. Machinima is the practice of making short films using computer graphics.
8. Melanie Kennedy, "'If the Rise of the TikTok Dance and E-Girl Aesthetic Has Taught Us Anything, It's That Teenage Girls Rule the Internet Right Now': TikTok Celebrity, Girls and the Coronavirus Crisis," *European Journal of Cultural Studies* 23, no. 6 (2020): 1069–76; and Trevor Boffone, *Renegades: Digital Dance Cultures from Dubsmash to TikTok* (New York: Oxford University Press, 2021).
9. Barrie Gelles, "*Glee* and the 'Ghosting' of the Musical Theatre Canon," *Popular Entertainment Studies* 2, no. 2 (2011): 92–93.
10. Henry Bial, *Acting Jewish: Negotiating Ethnicity on the American Stage and Screen* (Ann Arbor: University of Michigan Press, 2005), 17.
11. Gelles, "*Glee* and the 'Ghosting,'" 92.
12. Marvin Carlson, *The Haunted Stage: The Theatre as Memory Machine* (Ann Arbor: University of Michigan Press, 2001), 7.
13. After its off-Broadway run, *Heathers* played off–West End in 2018, before transferring to the West End for a limited engagement.
14. This mirrors previous generations' fascination with high school dramas such as Millennials' love for *Dawson's Creek*, *The O.C.*, *One Tree Hill*, *The Hills*, and *Gossip Girl*.
15. Of course, it's impossible to pin this rise on TikTok alone. (For example, the March 20, 2019, episode of *Riverdale*, "Chapter Fifty-One: Big Fun," was a musical episode of the hit TV series that saw Riverdale High School produce *Heathers: The Musical*. In addition to the production numbers that lived within the musical production, songs from

the musical were sung by Archie, Betty, Veronica, and company in scenes external to the production, advancing the plot of the episode.) Even so, it's no secret that TikTok is a critical site to disseminate music and culture in general, having made songs (including showtunes) into hits and recording artists into household names. See Boffone, *Renegades*; and D. Bondy Valdovinos Kaye, "Make This Go Viral: Building Musical Careers through Accidental Virality On TikTok," *Flow Journal* 27, no. 1 (2020), https://www.flowjournal.org/2020/09/make-this-go-viral/.

16. See Laurence O'Keefe and Kevin Murphy, "Big Fun" from *Heathers: The Musical*, Genius, accessed February 22, 2023, https://genius.com/Heathers-the-musical-ensemble-big-fun-lyrics.
17. Even clicking on the sound does not necessarily reveal that "Big Fun" is from a musical. The thumbnail is the cover of the original cast recording, but it remains small and difficult to read. Only the song title and actors' names are listed.
18. For more on the power of algorithms, see Safiya Umoja Noble, *Algorithms of Oppression: How Search Engines Reinforce Racism* (New York: New York University Press, 2018); and Ruha Benjamin, *Race after Technology: Abolitionist Tools for the New Jim Code* (Boston: Polity Press, 2019).
19. Kennedy, "If the Rise of the TikTok Dance and E-Girl Aesthetic Has Taught Us Anything," 1071.
20. Michelle Santiago Cortés, "Charli D'Amelio Now Has More Followers Than Anyone on TikTok," *Refinery29*, March 27, 2020, https://www.refinery29.com/en-us/2020/03/9612154/charli-damelio-most-followers-on-tiktok.
21. Boffone, *Renegades*, 2; Trevor Boffone, "The D'Amelio Effect: TikTok, Charli D'Amelio, and the Construction of Whiteness," in *TikTok Cultures in the United States*, ed. Trevor Boffone (London: Routledge, 2022), 17–27.
22. Kennedy, "If the Rise of the TikTok Dance and E-Girl Aesthetic Has Taught Us Anything," 1071.
23. Natalie Coulter, "'Frappés, Friends, and Fun': Affective Labor and the Cultural Identity of Girlhood," *Journal of Consumer Culture* 21, no. 3 (2018): 487–500.
24. Samantha Eve Marchiony, "Our Crowning Glory: *SIX* and the Path of the Modern Progressive Musical" (MA thesis, University of Houston, 2020), 2.
25. For example, during the show's post-curtain encore, "Six," audiences are encouraged to do two things that are usually forbidden in live theatre: take out their phones to film the number, and take pictures to later share on social media.
26. Grace Barnes, "'My Sleeves May Be Green but My Lipstick's Red': Deconstructing the 'Feminism' in *Six*," *Studies in Musical Theatre* 14, no. 2 (2020): 138.
27. Barnes, 139, 146.
28. Lindsey Barr, "Theorizing a Narrative Patriarchal (re/dis)Placement in Contemporary Musical Theatre," *Telephone Hour: A Quarantine Colloquium*, Musical Theatre/Dance Focus Group, Association for Theatre in Higher Education, April 13, 2020. While admitting the competitiveness between the queens that at times gets ugly, Samantha Eve Marchiony still proposes that *Six* has a feminist message in the way that it underscores the pervasiveness of violence against women throughout history, and women's responses to these violent acts. See Marchiony, "Our Crowning Glory," 83.

29. Lyrics from Toby Marlow and Lucy Moss, "All You Wanna Do" from *Six: The Musical*, Genius, accessed February 22, 2023, https://genius.com/Six-cast-all-you-wanna-do-lyrics.
30. Marchiony sees Katherine Howard as inspired by both Ariana Grande and Britney Spears. See Marchiony, "Our Crowning Glory," 153.
31. Barnes, "My Sleeves May Be Green but My Lipstick's Red," 142.
32. Barr, "Theorizing a Narrative Patriarchal (re/dis)Placement."
33. Marchiony, "Our Crowning Glory," 157.
34. Marlow and Moss, "All You Wanna Do."
35. Barnes, "My Sleeves May Be Green but My Lipstick's Red," 146.
36. Quoted in Tatiana Walk-Morris, "TikTok's Digital Blackface Problem," *One Zero* (blog), *Medium*, February 12, 2020, https://onezero.medium.com/tiktoks-digital-blackface-problem-409571589a8.
37. Gelles, "*Glee* and the 'Ghosting,'" 102.

Interlude

1. Cienna Davis, "Digital Blackface and the Troubling Intimacies of TikTok Dance Challenges," in *TikTok Cultures in the United States*, ed. Trevor Boffone (London: Routledge, 2022), 28.
2. JJ Niemann, interview by author, February 10, 2022.
3. Mike Isaacson, interview by author, February 8, 2022.
4. Isaacson, interview by author.
5. The "Rich Man's Frug" challenge amassed around a thousand videos of dancers and musical fans executing Bob Fosse's choreography to the scene of the same name from the 1969 *Sweet Charity* film. Much like the Muny *Legally Blonde* dance call, the conversation beyond TikTok gave the illusion that *all* of TikTok was doing the challenge, when in reality it was such a small collection of videos that it didn't truly permeate TikTok's mainstream. Yet, just like with the Muny dance call, even a micro challenge like "Rich Man's Frug" can move the needle. *Hairspray*'s "The New Girl in Town" was more expansive with over 25,000 videos as of March 2023.
6. For more on TikTok's dance challenge culture, see Alexandra Harlig et al., "TikTok and Short-Form Screendance before and after Covid," *International Journal of Screendance* 12 (2021), https://screendancejournal.org/index.php/screendance/issue/view/279; Trevor Boffone, *Renegades: Digital Dance Cultures from Dubsmash to TikTok* (New York: Oxford University Press, 2021); Trevor Boffone, "The D'Amelio Effect: TikTok, Charli D'Amelio, and the Construction of Whiteness," in Boffone, *TikTok Cultures in the United States*, 17–27; and Davis, "Digital Blackface."
7. Although aspiring dancers post dance call videos from nearly every show, from high school theatre to Broadway, *Hamilton* and *Moulin Rouge!* have accumulated the most dance-call videos on TikTok. Notably, these videos don't trend so much as they are commonplace on the app, with frequent waves of new videos being routinely posted.

NOTES 183

8. Ali Sousa (@alisousa4), "why am i on 'muny legally blonde dance call self tape' [. . .]," Twitter, January 29, 2022, 5:34 p.m., https://twitter.com/alisousa4/status/1487569757503213568.
9. Julia Capizzi (@julia_capizzi), "The way I haven't been to a dance call [. . .]," Twitter, January 30, 2022, 12:33 p.m., https://twitter.com/julia_capizzi/status/1487856610022207493.
10. William Carlos Angulo, interview by author, February 8, 2022.
11. Angulo, interview by author.
12. Isaacson, interview by author.
13. Niemann, interview by author.
14. Isaacson, interview by author.
15. Isaacson, interview by author.

Chapter 3

1. True story: During my sophomore year of college I found myself driving east on I-20 somewhere between Dallas and Shreveport. As was common at the time, I found myself listening to the *Wicked* Broadway cast recording. By the time I got to the crescendo of "Defying Gravity," my foot fell heavily on the gas (without me realizing it, of course). Whether Stephen Schwartz, Idina Menzel, or myself is to blame, I was going twenty miles over the speed limit. My jam sesh was abruptly cut short by police sirens and my first speeding ticket in Texas. I'd say it has been my only speeding ticket in the Lone Star State, but my move to Houston in 2012 would prove otherwise.
2. For a comprehensive overview of *The Wizard of Oz*, see Ryan Bunch, *Oz and the Musical: Performing the American Fairy Tale* (New York: Oxford University Press, 2022).
3. Jane Barnette, "What Is Wanda but Witches Persevering? Palimpsests of American Witches in *WandaVision*," *Theatre Journal* 74, no. 1 (2022): 44.
4. Of course, there are numerous reasons explaining queer men's fascination with Judy Garland. Garland is also widely considered a camp figure. "Somewhere Over the Rainbow" is a queer anthem. Garland's own struggles in life mirrored the struggles of many queer men at the time.
5. It is easy to see the metaphor of the closed-mindedness of small-town America versus the expansive inclusiveness of big cities like San Francisco and New York.
6. Baum even uses the word *queer* an inordinate number of times throughout the Oz series of books. And, I would be remiss to not mention Dorothy's queer relationship with Ozma.
7. Stacy Wolf, *Changed for Good: A Feminist History of the Broadway Musical* (New York: Oxford University Press, 2011), 221.
8. Wolf, 221–22.
9. Laura MacDonald and Myrtle Halman, "*Geen Grenzen Meer*: An American Musical's Unlimited Border Crossing," *Theatre Research International* 39, no. 3 (2014): 203.

10. Wolf, *Changed for Good*, 222. Although some scholars, most notably Wolf and Steven Greenwood, have done queer readings of *Wicked*, MacDonald and Halman propose that reading *Wicked* as queer is complicated given how, in the end, Elphaba chooses Fiyero and not Glinda: "The possibility of a queer reading is therefore also ultimately a failed promise." For more, see MacDonald and Halman, "Geen Grenzen Meer," 207.
11. Stacy Wolf, "'Defying Gravity': Queer Conventions in the Musical *Wicked*," *Theatre Journal* 60, no. 1 (2008): 11.
12. Quoted in Carol de Giere, *Defying Gravity: The Creative Career of Stephen Schwartz, from "Godspell" to "Wicked"* (New York: Applause Theater and Cinema, 2008), 275.
13. Claude J. Summers, *Queer Encyclopedia of Music, Dance and Musical Theater* (San Francisco: Cleis Press, 2004), 182.
14. The length of the green makeup application—the greenification, if you will—depends on the production of *Wicked* (Broadway, West End, touring, etc.) and the makeup designer in question. Some claim the process takes between ten and fifteen minutes, with some designers even saying they can achieve the look in around seven minutes. Even so, twenty-five to thirty minutes remains the standard.
15. Trevor Boffone, "TikTok Is Theatre, Theatre Is TikTok," *Theatre History Studies* 41 (2022): 42.
16. Boffone, 44.
17. Part of this popularity is due to the explosion of Beauty YouTube in the aughts and 2010s.
18. Krysten Stein, "YOU BETTER WORK! Drag Queen Storytelling and Performativity on TikTok," conference presentation, *TikTok and Social Movements Symposium*, TikTok Cultures Research Network, September 20, 2021.
19. Trevor Boffone, "The D'Amelio Effect: TikTok, Charli D'Amelio, and the Construction of Whiteness," in *TikTok Cultures in the United States*, ed. Trevor Boffone (London: Routledge, 2022), 17–27.
20. A "thirst follow" is when you follow someone on social media just because you think they are hot. Slang for "horny," thirst implies that the person in question is parched and must get their thirst quenched. Thirst follows are how we attempt to quench our thirst.
21. For critical perspectives on *In the Heights*, see Elena Machado Sáez, "Blackout on Broadway: Affiliation and Audience in *In the Heights* and *Hamilton*," *Studies in Musical Theatre* 12, no. 2 (2018): 181–97; Nicole Hodges Persley, *Sampling and Remixing Blackness in Hip-Hop Theater and Performance* (Ann Arbor: University of Michigan Press, 2021); Trevor Boffone, "Whitewashed Usnavi: Race, Power and Representation in *In the Heights*," *Studies in Musical Theatre* 13, no. 3 (2019): 235–50; and Trevor Boffone, "'World'-Traveling, Diversity, Inclusion, and the Making of Musicals in the Twenty-First Century," in *The Routledge Companion to Musical Theatre*, ed. Laura MacDonald and Ryan Donovan (London: Routledge, 2023), 567–81.
22. Curiously, *In the Heights* represents one of the few times in which TikTok virality did not necessarily translate to profit. Although trending sound bites on TikTok typically dominate the Billboard Hot 100 and the Billboard 200 album charts, *In the Heights* was an outlier. The album did achieve some modicum of success. It hit number 1 on

the US Billboard Soundtracks chart and reached number 45 on the Billboard 200. These achievements, however, pale in comparison to that of other music that has gone viral on TikTok.
23. Here, *af* is shorthand for "as fuck," meaning extremely, very, uber, the most, etc.
24. Ramos being shirtless is noteworthy in that the video also serves as a TikTok thirst trap.
25. Luis Loya and Elaine Almeida, "Things That Shouldn't Have Gay Energy But Do Anyways: CTI, Remixes and TikTok Duets," *Flow Journal* 27, no. 1 (2020), https://www.flowjournal.org/2020/09/cti-remixes-tiktok-duets/.
26. Loya and Almeida.
27. Of course, this list merely represents a handful of the upper echelon of Broadway leading ladies. Actors like Patti LuPone, Donna Murphy, Christine Ebersole, LaChanze, Victoria Clark, Katrina Lenk, and Adrienne Warren are highly revered in their own right.
28. Michelle Dvoskin, "Embracing Excess: The Queer Feminist Power of Musical Theatre Diva Roles," *Studies in Musical Theatre* 10, no. 1 (2016): 94.
29. D. A. Miller, *Place for Us: Essay on the Broadway Musical* (Cambridge, MA: Harvard University Press, 1998), 105.
30. As of this writing, early 2024, no out trans women have been cast as Elphaba on Broadway, on tour, or on the West End.
31. Jane Barnette, "Witch Fulfillment: Casting & Designing the Witch for Stage & Screen," public talk, University of Kansas, November 8, 2021; and see Jane Barnette, *Witch Fulfillment* (London: Routledge, 2023).
32. Kelsey Blair, "Broomsticks and Barricades: Performance, Empowerment, and Feeling in *Wicked* and *Les Misérables*," *Studies in Musical Theatre* 10, no. 1 (2016): 58.
33. Blair, "Broomsticks and Barricades," 59.
34. The phrase "baby witch" was popularized on WitchTok. For more, see Jane Barnette, "Hocus-Pocus: WitchTok Education for Baby Witches," in Boffone, *TikTok Cultures in the United States*, 97–107.
35. Barrie Gelles, "*Glee* and the 'Ghosting' of the Musical Theatre Canon," *Popular Entertainment Studies* 2, no. 2 (2011): 95–96.
36. For an in-depth analysis of *Wicked*'s score and orchestrations, see Paul Laird, *Wicked: A Musical Biography* (Lanham, MD: Scarecrow Press, 2011).
37. Wolf, *Changed for Good*, 5.
38. For more on how voice contributes to Elphaba's performance of power, see Michelle Boy, "Alto on a Broomstick: Voicing the Witch in the Musical *Wicked*," *American Music* 28, no. 1 (2010): 97–118.
39. Doris Raab, "From Book to Broadway: Elphaba's Gender Ambiguity and Her Journey into Heteronormativity in *Wicked*," *Studies in Musical Theatre* 5, no. 3 (2011): 248.
40. Blair, "Broomsticks and Barricades," 56.
41. danah boyd, "Why Youth (Heart) Social Media Network Sites: The Rise of Networked Publics in Teenage Life," in *Youth, Identity, and Digital Media*, ed. David Buckingham (Cambridge, MA: MIT Press), 2007.
42. Loya and Almeida, "Things That Shouldn't Have Gay Energy."

43. D. A. Miller, *Place for Us*, 90.
44. Warwick's TikTok account (@tyler_warwick) had 771,000 followers as of May 2022.
45. Gelles, "*Glee* and the 'Ghosting' of the Musical Theatre Canon," 96.
46. Raymond Knapp, *The American Musical and the Performance of Personal Identity* (Princeton, NJ: Princeton University Press, 2009), 164.
47. Schyvinck's TikTok account (@lowgy_) had 25,200 followers as of January 2022.
48. Blair, "Broomsticks and Barricades," 59.
49. Blair, "Broomsticks and Barricades," 59.
50. Wolf, *Changed for Good*, 226.
51. To *stan* is to support or "stand up" for something. The term was popularized by Eminem, who theorized "stans" as a mix of stalker and fan, a deranged fan who worships a celebrity. The term has since been given a life of its own, less problematic in meaning and far removed from Eminem.
52. Bootlegs of musical theatre performances and productions often live on YouTube with coded names such as "slime tutorial."

Interlude

1. Elsewhere, I offer an autoethnographic exploration of child/adult co-creation on TikTok, focusing on my niece and me. I explain how engaging in child-led creation creates a euphoric feeling that enables stronger relationships to develop and children to forge and perform identity. See Trevor Boffone, "Charli, Charlie, and I: An Autoethnographic Study of TikTok Dance and Child/Adult Collaborations," in *Creative Children and Children's Culture*, ed. Victoria Ford Smith and Peter C. Kunze (forthcoming).
2. The hashtag #MammaMia had 4.2 billion views as of March 2023, and there are numerous *Mamma Mia!*-inspired hashtags as well. It is also worth looking at TikTok activity for ABBA content (#ABBA: 5.4 billion views) in general, since so many TikTokers conflate the two properties. That is, *Mamma Mia!* lovers are ABBA lovers are *Mamma Mia!* lovers. The Venn diagram is nearly a circle.
3. Terence Tsai and Shubo Liu, "*Mamma Mia!* Made in China: Challenges in Developing the Musical Industry," *Asian Case Research Journal* 19, no. 2 (2015): 419.
4. The ABBA songbook is a regular feature across TikTok. Gen Z loves ABBA, and, as I've written throughout this book, Gen Z sets the tone on TikTok. TikTokers routinely choreograph dances to ABBA songs such as "Gimme! Gimme! Gimme!" and "Voulez-Vous," and they use ABBA songs for other trending challenges as well, such as was the case when TikTokers used audio from "Slipping through My Fingers" to take a trip down memory lane. Of course, as with every robust TikTok archive chronicled in this book, the expansiveness of ABBA TikTok can't be contained to a footnote.
5. Compared to other TikTok trends, which are often a flash in the pan, *Mamma Mia!* trends tend to have a longer shelf life. This signals the fandom's commitment to *Mamma Mia!* itself, more than simply an attempt to game the TikTok algorithm.

6. Malcolm Womack, "'Thank You for the Music': Catherine Johnson's Feminist Revoicings in *Mamma Mia!*," *Studies in Musical Theatre* 3, no. 2 (2009): 205.
7. Nicolle Lamerichs, "Stranger Than Fiction: Fan Identity in Cosplay," *Transformative Works and Cultures* 7 (2011), https://doi.org/10.3983/twc.2011.0246.
8. Melanie Kennedy and Katlin Marisol Sweeney-Romero propose that TikTok makes the traditionally private space of girls' bedrooms and bathrooms into public space. See Melanie Kennedy, "'If the Rise of the TikTok Dance and E-Girl Aesthetic Has Taught Us Anything, It's That Teenage Girls Rule the Internet Right Now': TikTok Celebrity, Girls and the Coronavirus Crisis," *European Journal of Cultural Studies* 23, no. 6 (2020): 1069–76; and Katlin Marisol Sweeney-Romero, "Wellness TikTok Morning Routines, Eating Well, and Getting Ready to Be 'That Girl,'" in *TikTok Cultures in the United States*, ed. Trevor Boffone (London: Routledge, 2022), 108–16.
9. Shauna Pomerantz and Miriam Field, "A TikTok Assemblage: Girlhood, Radical Media Engagement, and Parent-Child Generativity," in *Visual and Cultural Identity Constructs of Global Youth and Young Adults: Situated, Embodied and Performed Ways of Being, Engaging and Belonging*, ed. Fiona Blaikie (New York: Routledge, 2021), 139–57; and Shauna Pomerantz and Miriam Field, "Watching TikTok, Feeling Feminism: Intergenerational Flows of Feminist Knowledge," in Boffone, *TikTok Cultures in the United States*, 61–71.
10. Jen Gunnels, "'A Jedi like My Father before Me': Social Identity and the New York Comic Con," *Transformative Works and Cultures* 3 (2009), https://doi.org/10.3983/twc.2009.0161.
11. BroadwayCon is an annual three-day celebration of musical theatre held in New York City that began in 2018 and was founded by Melissa Anelli, Stephanie Dornhelm, and Anthony Rapp. Despite the inaugural BroadwayCon taking place in January (arguably the least lucrative time to visit New York), the festival proved to be a hit with musical fans from its first iteration. As musical theatre fans quickly revealed, no amount of inclement weather, exuberant prices, and overcrowded spaces can keep them from expressing their fandom. BroadwayCon has meant getting to take digital fandom into in-person physical spaces. Attendees relish the chance to unabashedly engage with other musical fans in a space exclusively dedicated to all things Broadway. BroadwayCon is host to a vast array of panels with major Broadway celebrities, conversations about the making of everyone's favorite musicals, dance workshops, autograph tables, musical sing-a-longs, trivia challenges, and, of course, performances from musicals currently playing on Broadway. By any account, BroadwayCon has something for die-hard Broadway enthusiasts of all ages and identities. And, of course, musical cosplayers have flocked to BroadwayCon. I mean where else can *Sweeney Todd* fans dress up as Mrs. Lovett and be immediately recognized by thousands of people? How many opportunities do theatre nerds have to dress in a full Fosca costume and be immediately recognizable as Donna Murphy's Tony Award–winning character from *Passion*? Let's be honest, the opportunities rarely exist. While many festival attendees engage in varying degrees of cosplay, BroadwayCon also includes an official cosplay contest, with the winner receiving free admission to the next year's festival. Cosplay is everywhere.

12. Although not a musical, *Harry Potter and the Cursed Child* is also regularly attended by spectators in cosplay. Wizards will frequently cosplay in robes or wear the colors of their house: Gryffindor, Ravenclaw, Hufflepuff, or Slytherin. Moreover, for any popular musical on Broadway, it is common to see a handful of audience members engaged in some level of cosplay, even if not in elaborate costumes.
13. Lamerichs, "Stranger Than Fiction."
14. Gunnels, "A Jedi like My Father before Me."
15. While our "Angel Eyes" TikTok didn't go viral by definition, it amassed over twice as many views as my follower count at the time, showing a significant impact on the TikTok algorithm.
16. Joli Jensen, "Fandom as Pathology: The Consequences of Characterization," in *The Adoring Audience: Fan Culture and Popular Media*, ed. Lisa A. Lewis (London: Routledge, 1992), 22.
17. "Angel Eyes" is not on the *ABBA Gold* (1992) track list. The song does, however, appear on *More ABBA Gold: More ABBA Hits* (1993). I classify it as a part of *ABBA Gold* here for comedic effect.

Chapter 4

1. During the benefit concert, in a musical theatre scholar group chat between Barrie Gelles, Amy Osatinski, Bryan M. Vandevender, and myself, Gelles used the term *rataturgy*. It immediately stuck in our group chat, with Osatinski even declaring herself a "rataturg."
2. The Actors Fund is a nonprofit that supports performers and other workers in the performing arts community. The organization provides emergency financial assistance, affordable housing, and health care, among other services. For reviews of *Ratatouille: The TikTok Musical*, see Trevor Boffone, rev. of *Ratatouille: The TikTok Musical*, dir. Lucy Moss, *Studies in Musical Theatre* 15, no. 2 (2021): 153–55; Lusie Cuskey, "Not Writing New Rules, Merely Rat-ifying: Musical Theatre Goes Digital in *Ratatouille*," rev. of *Ratatouille: The TikTok Musical*, dir. Lucy Moss, *PARtake: The Journal of Performance as Research* 4, no. 1 (2021): 1–9; and Christian Lewis, rev. of *Ratatouille: The Tiktok Musical*, dir. Lucy Moss, *Theatre Journal* 73, no. 3 (2021): 432–33.
3. For more on how musical theatre fans hate-watch, see Kelly Kessler, "'Rash Talk and Virtual Protests': The Musical Genre's Personal and Political Interactivity in the Age of Social Media," in *The Routledge Companion to the Contemporary Musical*, ed. Jessica Sternfeld and Elizabeth L. Wollman (London: Routledge, 2020), 335–44.
4. Lewis, rev. of *Ratatouille*, 433.
5. Jesse Green, "What's Small and Hairy with Big Dreams?," rev. of *Ratatouille: The TikTok Musical*, dir. Lucy Moss, *New York Times*, January 3, 2021, https://www.nytimes.com/2021/01/03/theater/ratatouille-tiktok-musical-review.html.
6. In early 2020, *Ratatouille* entered the TikTok mainstream. The song "Le Festin" from the film became a popular trend that encouraged creators to show off their skill in the

kitchen. The trend accumulated more than 314,000 videos. Later, a parody of the song, "CEO of Speaking French," went viral. "CEO of Speaking French" featured a female vocalist singing nonsensical French gibberish to the tune of "Le Festin." As opposed to the original "Le Festin" trend, which featured haute cuisine, "CEO of Speaking French" videos showcased extraordinarily bad cooking, with the creator being in on the joke. Although it is impossible to know the extent to which TikTokers knew that "Le Festin" came from the *Ratatouille* soundtrack, the trend's popularity does reveal the critical role that the Pixar film played on TikTok, even before *Ratatouille* the musical was an idea.

7. Laure Murat, "What's Queer about Remy, *Ratatouille*, and French Cuisine?," in *What's Queer about Europe? Productive Encounters and Re-Enchanting Paradigms*, ed. Mireille Rosello and Sudeep Dasgupta (New York: Fordham University Press, 2014), 136–47.
8. Daren C. Brabham, *Crowdsourcing* (Cambridge, MA: MIT Press, 2013), xv–xvi, 1.
9. Cuskey, "Not Writing New Rules," 3.
10. Luis Loya and Elaine Almeida, "Things That Shouldn't Have Gay Energy but Do Anyways: CTI, Remixes and TikTok Duets," *Flow Journal* 27, no 1 (2020), http://www.flowjournal.org/2020/09/cti-remixes-tiktok-duets/.
11. Brabham, *Crowdsourcing*, 12.
12. For example, Khabane Lame (@khaby.lame), who had TikTok's most followed account as of March 2024 (161 million), rose to fame primarily from reaction videos.
13. This submission was uploaded by a user with the handle @molle89. Since posting, she has changed her handle, making the video particularly difficult to track down. While not especially pertinent to this book, this habit of changing social media handles is common among Zoomers. I became aware of this issue while writing *Renegades: Digital Dance Cultures from Dubsmash to TikTok* (New York: Oxford University Press, 2021) and while working with teens as a high school teacher.
14. Emma Lynn (@emmaspacelynn), "This thread is evidence of the way TikTok's duet feature [. . .], Twitter, October 4, 2020, 10:07 p.m., https://twitter.com/emmaspacelynn/status/1312952644193996800.
15. *Thanksgiving: The Musical* premiered on the Tuesday, November 24, 2020, episode of *The Late Late Show with James Corden*. It began as a duet collaboration between Corden and Mertzlufft, before Corden surprised him with a chain of duets featuring some of Broadway's biggest names: Patti LuPone, Audra McDonald, Josh Groban, Kristin Chenoweth, and Josh Gad.
16. Eric Herhuth, *Pixar and the Aesthetic Imagination: Animation, Storytelling, and Digital Culture* (Berkeley: University of California Press, 2017), 158.
17. Birgitta Edelman, "From Trap to Lap: The Changing Sociogenic Identity of the Rat," in *Animals in Person: Cultural Perspectives on Human-Animal Intimacy*, ed. John Kohnt (Oxford: Berg, 2005), 119.
18. With this in mind, Stanley Brandes and Thor Anderson propose that *Ratatouille* holds much anthropological value, specifically in its questioning of what humanity and being human mean. Stanley Brandes and Thor Anderson, "*Ratatouille*: An Animated Account of Cooking, Taste, and Human Evolution," *Ethnos* 76, no. 3 (2011): 277–99.

19. For more on how guests interact with Disney Parks and, ultimately, become performers themselves, see Jennifer A. Kokai and Tom Robson, eds., *Performance and the Disney Theme Park Experience: The Tourist as Actor* (London: Palgrave Macmillan, 2019).
20. Quoted in Alyssa Bereznak, "Anyone Can Cook: The Oral History of *Ratatouille: The Musical*," *Ringer*, December 31, 2020, https://www.theringer.com/movies/2020/12/31/22206943/.
21. Quoted in Diep Tran, "How 'Ratatouille' the TikTok Musical Became 'Ratatouille' the Broadway Musical," *Backstage*, December 30, 2020, https://www.backstage.com/magazine/article/ratatouille-tiktok-musical-broadway-the-actors-fund-72365/.
22. Quoted in Tran.
23. Brittany Broski (@brittany_broski) went viral in August 2019. She posted a TikTok of herself drinking kombucha and reacting to the taste. In the short video, dated August 6, 2019, she flip-flops between disgust and pleasure. The video quickly became an internet meme that circulated across nearly every social media platform, made Broski TikTok famous, and eventually led to her being fired from work, which prompted her to move to Los Angeles to become a comedian.
24. Quoted in Bereznak, "Anyone Can Cook."
25. One popular comment on Mertzlufft's video, from @leah_camden, even noted the classic Disney sound: "why does this sound like a melody from frozen." This comment was liked over 37,000 times by the time of the Actors Fund benefit concert.
26. To achieve this effect, Mertzlufft asked his friends to record themselves singing the arrangement. He then used each recording multiple times, layering them on top of one another to create a cohesive—and sonically impressively—forty-person choir.
27. Due to space constraints, this chapter primarily focuses on the score to *Ratatouille: The TikTok Musical*. This does not discredit the work of designers, dancers, artists, directors, producers, and other theatre-makers who contributed to the show's rataturgy.
28. Brabham, *Crowdsourcing*, 49.
29. Laura MacDonald, "Off Off Off Off Broadway: Musical Development Out of Town and Regionally," in *A Critical Companion to the American Stage Musical*, by Elizabeth L. Wollman (London: Methuen Drama, 2017), 215.
30. MacDonald, "Off Off Off Off Broadway," 216.
31. Quoted in Bereznak, "Anyone Can Cook."
32. Bereznak, "Anyone Can Cook."
33. Quoted in Bereznak, "Anyone Can Cook."
34. Quoted in Bereznak, "Anyone Can Cook."
35. Quoted in Tran, "How 'Ratatouille' the TikTok Musical."
36. Stacy Wolf, *Beyond Broadway: The Pleasure and Promise of Musical Theatre across America* (New York: Oxford University Press, 2019).
37. Patton Oswalt (@pattonoswalt), "My . . . God . . . [. . .]," Twitter, November 14, 2020, 8:38 p.m., https://twitter.com/pattonoswalt/status/1327803080302161920.
38. Pixar (@pixar), "The rat of all our dreams," Instagram, November 21, 2020, https://www.instagram.com/p/CH3Hn65nSsV.

39. Quoted in Bereznak, "Anyone Can Cook."
40. Amy S. Osatinski, *Disney Theatrical Productions: Producing Broadway Musicals the Disney Way* (London: Routledge, 2019), 4.
41. Quoted in Greg Evans, "'Ratatouille: The TikTok Musical': How Broadway Cooked Up the Perfect Appetizer for a New Year That Can't Start Soon Enough," *Deadline*, January 1, 2021, https://deadline.com/2021/01/ratatouille-tiktok-musical-benefit-disney-seaview-emily-jacobsen-tituss-burgess-actors-fund-1234663746/.
42. Founded in 2012, Seaview is primarily a Broadway producing company, but it also has its hands in different mediums. One goal of the company is to disrupt and reshape how stories are told. Seaview takes a radical approach to producing, which made it a perfect fit for *Ratatouille: The TikTok Musical*.
43. Christina Morales, "TikTok 'Ratatouille' Musical to Be Presented as Benefit Performance," *New York Times*, December 9, 2020, https://www.nytimes.com/2020/12/09/theater/ratatouille-tiktok-musical.html.
44. Osatinski, *Disney Theatrical Productions*, 5.
45. Evans, "Ratatouille."
46. Rebecca Jennings, "This Week in TikTok: How a *Ratatouille* Joke Led to a Broadway Musical," *Vox*, January 5, 2021, https://www.vox.com/the-goods/2021/1/5/22213890/. For more on the issue of artistic credit and intellectual property on TikTok, see Boffone, *Renegades*, 51–69.
47. The production did not release any salaries. These numbers come from interviews I conducted with members of the creative team, who wished to remain off the record regarding their salaries.
48. Lee Seymour, "What Broadway Can Learn from the Record-Breaking TikTok Musical 'Ratatouille,'" *Forbes*, January 21, 2021, https://www.forbes.com/sites/leeseymour/2021/01/21/what-broadway-can-learn-from-the-record-breaking-tiktok-musical-ratatouille/.
49. For more on *Circle Jerk*, see Trevor Boffone, "*Circle Jerk* by Michael Breslin and Patrick Foley," *Theatre Journal* 73, no. 1 (2021): 89–91; and Helen Shaw, "How *Ratatouille: The TikTok Musical* Came to Be (and Yes, Disney's Okay with It)," *Vulture*, December 31, 2020, https://www.vulture.com/2020/12/how-ratatouille-the-tiktok-musical-came-to-be.html.
50. For more on Breslin and Foley's journey with *Ratatouille: The TikTok Musical*, see Bereznak, "Anyone Can Cook."
51. Quoted in Bereznak, "Anyone Can Cook."
52. For an in-depth study of Disney's Broadway musicals, see Osatinski, *Disney Theatrical Productions*.
53. For an in-depth study of these TikTok dance moves, see Boffone, *Renegades*.
54. Notably, while 499 seats is the maximum number for an Off-Broadway house, few of them actually have such a high capacity (they can have as few as 99 seats), and, although eight shows per week is the norm on Broadway, it is not as common Off-Broadway. With this in mind, the number of weeks for an Off-Broadway run of *Ratatouille* to reach 350,000 audience members is likely much higher than calculated here.

55. While most of these streaming events experienced only momentary success, *Hamilton*'s debut on Disney+ was perhaps 2020's most successful digital theatre offering.
56. For more on *Show Boat*, see Todd Decker, *Show Boat: Performing Race in an American Musical* (New York: Oxford University Press, 2012). For more on *Hair*, see Elizabeth Wollman, *The Theater Will Rock: A History of the Rock Musical, from "Hair" to "Hedwig"* (Ann Arbor: University of Michigan Press, 2006); and Bryan M. Vandevender, "Splitting *HAIR*: Reviving the American Tribal Love-Rock Musical in the 1970s," *New England Theatre Journal* 29, no. 1 (2018): 31–53.
57. Herhuth, *Pixar and the Aesthetic Imagination*, 158.
58. Quoted in Tran, "How 'Ratatouille' the TikTok Musical."
59. Quoted in Tran, "How 'Ratatouille' the TikTok Musical."
60. Quoted in Bereznak, "Anyone Can Cook."
61. Jonathan Mandell, "Many Cooks for This Flavorful Broadway Broth," rev. of *Ratatouille: The TikTok Musical*, dir. Lucy Moss, *New York Theater*, January 2, 2021, https://newyorktheater.me/2021/01/02/review-ratatouille-the-tik-tok-musical-many-cooks-for-this-flavorful-broadway-broth/.
62. Green, "What's Small and Hairy with Big Dreams?"
63. Green, "What's Small and Hairy with Big Dreams?"
64. Quoted in Brent Lang, "Daniel J. Mertzlufft, TikTok Musical Star, Signs with CAA, Kraft-Engel Management," *Variety*, January 12, 2021, https://variety.com/2021/digital/news/daniel-j-mertzlufft-tiktok-caa-kraft-engel-management-1234883925/.
65. Subsequently, Mertzlufft was commissioned by TikTok to write *For You, Paige*, an original musical that streamed live on TikTok on April 14, 2022. Mertzlufft used TikTok Live sessions to document the creation of the musical from January 2022 until its debut. *For You, Paige* follows Landon, a teen music lover who collaborates with his bestie, Paige, to create a TikTok song inspired by one of her favorite books. Landon's video goes viral, engaging Paige and the TikTok community, who help him finish creating the musical (not unlike how *Ratatouille: The TikTok Musical* was created). The commissioning of *For You, Paige* demonstrates TikTok's recognition of the import of theatre on the platform.
66. Another deliciously ridiculous example of TikTok as a musical platform is *Mexican Pizza: The Musical*. This new musical, which was produced by Taco Bell and streamed on TikTok on May 26, 2022, celebrated the return of the beloved Mexican Pizza menu item. The musical was penned by Abigail Barlow and Emily Bear, and featured Dolly Parton and Doja Cat.
67. For more on *Bridgerton: The Musical*, see Felicia Fitzpatrick, "*Bridgerton* Is TikTok's Latest Musical—The Writers Share a Track and Discuss Future Plans," *Playbill*, January 22, 2021, https://playbill.com/article/exclusive-bridgerton-tiktok-musical-writers-share-track-and-discuss-future-plans.
68. At twenty-three and twenty years old, Barlow and Bear also made history as the youngest nominees in the musical theatre Grammy category.
69. Sarah Bay-Cheng, "'The Unofficial Bridgerton Musical' as TikTok Grammy-Winning Sensation: Is the Future of Musical Theatre Online?," *Conversation*, April 28, 2022,

https://theconversation.com/the-unofficial-bridgerton-musical-as-tiktok-grammy-winning-sensation-is-the-future-of-musical-theatre-online-181776.
70. Gene Maddaus, "Netflix Settles Copyright Lawsuit over 'Unofficial Bridgerton Musical,'" *Variety*, September 23, 2022, https://variety.com/2022/music/news/netflix-bridgerton-musical-lawsuit-dropped-barlow-bear-1235382454/.
71. Quoted in Maddaus, "Netflix Settles Copyright Lawsuit."

Interlude

1. Don't worry, dear reader. I soon fixed this by hosting a film screening of *In the Heights* in the school auditorium, so that all of my students were able to watch the film on the big screen. During the film screening, students sang along to the TikTok section of "Fireworks."
2. Trevor Boffone, "The Rise of TikTok in US Culture," in *TikTok Cultures in the United States*, ed. Trevor Boffone (London: Routledge, 2022), 1–12; Cienna Davis, "Digital Blackface and the Troubling Intimacies of TikTok Dance Challenges," in Boffone, *TikTok Cultures in the United States*, 28–38.
3. Despite being an exposition-heavy Disney song, "We Don't Talk about Bruno" did become a club staple in early 2022. As the song gained popularity, videos surfaced of the song being played in clubs while throngs of tipsy night owls danced and sang their hearts out.
4. As Mirabel learns in *Encanto*, Bruno goes into hiding to protect her. After seeing a prophecy of Mirabel in front of a broken Casa Madrigal, Bruno believes that the prophecy indicates she will be the fall of the family's encanto. Later, Bruno and Mirabel learn that this couldn't have been further from the truth. As the family's encanto begins to die out, it is Mirabel who repairs the family's resilient bonds, thus extending their encanto into the future. Bruno then returns home to live with the family he has so dearly missed.
5. As has become customary with Lin-Manuel Miranda, the composer found inspiration from the musical theatre canon. In the case of "We Don't Talk about Bruno," Miranda was inspired by "A Weekend in the Country" from *A Little Night Music* and "Christmas Bells" from *Rent*.
6. Esperon's TikTok account (@besperon) had 3.2 million followers as of March 2024.

Conclusion

1. A collaboration among Jason Kim, Helen Park, and Max Vernon, *KPOP* brought the exciting world of K-pop—and Korean culture to boot—to Broadway. The musical chronicles a group of fictional K-pop stars who are preparing for a one-night-only concert debut in the United States. Throughout the two-act musical, audiences learn about the personal struggles of solo artist MwE, boy band F8, and girl group RTMS.

The musical was notable for being the first Broadway musical to feature Korean stories written by Korean American theatre-makers. *KPOP* featured eighteen Broadway debuts, all of whom were Asian American.
2. Jordan E. Cooper's play *Ain't No Mo'* faced similar financial struggles as *KPOP*. After playing to low capacity and anemic weekly grosses, *Ain't No Mo'* closed, having only played twenty-eight performances despite being one of the most critically acclaimed new plays of the 2022–23 season. *Ain't No Mo'* is a series of comedy sketches in an alternate reality in which the US government buys every Black person a one-way ticket to Africa should they accept the program's offer.
3. Monica Chin, "Broadway's K-Pop Musical Showed How Hard It Is to Create Internet Fame," *Verge*, December 8, 2022, https://www.theverge.com/23498194/kpop-broadway-musical-instagram-tiktok.
4. The fifteen-minute mark falls within what is allowed for marketing purposes.
5. Brandon Powers (@bpowtweets), "SO glad we got to make this happen [. . .]," Twitter, December 11, 2022, 6:38 p.m., https://twitter.com/bpowtweets/status/1602100660438269952.
6. Jared Mezzocchi (@JaredMezzocchi), "Two phones from different angles [. . .]," Twitter, December 11, 2022, 4:37 p.m., https://twitter.com/JaredMezzocchi/status/1602070190115749888.
7. Jared Mezzocchi (@jaredmezzocchi), "The act of just DOING THIS [. . .]," Twitter, December 11, 2022, 4:39 p.m., https://twitter.com/JaredMezzocchi/status/1602070537408512000.
8. For more on digital theatre during the pandemic, see Jared Mezzocchi, "The Technological Theatre Experimenters," *HowlRound*, February 18, 2021, https://howlround.com/technological-theatre-experimenters; Gemma Kate Allred, Benjamin Broadribb, and Erin Sullivan, eds., *Lockdown Shakespeare: New Evolutions in Performance and Adaptation* (New York: Bloomsbury, 2022); Dani Snyder-Young, "We're All in This Together: Digital Performances and Socially Distanced Spectatorship," *Theatre Journal* 74, no. 1 (2022): 1–15; Isaiah Matthew Wooden, "Effective Dreaming in the Time of Zoom Theatre: Reflections on Directing *The Lathe of Heaven*," *Theatre Topics* 32, no. 3 (2022), 127–37.
9. It is worth noting that *KPOP* was not the first musical to live-stream on TikTok. On September 14, 2021, *The Lion King* partnered with TikTok to live stream the opening number, "The Circle of Life," to celebrate the musical's return to Broadway following the COVID-19 shutdown. And, of course, there is the adjacent question of pro-shots of Broadway musicals (such as *Hamilton* on Disney+, *Come from Away* on Apple TV, and *Diana* on Netflix), which can run concurrent to their Broadway runs. Notably, the Lynn Nottage play *Clyde's* did sell a limited number of tickets to special live-streamed performances in 2021. Although the *Clyde's* live stream was a landmark moment for Broadway theatre, there was still criticism at the cost of tickets, which were considerably higher than nearly every other competitive example of live-streamed theatre in 2021.
10. Gemma Kate Allred, "Notions of Liveness in Lockdown Performance," in Allred, Broadribb, and Sullivan, *Lockdown Shakespeare*, 65–86.
11. Broadway League, "Broadway Grosses Week Ending December 11, 2022," *Playbill*, December 12, 2022, https://www.playbill.com/grosses.

Bibliography

Abidin, Crystal. "Mapping Internet Celebrity on TikTok: Exploring Attention Economies and Visibility Labours." *Cultural Science* 12, no. 1 (2021): 77–103.
Abidin, Crystal. *TikTok and Youth Cultures*. Bingley, UK: Emerald, 2024.
Allred, Gemma Kate. "Notions of Liveness in Lockdown Performance." In *Lockdown Shakespeare: New Evolutions in Performance and Adaptation*, edited by Gemma Kate Allred, Benjamin Broadribb, and Erin Sullivan, 65–86. New York: Bloomsbury, 2022.
Allred, Gemma Kate, Benjamin Broadribb, and Erin Sullivan, eds. *Lockdown Shakespeare: New Evolutions in Performance and Adaptation*. New York: Bloomsbury, 2022.
Barnes, Grace. "'My Sleeves May Be Green but My Lipstick's Red': Deconstructing the 'Feminism' in *Six*." *Studies in Musical Theatre* 14, no. 2 (2020): 137–48.
Barnette, Jane. "Hocus-Pocus: WitchTok Education for Baby Witches." In *TikTok Cultures in the United States*, edited by Trevor Boffone, 97–107. London: Routledge, 2022.
Barnette, Jane. "What Is Wanda but Witches Persevering? Palimpsests of American Witches in *WandaVision*." *Theatre Journal* 74, no. 1 (2022): 41–57.
Barnette, Jane. *Witch Fulfillment*. London: Routledge, 2023.
Barnette, Jane. "Witch Fulfillment: Casting & Designing the Witch for Stage & Screen." Public talk, University of Kansas, November 8, 2021.
Barr, Lindsey. "Theorizing a Narrative Patriarchal (re/dis)Placement in Contemporary Musical Theatre." *Telephone Hour: A Quarantine Colloquium*, Musical Theatre/Dance Focus Group, Association for Theatre in Higher Education, April 13, 2020.
Bay-Cheng, Sarah. "'The Unofficial Bridgerton Musical' as TikTok Grammy-Winning Sensation: Is the Future of Musical Theatre Online?" *Conversation*, April 28, 2022. https://theconversation.com/the-unofficial-bridgerton-musical-as-tiktok-grammy-winning-sensation-is-the-future-of-musical-theatre-online-181776.
Benjamin, Ruha. *Race after Technology: Abolitionist Tools for the New Jim Code*. Boston: Polity Press, 2019.
Bennett, Lucy. "Surveying Fandom: The Ethics, Design, and Use of Surveys in Fan Studies." In *The Routledge Companion to Media Fandom*, edited by Melissa A. Click and Suzanne Scott, 36–44. London: Routledge, 2018.
Bereznak, Alyssa. "Anyone Can Cook: The Oral History of *Ratatouille: The Musical*." *Ringer*, December 31, 2020. https://www.theringer.com/movies/2020/12/31/22206943/.
Bial, Henry. *Acting Jewish: Negotiating Ethnicity on the American Stage and Screen*. Ann Arbor: University of Michigan Press, 2005.
Biddle, Sam, Paulo Victor Ribeiro, and Tatian Dias. "Invisible Censorship." *Intercept*, March 16, 2020. https://theintercept.com/2020/03/16/tiktok-app-moderators-users-discrimination/.
Blair, Kelsey. "Broomsticks and Barricades: Performance, Empowerment, and Feeling in *Wicked* and *Les Misérables*." *Studies in Musical Theatre* 10, no. 1 (2016): 55–67.

Blake, Bill. *Theatre and the Digital*. London: Red Globe Press, 2014.
Boffone, Trevor. "Charli, Charlie, and I: An Autoethnographic Study of TikTok Dance and Child/Adult Collaborations." In *Creative Children and Children's Culture*, edited by Victoria Ford Smith and Peter C. Kunze. Forthcoming.
Boffone, Trevor. "*Circle Jerk* by Michael Breslin and Patrick Foley." *Theatre Journal* 73, no. 1 (2021): 89–91.
Boffone, Trevor. "The D'Amelio Effect: TikTok, Charli D'Amelio, and the Construction of Whiteness." In *TikTok Cultures in the United States*, edited by Trevor Boffone, 17–27. London: Routledge, 2022.
Boffone, Trevor. "Do You Want to Make a TikTok? Is It Time to BeReal? Gen Z, Social Media, and Digital Literacies." *Journal of Language and Literacy Education* 18, no. 2 (2022). http://jolle.coe.uga.edu/volume-18-2/.
Boffone, Trevor. *Renegades: Digital Dance Cultures from Dubsmash to TikTok*. New York: Oxford University Press, 2021.
Boffone, Trevor. Review of *Ratatouille: The TikTok Musical*, directed by Lucy Moss. *Studies in Musical Theatre* 15, no. 2 (2021): 153–55.
Boffone, Trevor. "The Rise of TikTok in US Culture." In *TikTok Cultures in the United States*, edited by Trevor Boffone, 1–12. London: Routledge, 2022.
Boffone, Trevor. "Taking *Hamilton* to the Streets: Lin-Manuel Miranda, Latinidad, and the Aesthetics of Accessibility." In *Dueling Grounds: Revolution and Revelation in the Musical "Hamilton*,*"* edited by Paul Laird and Mary Jo Lodge, 88–102. New York: Oxford University Press, 2021.
Boffone, Trevor, ed. *TikTok Cultures in the United States*. London: Routledge, 2022.
Boffone, Trevor. "TikTok Is Theatre, Theatre Is TikTok." *Theatre History Studies* 41 (2022): 41–48.
Boffone, Trevor. "Whitewashed Usnavi: Race, Power and Representation in *In the Heights*." *Studies in Musical Theatre* 13, no. 3 (2019): 235–50.
Boffone, Trevor. "'World'-Traveling, Diversity, Inclusion, and the Making of Musicals in the Twenty-First Century." In *The Routledge Companion to Musical Theatre*, edited by Laura MacDonald and Ryan Donovan, 567–81. London: Routledge, 2022.
Boffone, Trevor, and Sarah Jerasa. "Toward a (Queer) Reading Community: BookTok, Teen Readers, and the Rise of TikTok Literacies." *Talking Points* 33, no. 1 (2021): 10–16.
Booth, Paul. *Digital Fandom: New Media Studies*. London: Peter Lang, 2010.
Boy, Michelle. "Alto on a Broomstick: Voicing the Witch in the Musical *Wicked*." *American Music* 28, no. 1 (2010): 97–118.
boyd, danah. "Why Youth (Heart) Social Media Network Sites: The Rise of Networked Publics in Teenage Life." In *Youth, Identity, and Digital Media*, edited by David Buckingham, 119–42. Cambridge: MIT Press, 2007.
Brabham, Daren C. *Crowdsourcing*. Cambridge: MIT Press, 2013.
Brandes, Stanley, and Thor Anderson. "*Ratatouille*: An Animated Account of Cooking, Taste, and Human Evolution." *Ethnos* 76, no. 3 (2011): 277–99.
Brantley, Ben. "In 'Beetlejuice,' the Afterlife Is Exhausting." Review of *Beetlejuice*, directed by Alex Timbers. *New York Times*, April 25, 2019. https://www.nytimes.com/2019/04/25/theater/beetlejuice-review-broadway.html.
Broadway League. "Broadway Grosses Week Ending December 11, 2022." *Playbill*, December 12, 2022. https://www.playbill.com/grosses.

Brooker, Will, Mark Duffett, and Karen Hellekson. "Fannish Identities and Scholarly Responsibilities: A Conversation." In *The Routledge Companion to Media Fandom*, edited by Melissa A. Click and Suzanne Scott, 63–74. London: Routledge, 2018.

Bunch, Ryan. *Oz and the Musical: Performing the American Fairy Tale*. New York: Oxford University Press, 2022.

Bunch, Ryan. "'You Can't Stop the Tweet': Social Media and Networks of Participation in the Live Television Musical." In *iBroadway: Musical Theatre in the Digital Age*, edited by Jessica Hillman-McCord, 173–205. London: Palgrave Macmillan, 2017.

Busse, Kristina. "The Ethics of Studying Online Fandom." In *The Routledge Companion to Media Fandom*, edited by Melissa A. Click and Suzanne Scott, 9–17. London: Routledge, 2018.

Carlson, Marvin. *The Haunted Stage: The Theatre as Memory Machine*. Ann Arbor: University of Michigan Press, 2001.

Causey, Matthew. *Theatre and Performance in Digital Culture*. London: Routledge, 2006.

Chin, Monica. "Broadway's K-Pop Musical Showed How Hard It Is to Create Internet Fame." *Verge*, December 8, 2022. https://www.theverge.com/23498194/kpop-broadway-musical-instagram-tiktok.

Click, Melissa A., and Suzanne Scott, eds. *The Routledge Companion to Media Fandom*. London: Routledge, 2020.

Cortés, Michelle Santiago. "Charli D'Amelio Now Has More Followers Than Anyone on TikTok." *Refinery29*, March 27, 2020. https://www.refinery29.com/en-us/2020/03/9612154/charli-damelio-most-followers-on-tiktok.

Corts, Alicia. "(Un)limited: Virtual Performance Spaces and Digital Identity." *Theatre Symposium* 24 (2016): 113–28.

Coulter, Natalie. "'Frappés, Friends, and Fun': Affective Labor and the Cultural Identity of Girlhood." *Journal of Consumer Culture* 21, no. 3 (2018): 487–500.

Craft, Elizabeth Titrington. "'Is This What It Takes Just to Make It to Broadway?!': Marketing *In the Heights* in the Twenty-First Century." *Studies in Musical Theatre* 5, no. 1 (2011): 49–69.

CubbyBernstein, "Cubby Bernstein—Xanadu—Episode One," YouTube video, uploaded May 12, 2008, 3:34, https://www.youtube.com/watch?v=qa8sPwfdn9g.

Cuskey, Lusie. "Not Writing New Rules, Merely Rat-ifying: Musical Theatre Goes Digital in *Ratatouille*." Review of *Ratatouille: The TikTok Musical*, directed by Lucy Moss, *PARtake: The Journal of Performance as Research* 4, no. 1 (2021): 1–9.

Davis, Cienna. "Digital Blackface and the Troubling Intimacies of TikTok Dance Challenges." In *TikTok Cultures in the United States*, edited by Trevor Boffone, 28–38. London: Routledge, 2022.

Davis, Fred. *Fashion, Culture, and Identity*. Chicago: University of Chicago Press, 1992.

Deaville, James. "Play It Again (and Again, and Again): The Superfan and Musical Theater." In *The Routledge Companion to the Contemporary Musical*, edited by Jessica Sternfeld and Elizabeth L. Wollman, 355–63. London: Routledge, 2020.

Decker, Todd. *Show Boat: Performing Race in an American Musical*. New York: Oxford University Press, 2012.

De Giere, Carol. *Defying Gravity: The Creative Career of Stephen Schwartz, from "Godspell" to "Wicked."* New York: Applause Theater and Cinema, 2008.

Dickson, EJ. "Can TikTok Save 'Beetlejuice,' the Broadway Musical?" *Rolling Stone*, December 16, 2019. https://www.rollingstone.com/culture/culture-features/beetlejuice-broadway-musical-tiktok-trend-920184/.

Divon, Tom, and Tobias Ebbrecht-Hartmann. "#JewishTikTok: The JewToks' Fight against Antisemitism." In *TikTok Cultures in the United States*, edited by Trevor Boffone, 47–58. London: Routledge, 2022.

Donovan, Ryan. *Broadway Bodies: A Critical History of Conformity*. New York: Oxford University Press, 2023.

Drotner, Kirsten. "Leisure Is Hard Work: Digital Practices and Future Competences." In *Youth, Identity, and Digital Media*, edited by David Buckingham, 167–84. Cambridge: MIT Press, 2008.

Dvoskin, Michelle. "Embracing Excess: The Queer Feminist Power of Musical Theatre Diva Roles." *Studies in Musical Theatre* 10, no. 1 (2016): 93–103.

Edelman, Birgitta. "From Trap to Lap: The Changing Sociogenic Identity of the Rat." In *Animals in Person: Cultural Perspectives on Human-Animal Intimacy*, edited by John Kohnt, 119–40. Oxford: Berg, 2005.

Edelstein, David. "'Beetlejuice': Tim Burton, Michael Keaton on the Ghoulish Masterpiece." *Rolling Stone*, June 2, 1988. https://www.rollingstone.com/movies/movie-features/mixing-beetlejuice-78733/.

Edney, Kathryn. "Let's Misbehave: Cell Phone Technology and Audience Behaviors." In *iBroadway: Musical Theatre in the Digital Age*, edited by Jessica Hillman-McCord, 95–117. London: Palgrave Macmillan, 2017.

Ellcessor, Elizabeth. "Accessing Fan Culture: Disability, Digital Media, and Dreamwidth." In *The Routledge Companion to Media Fandom*, edited by Melissa A. Click and Suzanne Scott, 202–11. London: Routledge, 2018.

Evans, Greg. "'Ratatouille: The TikTok Musical': How Broadway Cooked Up the Perfect Appetizer for a New Year That Can't Start Soon Enough." *Deadline*, January 1, 2021. https://deadline.com/2021/01/ratatouille-tiktok-musical-benefit-disney-seaview-emily-jacobsen-tituss-burgess-actors-fund-1234663746/.

Farley, Shannon K. "Translation, Interpretations, Fan Fiction: A Continuum of Meaning Production." *Transformative Works and Cultures* 14 (2013). https://doi.org/10.3983/twc.2013.0517.

Fazel, Valerie M., and Louise Geddes, eds., *The Shakespeare Multiverse Fandom as Literary Praxis*. London: Routledge, 2021.

Fitzpatrick, Felicia. "*Bridgerton* Is TikTok's Latest Musical—The Writers Share a Track and Discuss Future Plans." *Playbill*, January 22, 2021. https://playbill.com/article/exclusive-bridgerton-is-tiktoks-latest-musical-the-writers-share-a-track-and-disc uss-future-plans.

Gardner, Howard, and Katie Davis. *The App Generation: How Today's Youth Navigate Identity, Intimacy, and Imagination in a Digital World*. New Haven, CT: Yale University Press, 2013.

Gaunt, Kyra D. "YouTube, Twerking & You: Context Collapse and the Handheld Co-Presence of Black Girls and Miley Cyrus." *Journal of Popular Music Studies* 27, no. 3 (2015): 244–73.

Gelles, Barrie. "*Glee* and the 'Ghosting' of the Musical Theatre Canon." *Popular Entertainment Studies* 2, no. 2 (2011): 89–111.

Giannachi, Gabriella. *Virtual Theatre: An Introduction*. London: Routledge, 2004.

Green, Jesse. "What's Small and Hairy with Big Dreams?" Review of *Ratatouille: The TikTok Musical*, directed by Lucy Moss. *New York Times*, January 3, 2021. https://www.nytimes.com/2021/01/03/theater/ratatouille-tiktok-musical-review.html.

Greenwood, Steven. "Say There's No Future: The Queer Potential of *Wicked*'s Fiyero." *Studies in Musical Theatre* 12, no. 3 (2018): 305–317.

Gunnels, Jen. "'A Jedi like My Father before Me': Social Identity and the New York Comic Con." *Transformative Works and Cultures* 3 (2009). https://doi.org/10.3983/twc.2009.0161.

Halliday, Aria S. *Buy Black: How Black Women Transformed US Pop Culture*. Urbana: University of Illinois Press, 2022.

Halliday, Aria S. "Twerk Sumn! Theorizing Black Girl Epistemology in the Body." *Cultural Studies* 34, no. 6 (2020): 874–91.

Harlig, Alexandra, Crystal Abidin, Trevor Boffone, Kelly Bowker, Colette Eloi, Pamela Krayenbuhl, and Chuyun Oh. "TikTok and Short-Form Screendance before and after Covid." *International Journal of Screendance* 12 (2021). https://screendancejournal.org/index.php/screendance/issue/view/279.

Hayashi, Aya Esther. "'YouTube! Musicals! YouTubesicals!': Cultivating Theater Fandom through New Media." In *The Routledge Companion to the Contemporary Musical*, edited by Jessica Sternfeld and Elizabeth L. Wollman, 374–83. London: Routledge, 2020.

Herhuth, Eric. *Pixar and the Aesthetic Imagination: Animation, Storytelling, and Digital Culture*. Berkeley: University of California Press, 2017.

Herrera, Brian Eugenio. *Latin Numbers: Playing Latino in Twentieth-Century U.S. Popular Performance*. Ann Arbor: University of Michigan Press, 2015.

Herrera, Brian Eugenio. "Little Steps: The Absurdity of *A Chorus Line*." *Studies in Musical Theatre* 10, no. 1 (2016): 105–15.

Hershberg, Marc. "Broadway Marketers Fear TikTok Ban." *Forbes*, July 19, 2020. https://www.forbes.com/sites/marchershberg/2020/07/19/broadway-marketers-fear-tiktok-ban/.

Hillman-McCord, Jessica. "Digital Fandom: *Hamilton* and the Participatory Spectator." In *iBroadway: Musical Theatre in the Digital Age*, edited by Jessica Hillman-McCord, 119–44. London: Palgrave Macmillan, 2017.

Hillman-McCord, Jessica. "Lin-Manuel Miranda: Digital Diva." *Studies in Musical Theatre* 12, no. 1 (2018): 109–22.

Hillman-McCord, Jessica. "Musical Theatre in the Digital Age." In *iBroadway: Musical Theatre in the Digital Age*, edited by Jessica Hillman-McCord, 1–13. London: Palgrave Macmillan, 2017.

Hills, Matt. *Fan Cultures*. London: Routledge, 2002.

Hodges Persley, Nicole. *Sampling and Remixing Blackness in Hip-Hop Theater and Performance*. Ann Arbor: University of Michigan Press, 2021.

Hoffman, Warren. *The Great White Way: Race and the Broadway Musical*. New Brunswick, NJ: Rutgers University Press, 2014.

Holdren, Sara. "Beetlejuice Is Best When It's at Its Most Antic." Review of *Beetlejuice*, directed by Alex Timbers. *Vulture*, April 25, 2019. https://www.vulture.com/2019/04/review-beetlejuice-is-best-when-its-at-its-most-antic.html.

Jenkins, Henry. *Convergence Culture: Where Old and New Media Collide*. New York: New York University Press, 2006.

Jenkins, Henry. *Textual Poachers: Television Fans and Participatory Culture*. London: Routledge, 1992.

Jennings, Kyesha. "City Girls, Hot Girls and the Re-Imagining of Black Women in Hip Hop and Digital Spaces." *Global Hip Hop Studies* 1, no. 1 (2020): 47–70.

Jennings, Rebecca. "This Week in TikTok: How a *Ratatouille* Joke led to a Broadway Musical." *Vox*, January 5, 2021. https://www.vox.com/the-goods/2021/1/5/22213890/.

Jensen, Amy Petersen. *Theatre in a Media Culture: Production, Performance and Perception since 1970*. Jefferson, NC: McFarland, 2007.

Jensen, Joli. "Fandom as Pathology: The Consequences of Characterization." In *The Adoring Audience: Fan Culture and Popular Media*, edited by Lisa A. Lewis, 9–26. London: Routledge, 1992.

Jerasa, Sarah, and Trevor Boffone. "BookTok 101: TikTok, Digital Literacies, and Out-of-School Reading Practices." *Journal of Adolescent & Adult Literacy* 65, no. 3 (2021): 219–26.

Kant, Tanya. *Making It Personal: Algorithmic Personalization, Identity, and Everyday Life*. Oxford: Oxford University Press, 2020.

Kaye, D. Bondy Valdovinos. "Make This Go Viral: Building Musical Careers through Accidental Virality on TikTok." *Flow Journal* 27, no. 1 (2020). https://www.flowjournal.org/2020/09/make-this-go-viral/.

Kaye, D. Bondy Valdovinos, Jing Zeng, and Patrik Wikstrom. *TikTok: Creativity and Culture in Short Video*. Cambridge: Polity Press, 2022.

Kennedy, Melanie. "'If the Rise of the TikTok Dance and E-Girl Aesthetic Has Taught Us Anything, It's That Teenage Girls Rule the Internet Right Now': TikTok Celebrity, Girls and the Coronavirus Crisis." *European Journal of Cultural Studies* 23, no. 6 (2020): 1069–76.

Kessler, Kelly. "'Rash Talk and Virtual Protests': The Musical Genre's Personal and Political Interactivity in the Age of Social Media." In *The Routledge Companion to the Contemporary Musical*, edited by Jessica Sternfeld and Elizabeth L. Wollman, 335–44. London: Routledge, 2020.

Klich, Rosemary, and Edward Scheer. *Multimedia Performance*. London: Red Globe Press, 2011.

Knapp, Raymond. *The American Musical and the Performance of Personal Identity*. Princeton, NJ: Princeton University Press, 2009.

Kokai, Jennifer A., and Tom Robson, eds. *Performance and the Disney Theme Park Experience: The Tourist as Actor*. London: Palgrave Macmillan, 2019.

Kunze, Peter C. "Bootlegs over Broadway: Musical Theatre (Re)Productions, Digital Circulation, and the Informal Media Economy." *Creative Industries Journal* 16, no. 2, 2021. https://doi.org/10.1080/17510694.2021.1996984.

Kustow, Michael. *Theatre@Risk*. London: Methuen Drama, 2007.

Laird, Paul. *Wicked: A Musical Biography*. Lanham, MD: Scarecrow Press, 2011.

Lamerichs, Nicolle. "Stranger Than Fiction: Fan Identity in Cosplay." *Transformative Works and Cultures* 7 (2011). https://doi.org/10.3983/twc.2011.0246.

Lamont, Tom. "'It's Hard to Put the Brakes on It. We Doubled Down': Charli D'Amelio and the First Family of TikTok." *Guardian*, June 6, 2020. https://www.theguardian.com/lifeandstyle/2020/jun/06/its-hard-to-put-the-brakes-on-it-we-doubled-down-charli-damelio-and-the-first-family-of-tiktok.

Lang, Brent. "Daniel J. Mertzlufft, TikTok Musical Star, Signs with CAA, Kraft-Engel Management." *Variety*, January 12, 2021. https://variety.com/2021/digital/news/daniel-j-mertzlufft-tiktok-caa-kraft-engel-management-1234883925/.

Lang, Brent. "How 'Beetlejuice: The Musical' Became a Broadway Turnaround Story." *Variety*, November 18, 2019. https://variety.com/2019/legit/news/beetlejuice-the-musical-broadway-1203407953/.

Leskin, Paige. "The Ultimate Guide to TikTok, the Hot App Gen Z Is Obsessed with and Facebook Is Terrified Of." *Business Insider*, October 24, 2019. https://markets.business insider.com/news/stocks/tiktok-how-to-use-short-form-video-app-gen-z-2019-6-1028319047.

Lewis, Christian. Review of *Ratatouille: The Tiktok Musical*, directed by Lucy Moss. *Theatre Journal* 73, no. 3 (2021): 432–33.

Lonergan, Patrick. *Theatre and Social Media*. London: Red Globe Press, 2016.

Loya, Luis, and Elaine Almeida. "Things That Shouldn't Have Gay Energy but Do Anyways: CTI, Remixes and TikTok Duets." *Flow Journal* 27, no. 1 (2020). https://www.flowjournal.org/2020/09/cti-remixes-tiktok-duets/.

MacDonald, Laura. "The Border and Boundary Crossings of Musical Theatre Fans in Europe and East Asia." In *Theatre Fandom*, edited by Kirsty Sedgman. Forthcoming.

MacDonald, Laura. "Connection in an Isolating Age: Looking Back on Twenty Years of Engaging Audiences and Marketing Musical Theatre Online." In *iBroadway: Musical Theatre in the Digital Age*, edited by Jessica Hillman-McCord, 17–42. London: Palgrave Macmillan, 2017.

MacDonald, Laura. "Have I Done Enough? Lin-Manuel Miranda and *Hamilton*'s Culture of Generosity." *Performance Research* 23, no. 6 (2018): 40–49.

MacDonald, Laura. "Off Off Off Off Broadway: Musical Development Out of Town and Regionally." In *A Critical Companion to the American Stage Musical*, by Elizabeth L. Wollman, 214–25. London: Methuen Drama, 2017.

MacDonald, Laura. "Rising in the East: Disney Rehearses Chinese Consumers at a Glocalised Shanghai Disneyland." In *Performance and the Disney Theme Park Experience: The Tourist as Actor*, edited by Jenny Kokai and Tom Robson, 127–48. London: Palgrave Macmillan, 2019.

MacDonald, Laura. "Seasons of Love: Chinese Millennials' Affective Amateur Musical Theatre Performance." *Performance Research* 25, no. 1 (2020): 112–20.

MacDonald, Laura, and Myrtle Halman. "*Geen Grenzen Meer*: An American Musical's Unlimited Border Crossing." *Theatre Research International* 39, no. 3 (2014): 198–216.

Machado Sáez, Elena. "Blackout on Broadway: Affiliation and Audience in *In the Heights* and *Hamilton*." *Studies in Musical Theatre* 12, no. 2 (2018): 181–97.

Machado Sáez, Elena. "Debt of Gratitude: Lin-Manuel Miranda and the Politics of US Latinx Twitter." *archipelagos: a journal of Caribbean digital praxis* 4 (2020). https://archipelagosjournal.org/issue04/machado-gratitude.html.

Machado Sáez, Elena. "Hype It Up: US Latinx Theater on TikTok." In *TikTok Cultures in the United States*, edited by Trevor Boffone, 117–25. London: Routledge, 2022.

Maddaus, Gene. "Netflix Settles Copyright Lawsuit over 'Unofficial Bridgerton Musical.'" *Variety*, September 23, 2022. https://variety.com/2022/music/news/netflix-bridgerton-musical-lawsuit-dropped-barlow-bear-1235382454/.

Mandell, Jonathan. "Many Cooks for This Flavorful Broadway Broth." Review of *Ratatouille: The TikTok Musical*, directed by Lucy Moss. *New York Theater*, January 2, 2021. https://newyorktheater.me/2021/01/02/review-ratatouille-the-tik-tok-musical-many-cooks-for-this-flavorful-broadway-broth/.

Marchiony, Samantha Eve. "Our Crowning Glory: *SIX* and the Path of the Modern Progressive Musical." MA thesis, University of Houston, 2020.

Marks, Peter. "'Beetlejuice' Cleans Up Its Act for Broadway. It's Not a Raging Success, but It'll Do." Review of *Beetlejuice*, directed by Alex Timbers. *Washington Post*, April 25, 2019.

Marlow, Toby, and Lucy Moss. "All You Wanna Do" from *Six: The Musical*. Genius, accessed February 22, 2023. https://genius.com/Six-cast-all-you-wanna-do-lyrics.

Martinez, Wendyliz. "TikTok for Us by Us: Black Girlhood, Joy, and Self-Care." In *TikTok Cultures in the United States*, edited by Trevor Boffone, 39–46. London: Routledge, 2022.

Mezzocchi, Jared. "The Technological Theatre Experimenters." *HowlRound*, February 18, 2021. https://howlround.com/technological-theatre-experimenters.

Miller, Chris. "How Modern Witches Enchant TikTok: Intersections of Digital, Consumer, and Material Culture(s) on #WitchTok." *Religions* 13, no. 2 (2022): article 118. https://doi.org/10.3390/rel13020118.

Miller, D. A. *Place for Us: Essay on the Broadway Musical*. Cambridge, MA: Harvard University Press, 1998.

Miller, Jonathan. *Subsequent Productions*. New York: Viking Adult, 1986.

Miranda, Lin-Manuel, and Jeremy McCarter. *Hamilton: The Revolution*. Hachette UK, 2016.

Morales, Christina. "TikTok 'Ratatouille' Musical to Be Presented as Benefit Performance." *New York Times*, December 9, 2020. https://www.nytimes.com/2020/12/09/theater/ratatouille-tiktok-musical.html.

Mullen, Caitlin. "Brands Look to Employees to Engage Gen Z on TikTok." *Biz Women*, November 13, 2020. https://www.bizjournals.com/bizwomen/news/latest-news/2020/11/brands-look-to-employees-to-engage-gen-z-on-tiktok.html.

Murat, Laure. "What's Queer about Remy, *Ratatouille*, and French Cuisine?" In *What's Queer about Europe? Productive Encounters and Re-Enchanting Paradigms*, edited by Mireille Rosello and Sudeep Dasgupta, 136–47. New York: Fordham University Press, 2014.

Noble, Safiya Umoja. *Algorithms of Oppression: How Search Engines Reinforce Racism*. New York: New York University Press, 2018.

O'Connell, Sam. "Mediated Musical Theatre." In *The Routledge Companion to Musical Theatre*, edited by Laura MacDonald and Ryan Donovan, 464–77. London: Routledge, 2022.

O'Keefe, Laurence, and Kevin Murphy. "Big Fun" from *Heathers: The Musical*. Genius, accessed February 22, 2023. https://genius.com/Heathers-the-musical-ensemble-big-fun-lyrics.

Onion. "TikTok Apologizes after Inadvertently Giving Platform to Thousands of Theater Kids." June 8, 2020. https://www.theonion.com/tiktok-apologizes-after-inadvertently-giving-platform-t-1843955237.

Osatinski, Amy S. *Disney Theatrical Productions: Producing Broadway Musicals the Disney Way*. London: Routledge, 2019.

Paskett, Zoe. "From *Six* to *Heathers*, the Best Musical Theatre TikToks." *Evening Standard*, February 26, 2020. https://www.standard.co.uk/culture/theatre/best-musical-theatre-tiktoks-six-heathers-hamilton-a4372251.html.

Pincus-Roth. Zachary. "The Most Exciting Theater Now Is a Figment of Our Imagination." *Washington Post*, December 22, 2020. https://www.washingtonpost.com/arts-entertainment/2020/12/22/tiktok-broadway-musical-theater-ratatouille/.

Pomerantz, Shauna, and Miriam Field. "A TikTok Assemblage: Girlhood, Radical Media Engagement, and Parent-Child Generativity." In *Visual and Cultural Identity Constructs of Global Youth and Young Adults: Situated, Embodied and Performed Ways of Being, Engaging and Belonging*, edited by Fiona Blaikie, 139–57. New York: Routledge, 2021.

Pomerantz, Shauna, and Miriam Field. "Watching TikTok, Feeling Feminism: Intergenerational Flows of Feminist Knowledge." In *TikTok Cultures in the United States*, edited by Trevor Boffone, 61–71. London: Routledge, 2022.

Raab, Doris. "From Book to Broadway: Elphaba's Gender Ambiguity and Her Journey into Heteronormativity in *Wicked*." *Studies in Musical Theatre* 5, no. 3 (2011): 245–56.

Rauchberg, Jessica Sage. "#SHADOWBANNED: Queer, Trans, and Disabled Creator Responses to Algorithmic Oppression on TikTok." In *LGBTQ Digital Cultures: A Global Perspective*, edited by Paromita Pain, 196–209. London: Routledge, 2022.

Rauchberg, Jessica Sage. "TikTok's Digital Eugenics: Challenging Ableism and Algorithmic Erasure through Disability Activism." *Flow Journal* 27, no. 1 (2020). http://www.flowjournal.org/2020/09/tiktok-digital-eugenics/.

Replogle-Wong, Holley. "The Great Generational Divide: Stage-to-Screen Hollywood Musical Adaptations and the Enactment of Fandom." In *The Routledge Companion to the Contemporary Musical*, edited by Jessica Sternfeld and Elizabeth L. Wollman, 345–54. London: Routledge, 2020.

Rizvic, Sejla. "Everybody Hates Millennials: Gen Z and the TikTok Generation Wars." *Walrus*, February 9, 2021. https://thewalrus.ca/everybody-hates-millennials-gen-z-and-the-tiktok-generation-wars/.

Rizzo, Frank. Review of *Beetlejuice*, directed by Alex Timbers. *Variety*, April 26, 2019. https://variety.com/2019/legit/reviews/beetlejuice-review-broadway-musical-1203194763/.

Rochford, Elle, and Zachary D. Palmer. "Trans TikTok: Sharing Information and Forming Community." In *TikTok Cultures in the United States*, edited by Trevor Boffone, 84–94. London: Routledge, 2022.

Rodgers, Richard, and Oscar Hammerstein II. "In My Own Little Corner" from *Cinderella*. Genius, accessed February 20, 2023. https://genius.com/The-original-broadway-cast-of-cinderella-in-my-own-little-corner-lyrics.

Roman, David. *Performance in America: Contemporary US Culture and the Performing Arts*. Durham, NC: Duke University Press, 2005.

Ruehlicke, Andrea. "All the Content, Just for You: TikTok and Personalization." *Flow Journal* 27, no. 1 (2020). http://www.flowjournal.org/2020/10/content-just-for-you/.

Rush, Adam. "#YouWillBeFound: Participatory Fandom, Social Media Marketing and *Dear Evan Hansen*." *Studies in Musical Theatre* 15, no. 2 (2021): 119–32.

Rush, Adam, and Stephanie Lim. "From Stage Door to Cyber Space: The Digital Evolution of Musical Theatre Fandom." In *The Routledge Companion to Musical Theatre*, edited by Laura MacDonald and Ryan Donovan, 231–46. London: Routledge, 2022.

Salisbury, Mark, and Tim Burton. *Burton on Burton*. London: Faber and Faber, 2006.

Schellewald, Andreas. "Communicative Forms on TikTok: Perspectives from Digital Ethnography." *International Journal of Communication* 15 (2021): 1437–57.

Sedgman, Kirsty. "No-Object Fandom: *Smash*-ing Kickstarter and Bringing *Bombshell* to the Stage." In *iBroadway: Musical Theatre in the Digital Age*, edited by Jessica Hillman-McCord, 145–72. London: Palgrave Macmillan, 2017.

Seymour, Lee. "What Broadway Can Learn from the Record-Breaking TikTok Musical 'Ratatouille.'" *Forbes*, January 21, 2021. https://www.forbes.com/sites/leeseymour/2021/01/21/what-broadway-can-learn-from-the-record-breaking-tiktok-musical-ratatouille/.

Shaw, Helen. "How *Ratatouille: The TikTok Musical* Came to Be (and Yes, Disney's Okay with It)." *Vulture*, December 31, 2020. https://www.vulture.com/2020/12/how-ratatouille-the-tiktok-musical-came-to-be.html.

Shifman, Limor. "Memes in a Digital World: Reconciling with a Conceptual Troublemaker." *Journal of Computer-Mediated Communication* 18, no. 3 (2013): 362–77.

Sibirtseva, Maria. "Insightful Tips on TikTok Marketing to Reach Generation Z and Millennials." *Deposit Photos* (blog), August 4, 2020. https://blog.depositphotos.com/tips-on-tiktok-marketing.html.

Siegal, Alan. "How 'Beetlejuice' Was Born." *Ringer*, March 30, 2018. https://www.theringer.com/movies/2018/3/30/17178786/.

Snyder-Young, Dani. "We're All in This Together: Digital Performances and Socially Distanced Spectatorship." *Theatre Journal* 74, no. 1 (2022): 1–15.

Stein, Krysten. "YOU BETTER WORK! Drag Queen Storytelling and Performativity on TikTok." Conference presentation, *TikTok and Social Movements Symposium*, TikTok Cultures Research Network, September 20, 2021.

Stein, Louisa Ellen. *Millennial Fandom: Television Audiences in the Transmedia Age.* Des Moines: University of Iowa Press, 2015.

Stein, Louisa Ellen. "Tumblr Fan Aesthetics." In *The Routledge Companion to Media Fandom*, edited by Melissa A. Click and Suzanne Scott, 86–97. London: Routledge, 2018.

Sternfeld, Jessica, and Elizabeth L. Wollman. Introduction to *The Routledge Companion to the Contemporary Musical*, edited by Jessica Sternfeld and Elizabeth L. Wollman, 1–4. London: Routledge, 2020.

Sternfeld, Jessica, and Elizabeth L. Wollman, eds. *The Routledge Companion to the Contemporary Musical.* London: Routledge, 2020.

Stokel-Walker, Chris. "Presley Ryan's TikToks Have Made *Beetlejuice* Broadway's Hottest Ticket." *FFWD* (blog), *Medium*, December 20, 2019. https://ffwd.medium.com/presley-ryans-tiktoks-have-made-beetlejuice-broadway-s-hottest-ticket-fa9c76b1f123.

Stolworthy, Jacob. "Day-O: How Beetlejuice Conquered Its Strangeness to Become a Cult Classic." *Independent*, October 28, 2018. https://www.independent.co.uk/arts-entertainment/films/features/beetlejuice-30-years-michael-keaton-tim-burton-winona-ryder-cinema-release-film-a8602251.html.

Summers, Claude J. *Queer Encyclopedia of Music, Dance and Musical Theater.* San Francisco: Cleis Press, 2004.

Sunday Times. "TikTok: Everything You Need to Know." May 10, 2020. https://www.thetimes.co.uk/article/tiktok-everything-you-need-to-know-692pnxdb2.

Sweeney-Romero, Katlin Marisol. "Wellness TikTok Morning Routines, Eating Well, and Getting Ready to Be 'That Girl.'" In *TikTok Cultures in the United States*, edited by Trevor Boffone, 108–16. London: Routledge, 2022.

Ting, Deanna. "'Every Kid Wants to Be an Influencer': Why TikTok Is Taking Off with Gen Z." *Digiday*, February 7, 2020. https://digiday.com/marketing/every-kid-wants-influencer-tiktok-taking-off-gen-z/.

Tran, Diep. "How 'Ratatouille' the TikTok Musical Became 'Ratatouille' the Broadway Musical." *Backstage*, December 30, 2020. https://www.backstage.com/magazine/article/ratatouille-tiktok-musical-broadway-the-actors-fund-72365/.

Tsai, Terence, and Shubo Liu. "*Mamma Mia!* Made in China: Challenges in Developing the Musical Industry." *Asian Case Research Journal* 19, no. 2 (2015): 419–42.

Van Dijck, José. *The Culture of Connectivity: Critical History of Social Media.* Oxford: Oxford University Press, 2013.

Vandevender, Bryan M. "Splitting *HAIR*: Reviving the American Tribal Love-Rock Musical in the 1970s." *New England Theatre Journal* 29, no. 1 (2018): 31–53.
Vandevender, Bryan M. "They're Playing My Song: The American Musical in the Me-Decade." In *The Routledge Companion to the Contemporary Musical*, edited by Jessica Sternfeld and Elizabeth L. Wollman, 29–38. London: Routledge, 2020.
Vizcaíno-Verdú, Arantxa, and Crystal Abidin. "Music Challenge Memes on TikTok: Understanding In-Group Storytelling Videos." *International Journal of Communication* 16 (2022): 883–908.
Vizcaíno-Verdú, Arantxa, and Ignacio Aguaded. "#ThisIsMeChallenge and Music for Empowerment of Marginalized Groups on TikTok." *Media and Communication* 10, no. 1 (2022): 157–72.
Vuocolo, Alexander. "Gen Z Looks for Authenticity in TikTok Viral Marketing, Says Creative Agency CEO." *Cheddar*, December 28, 2020. https://cheddar.com/media/gen-z-looks-for-authenticity-in-tiktok-viral-marketing-says-creative-agency-ceo.
Walk-Morris, Tatiana. "TikTok's Digital Blackface Problem." *One Zero* (blog), *Medium*, February 12, 2020. https://onezero.medium.com/tiktoks-digital-blackface-problem-409571589a8.
Wallaroo. "TikTok Statistics." Last updated February 6, 2021. https://wallaroomedia.com/blog/social-media/tiktok-statistics/.
Wei, Eugene. "TikTok and the Sorting Hat." *Remains of the Day*, August 4, 2020. https://www.eugenewei.com/blog/2020/8/3/tiktok-and-the-sorting-hat.
Wetmore, Brendan. "'Beetlejuice' on Broadway Is Breaking TikTok." *Paper Mag*, October 3, 2019. https://www.papermag.com/beetlejuice-broadway-tiktok-trend-1-2640689936.html.
Williams, Raymond. *Culture*. London: Fontana Press, 1981.
Willis, Ika. "Keeping Promises to Queer Children: Making Space (for Mary Sue) at Hogwarts." In *Fan Fiction and Fan Communities in the Age of the Internet*, edited by Karen Hellekson and Kristina Busse, 153–70. Jefferson, NC: McFarland, 2006.
Wolf, Stacy. *Beyond Broadway: The Pleasure and Promise of Musical Theatre across America*. New York: Oxford University Press, 2019.
Wolf, Stacy. *Changed for Good: A Feminist History of the Broadway Musical*. New York: Oxford University Press, 2011.
Wolf, Stacy. "'Defying Gravity': Queer Conventions in the Musical *Wicked*." *Theatre Journal* 60, no. 1 (2008): 1–21.
Wollman, Elizabeth L. *A Critical Companion to the American Stage Musical*. London: Methuen Drama, 2017.
Wollman, Elizabeth. *The Theater Will Rock: A History of the Rock Musical, from "Hair" to "Hedwig."* Ann Arbor: University of Michigan Press, 2006.
Womack, Malcolm. "'Thank You for the Music': Catherine Johnson's Feminist Revoicings in *Mamma Mia!*" *Studies in Musical Theatre* 3, no. 2 (2009): 201–11.
Wooden, Isaiah Matthew. "Effective Dreaming in the Time of Zoom Theatre: Reflections on Directing *The Lathe of Heaven*." *Theatre Topics* 32, no. 3 (2022): 127–37.
Zeng, Jing, Crystal Abidin, and Mike S. Schäfer. "Research Perspectives on TikTok and Its Legacy Apps." *International Journal of Communications* 15 (2021): 3161–72.
Zhang, Yunan, and Tom Dotan. "TikTok's U.S. Revenues Expected to Hit $500 Million This Year." *Information*, June 17, 2020. https://www.theinformation.com/articles/tiktoks-u-s-revenues-expected-to-hit-500-million-this-year.

Index

[title of show], 37, 130

ABBA, 14, 28, 32, 117–22, 165, 186n2, 186n4, 188n17
activist, 19–20, 172n55
Actors Fund, The, 124, 137, 141, 143, 188n2, 190n25
Addison Rae, 45, 76
agency, 7, 30, 36, 39, 51, 56, 79, 99, 112
Aladdin, 35, 55, 97, 154
algorithm, 2, 8–9, 11–12, 16–19, 26–27, 32, 49, 53, 66, 75, 77, 90, 92, 100, 105, 108, 120–21, 125, 134, 161, 164, 166, 186n5, 188n15
All That Chat, 8, 11
"All You Wanna Do," 79–83. See also Six
"Angel Eyes," 118–19, 122, 165, 188n15, 188n17. See also Mamma Mia! Here We Go Again
Angulo, William Carlos, 85–86, 88–90
Ardolino, Amber, 31, 59–66, 165, 179n2
auditions, 2, 6, 23, 31, 85, 87–90, 97, 140
authenticity, 10, 13, 16, 33, 37, 40–43, 55–58, 140, 145–47, 160–61, 164

Barlow, Abigail, 150–52, 192n66, 192n68. See also Bridgerton: The Musical
Barrera, Melissa, 103–4
Barth Feldman, Andrew, 136
Bear, Emily, 150–52, 192n66, 192n68. See also Bridgerton: The Musical
Beck, Noah, 101–102
Beetlejuice, ix, xi, 6–7, 20, 22, 24–25, 28–31, 34–58, 60, 68, 70, 72, 90, 92, 99, 109, 121, 153, 161, 175n2, 175n6
Be More Chill, 29, 35, 45, 55, 73
Benanti, Laura, xi, 2, 25, 148
Benjamin, Nell, 85
Bennett, Michael, 2, 5, 70
BeReal, 15

Billboard Hot 100, 7, 33, 60, 87, 154, 184–85n22
Black Lives Matter, 19
Black TikTok Strike, 19
Blankenbuehler, Andy, 9, 38, 59
Bolt, Gabbi, 137–38, 150
Bootleg, 8, 64–65, 97, 108, 111, 115, 179n10, 186n52
Brady, Wayne, 124, 146
Breslin, Michael, 144. See also Circle Jerk
Bridgerton: The Musical, 7, 90, 150–53
Brightman, Alex, 44–49
Broadway Bob, xi, 22, 24, 165, 173n74
BroadwayCon, 32, 120, 187n11
Broadway Shutdown, 2, 8, 25, 54, 56, 78, 194n9
Broski, Brittany, 134, 190n23
Bryan the Business Analyst, 24, 165, 173n79
Burgess, Titus, 124, 144, 146
Burton, Tim, 34–35, 44
Butler, Kerry, 46–47
ByteDance, x, 14

camp, 50, 89, 92–93, 100–101, 106, 109, 116, 145–46, 175n6, 183n4
casting, 87–90, 106, 168n13
Chamberlain, Kevin, 139, 141, 146–47
Chenoweth, Kristin, xi, 2, 25, 45, 60, 96–98, 105, 148, 189n15
Chicago, 40, 96–97, 166
choreography, xi, 2–6, 9, 21–22, 24–25, 49, 59, 63, 70, 85–6, 88–90, 118, 123, 140, 151, 155–56, 160, 162, 176n28, 182n5
Chorus Line, A, 2–8, 18, 56, 70, 88, 99, 124, 146, 168n2, 168n7
Christian, R. J., 138–39, 150
Cinderella, 18
Circle Jerk, 163
Clayton, Max, 4, 60

clout, x, 53, 61, 68, 76, 78, 88, 98, 101, 136, 150
cosplay, ix, 10, 32, 50–51, 70, 92–93, 117–22, 155, 165, 187n11, 188n12
Cost n' Mayor (Austin and Meredith Telenko), 64, 159
COVID-19 pandemic, 1, 7–9, 54, 60, 62, 68, 78, 94, 111, 121, 129, 194n9
crowdsource, 32, 70, 124–26, 129–31, 134, 136–37, 139, 141, 148, 150–51

D'Amelio, Charli, 45, 76, 78, 101, 127
D'Amelio, Dixie, 101
D'Amelio Effect, The, 76, 78, 101
dance call, 31, 85–91, 165, 182n5, 182n7
Dear Evan Hansen, 20, 25, 51, 56, 97, 136
"Defying Gravity," 32, 82, 92–94, 100, 106–9, 111, 113–15, 183n1. See also *Wicked*
democratization, 6–9, 16–20, 99, 111, 124–25, 149, 168n1
Devereaux, John, 65, 179n9
Disney, 13, 64, 123, 125, 133–34, 136, 138, 142–45, 153–55, 158, 165, 190n25, 193n3
Disney World, 123, 133
Disney+, 32, 65, 103, 153, 192n55, 194n9
DiTanna, Dominic, 67–68, 180n1
diva, 2, 31, 38, 96, 98, 105, 109, 111, 114–16, 130, 148
DIY Drag, 15, 31–32, 93–102, 104, 105–6, 108–10, 112–16, 121, 156, 159
"Don't Lose Ur Head," 77–79. See also *Six*
Dr. Horrible's Sing-Along Blog, 13
drag, 15, 22, 31–32, 71, 92–116, 118, 121, 156, 159
dramaturgy, 2–3, 14, 24, 30–31, 35–36, 39, 41, 44, 53, 57, 68–69, 71–75, 77, 79–80, 82–84, 87, 106, 108–9, 112, 122, 137, 141, 151, 155, 158, 176n19, 178–9n66
duets, 23, 32, 49, 51, 104, 120, 125, 127–31, 151, 159, 189n15

Eilish, Billie, 45–47
Encanto, 32–33, 97, 153–59, 193n4
EPIC, 152
Esperon, Brian, 60, 64, 155–59, 193n6

Facebook, 6–8, 16, 31, 41–42, 56, 61, 87, 90, 97, 120–21, 127–28, 149, 164

Fake Friends, 163. See also *Circle Jerk*
feminism, 79, 83, 118
Foley, Patrick, 144. See also *Circle Jerk*
Follies, 16, 28, 54, 166, 179n7
For You Page (FYP), xi, 6, 35, 92, 127, 159, 166
Foxberri, 50
Frozen, 20, 43, 154
Fun Home, ix–x, 28, 45, 179n10
Funny Girl, 60–62, 107, 179n2

ghosting, 72, 82
Glee, xvi, 71–72, 83
Godspell, 40
Golden Age of TikTok, ix, 8, 53, 67–68, 169n17
Goldsberry, Renée Elise, 61
Gray, Loren, 76–77
Grocery Store: A New Musical, 52, 126–32, 134

Hach, Heather, 85
Hairspray, 88, 182n5
Ham 4Ham, 41
Hamilton, ix, 2, 9, 13, 20–21, 25, 28, 31, 38, 40–41, 53, 56, 59–65, 71, 73, 78, 88, 103, 117, 140, 147, 155, 164, 178–79n66, 182n7, 192n55, 194n9
Hamlisch, Marvin, 2, 5
hashtag, 5, 16, 19, 21, 32, 41, 50, 74, 91, 108, 118, 120, 125, 150, 158, 179n4, 186n2
Heathers: The Musical, ix, 7, 20, 24, 28–29, 31, 42, 47, 56, 67–69, 71–77, 83–84, 87, 90, 99, 105, 109, 153, 180n13, 180n15
Hedwig and the Angry Inch, 51, 121
Henry VIII, 77–83. See also *Six*
Herman, Jerry, 145
Howard, Katherine, 77–83, 182n30. See also *Six*
Hufford, Ashley, 24, 165, 173n80

In the Heights, ix, 13, 37, 55, 87, 90, 102–3, 153, 155, 184n22, 193n1
Instagram, 7, 12, 15–16, 26–27, 41–42, 52, 65, 90, 97, 120, 127, 142, 149, 152, 158, 162

Jackson, Christopher, 61
Jacobsen, Emily, 123, 133–34, 136, 140–41, 143, 148–49. See also *Ratatouille: The TikTok Musical*

Kinky Boots, 71
KPOP, 33, 160–65, 193–94n1, 194n2, 194n9
Kritzer, Leslie, 45–47

La La Land, 69–70
Laucerica, Pablo David, 22, 173n74
Legally Blonde, 31, 38, 85–91, 165, 176n17, 182n5
Legally Brown: The Search for the Next Piragua Guy, 38, 176n17
Lighting Thief, The, 13, 20, 25, 29, 35, 45, 56–58
Lion King, The, 21, 35, 41, 55, 146–47, 154, 194n9
Liotine, Matthew Aaron, 4, 168n7
lip-sync, ix, 48, 73–74, 77, 92–93, 100, 108, 113, 118, 122, 155–56, 159, 165, 167n1
live stream, 8, 148, 163, 194n9
LuPone, Patti, xi, 1, 39, 185n27, 189n15

Mamma Mia!, 14, 20–21, 28, 32, 54, 117–22, 165, 186n2, 186n5
Mamma Mia! Here We Go Again, 118–19, 122
marketing, 9, 14, 25, 30–31, 34–58, 60–61, 64–65, 90, 123, 136, 160–61, 163–64, 194n4
Marlow, Toby, 78. See also *Six*
"Martha Dumptruck in the flesh" (Martha Dumptruck Challenge), ix, 29, 31, 47, 67–69, 72–77, 81–82, 87. See also *Heathers: The Musical*
Matilda, 165
McCarrell, Chris, 57
McClure, Rob, 46
Mean Girls, 11, 45, 55, 72–73, 76, 78
Menzel, Idina, 2, 25, 45, 96, 105, 108, 111, 113, 115, 183n1
Mertzlufft, Daniel, 123, 129–32, 134–37, 140–41, 148–50, 189n15, 190n26, 192n62. See also *Grocery Store: A New Musical*
Miranda, Lin-Manuel, 38, 40, 59, 61, 103–4, 154–55, 158–59, 193n5
Moss, Lucy, 78, 124, 139, 141, 145–47, 149
Moulin Rouge!, 60–61, 88, 182n7
MUNY, The, 31, 85–91, 165, 182n5

Murphy, Kevin, 73
Musical.ly, x, 14, 100, 180n4

Newsies, xi, 20–21, 55
Next to Normal, 20, 39, 176n20
Niemann, JJ, 23, 60, 85–87, 90, 146, 148, 173n75

"Ode to Remy," 123, 132–38, 140–42, 145, 150. See also *Ratatouille: The TikTok Musical*
O'Keefe, Laurence, 72, 85
Olivo, Karen, 38, 103–4
Orfeh, 87

Paget, Ian, 60, 148
Park, Helen, 162, 193n1. See also *KPOP*
Patinkin, Mandy, xi, 25, 60
Perfect, Eddie, 35, 43–44, 47, 50–51, 55–56. See also *Beetlejuice*
Pixar, 123, 132–33, 142, 188–89n6
Porter, Billy, 71
Powers, Brandon, 24, 33, 161–65, 173n81

Quinn, Katherine, 24, 165, 173n80

Ramos, Anthony, 103–4, 185n24
Ratatouille (film), 123, 125, 132–33, 135, 188–89n6
Ratatouille: The TikTok Musical, xi, xiii, 6, 20, 28–29, 32, 70, 90, 92, 105, 123–50, 152–53, 165, 173n75, 191n54, 192n65
Reinking, Kate, 24, 165, 173n80
Renegade Challenge, 41, 50, 68, 88, 117
Rent, 11, 28, 56, 96, 145, 193n5
Rhimes, Shonda, 151
Rice, Christopher, 2–4, 18, 60, 168n1
"Rich Man's Frug," 41, 88, 165, 176n28, 182n5
Riegler, Adam, 38
Rivera-Herrans, Jorge, 151–52. See also *EPIC*
Rock of Ages, 37, 39
Ruggieri, Andrew N., 4–5
RuPaul, 99–100
Ryan, Presley, 45–49, 56, 60, 177n38. See also *Beetlejuice*

"Say My Name," 9, 48–50, 53, 178n53. See also *Beetlejuice*
Schwartz, Stephen, 94–95, 98, 107, 125, 183n1
Schyvinck, Logan, 112–15, 186n47
Scott, Ellenore, 142, 146
Seaview Productions, 143–44, 148, 191n42
self-tapes, 85–91
Shoebox Musicals, 22, 173n76
Shucked, 41–42
Siswick, Jess, 140–41
Siwa, Jojo, 76, 127
Six, xi, 6–7, 9–10, 20, 24–25, 28, 31, 56, 67–69, 71, 77–84, 90, 92, 99, 109, 139, 146, 153, 165, 181n28
Snapchat, 15
Sondheim, Stephen, 10–11, 22, 24, 125, 145, 179n7
Song, Stage & Screen Conference, 15, 92–94, 108
Soo, Phillipa, 61
SpongeBob SquarePants: The Broadway Musical, 55, 145
SpotCo, 161
Spring Awakening, 37, 45
stagedoor, 39, 51
stealth musicals, 24, 31, 67–84, 121, 159
Steingold, Dana, 45–46
Straight TikTok, 89, 101, 108
Strange Loop, A, 160
Sweet Charity, 41, 88, 165, 176n28, 182n5

Testa, Mary, 124, 146
thirst trap, 108, 161, 185n24

Timbers, Alex, 49
Tony Awards, xi, 9, 21, 37–38, 59, 96, 139, 145, 168n4, 187n11
Tumblr, 7, 12, 26, 42, 61, 73, 94, 97, 99, 121, 166
Twitter, 6–8, 15–16, 26–27, 31, 39–42, 56, 61, 65, 87, 90, 99, 103, 120, 127–28, 131, 141, 143, 149, 163–64, 176n20

Vosk, Jessica, 108, 111, 114–15

Walker, Grace, 173n82
"WAP," 59–60, 63–64, 88, 155–56, 176n4
Warwick, Tyler, 110–16, 136, 186n44
Weber, Jennifer, 162
webseries, 38–39
"We Don't Talk About Bruno," 33, 87, 153–59, 193n3, 193n5. See also *Encanto*
West Side Story, 10, 13, 22, 56, 153, 158
Whiteness, 18–20, 76, 100–101, 108, 160, 180n5
Wicked, 6, 13, 20–22, 24–26, 28, 31, 38, 41, 43, 45, 92–116, 121, 183n1, 184n10, 184n14
Wizard of Oz, The,
Woah, 47, 68, 117, 146
Wong, Alex, 60
Woods, Joy, 146

Xanadu, 37–39

YouTube, 8, 12, 37–39, 41–42, 51, 53, 55, 61, 65, 70, 73, 87, 97, 141, 152, 161, 176n19, 184n17, 186n52